Praise for *One Day I Will Write ...*

"From an early age, Wainaina's outlook on the world around him was characterized by his vivid imagination, from his vision of the sun's rays poking through the grass as 'a thousand tiny suns' to the 'hot snails of thick feeling' that suffuse his body during a hot bath. Throughout it all, he is keenly in tune with those who are outsiders, particularly his mother, a Ugandan who is the subject of xenophobic attacks from her neighbors."   —*The New Republic*

"[A] very good, if not remarkable, book. If you are a Western reader it will remind you of two things: 1) Nothing you have ever heard of before; and 2) Dylan Thomas when writing about his own childhood. The language is similarly startling and luminous. . . . This book is important because it brings us news from a part of Kenya seldom heard from. And it brings us a new voice, one that is anthropomorphic, poetic and pointed."   —*Star Tribune* (Minneapolis)

"This self-portrait of the artist as a young African man is the story of an outsider coming into his own, but it's Wainaina's capacity for language that sets it apart. Growing up in a place where people use many tongues—Kiswahili, English, Kikuyu and dozens of others—interchangeably serves him well in weaving together lyrical, impressionistic scenes from his past. More than just pretty prose, however, *ODIWWATP* does justice to the complex place that's much more than the sum of tidy facts unenlightened Westerners may know about it."   —*Time Out New York*

"Harried reader, I'll save you precious time: skip this review and head directly to the bookstore for Binyavanga Wainaina's stand-up-and-cheer coming-of-age memoir, *One Day I Will Write About This Place*. Although written by an East African and set in East and Southern Africa, Wainaina's book is not just for Afrophiles or lovers of postcolonial literature. This is a book for anyone who still finds the nourishment of a well-written tale preferable to the empty-calorie jolt of a celebrity confessional or Swedish mystery."   —Alexandra Fuller, *The New York Times Book Review*

"*This* is how to write about Africa—with love and a sharp eye, with intimacy and risk, with patience and such superlative skills."   —Leila Aboulela

"Binyavanga Wainaina writes with an unparalleled grace, a language that burns with tenderness and a scorching melancholy and an honesty rarely encountered in a memoir. A long awaited and brilliant book."   —Chris Abani, author of *Graceland* and *The Virgin of Flames*

"Language is clearly the author's preferred mode of structuring the world, but it is also the plaything he uses with idiosyncratic grace and brilliant immediacy to capture 'the scattered, shifting sensations' of memories and emotions long past."

—*Kirkus Reviews*

"Wainaina paints pictures with words; his writing is reflective and playful and worth lingering over. . . . The Africa evoked is captivating and will be exotic and new to many readers. Wainaina's memoir is by turns funny, sad, hopeful and occasionally cynical, but always engaging. Fanciful abstractions of his environment and instructive tales of African politics combine to give us a fascinating vision of his world."

—*Shelf Awareness*

"A narrative with its own galloping rhythm. . . . Wainaina is driven by a need to absorb the experiences of those around him and then express them in his unique style, and he is at his best when he is face-to-face with his subject. The result is a rich and vivid depiction of the author's life and a joy to read."

—*New Pages*

"[An] insightful, emotionally rich memoir. . . . Wainaina provides the means for readers to experience Africa, in all its dimensions, with newly invigorated senses."

—*The Brooklyn Rail*

"An utterly convincing and radically original portrait of 21st century Africa."

—AllAfrica.com

"Original. Poetic. Surprising. Experimental. . . . Wainaina depicts an Africa where real people live—an Africa that will stay in your mind."

—*A Traveler's Library*

"Wainaina's path to becoming a writer is wrapped up in his quest to realize his identity, to belong to his family yet create a life uniquely his own. . . . *One Day I Will Write About This Place* is a hilarious, intelligent, and nuanced portrayal of what it means to be a Kenyan-Ugandan-Gikuyu-Mufumbira-son-brother-foreigner-citizen-artist in our world today."

—*Africa Is a Country*

"*One Day I Will Write About This Place* is profound and insightful, a must for anyone who wants a personal insight about the state of Kenya and the African continent."

—*Midwest Book Review*

"This memoir of Africa is lyrical, sometimes raw, always magical of language in its telling of the day-to-day life of a complex continent. I am savoring every word."

—*Hudson Valley News*

One Day I Will
Write About
This Place

One Day I Will Write About This Place

A Memoir

...

Binyavanga Wainaina

GRAYWOLF PRESS

Excerpt from *Search Sweet Country* by Bernard Kojo Laing copyright © Bernard Kojo Laing, 1986. Used by permission of The Wylie Agency (UK) Limited.

This publication is made possible in part by a grant provided by the Minnesota State Arts Board, through an appropriation by the Minnesota State Legislature from the Minnesota general fund and its arts and cultural heritage fund with money from the vote of the people of Minnesota on November 4, 2008, and a grant from the Wells Fargo Foundation Minnesota. Significant support has also been provided by the National Endowment for the Arts; Target; the McKnight Foundation; and other generous contributions from foundations, corporations, and individuals. To these organizations and individuals we offer our heartfelt thanks.

ART WORKS.
arts.gov

MINNESOTA
STATE ARTS BOARD

CLEAN
WATER
LAND &
LEGACY
AMENDMENT

WELLS
FARGO

TARGET.

This book is made possible through a partnership with the College of Saint Benedict, and honors the legacy of S. Mariella Gable, a distinguished teacher at the College. Support has been provided by the Manitou Fund as part of the Warner Reading Program.

Published by Graywolf Press
212 Third Avenue North, Suite 485
Minneapolis, Minnesota 55401

www.graywolfpress.org

Published in the United States of America

ISBN 978-1-55597-591-3 (cloth)
ISBN 978-1-55597-624-8 (paper)

6 8 10 12 11 9 7 5

Library of Congress Control Number: 2012936226

Cover design: Kapo Ng @ A-Men

To Mum in Heaven & Babs in Naks
To Jim, to Ciru (unajua ka-magic ketu kadogo), to Chiqy
To Wee William Wilberforce, to Bobo, to Mary Rose, to Emma, to Eddy
To AN—You will know . . .
Much much love and thanks.

Some names have been changed
to protect the privacy of individuals.

One Day I Will
Write About
This Place

Chapter One

It is afternoon. We are playing soccer near the clothesline behind the main house. Jimmy, my brother, is eleven, and my sister, Ciru, is five and a half. I am the goalie.

I am seven years old, and I still do not know why everybody seems to know what they are doing and why they are doing it.

"You are not fat." That's what Mum says to me all the time. "You are plump."

Ciru has the ball. She is small and thin and golden. She has sharp elbows, and a smile as clean as a pencil drawing. It cuts evenly into her cheeks. She runs toward Jimmy, who is tall and fit and dark.

She is the star of her class. It is 1978, and we are all in Lena Moi Primary School. Last term, Ciru was moved a year forward. Now she is in standard two, like me, in the class next door. Her first term in standard two, she beat everybody and topped the class. She is the youngest in her class. Everybody else is seven.

I stand still between the metal poles we use as a makeshift goal-mouth watching Ciru and Jim play. Warm breath pushes down my nostrils past my mouth and divides my chin. I can see the pink shining flesh of my eyelids. Random sounds fall into my ears: cars, birds, black mamba bicycle bells, distant children, dogs, crows, and afternoon national radio music. Congo rumba. People outside our compound are talking, in languages I know the sounds of, but do not understand or speak, Luhya, Gikuyu.

My laugh is far away inside, like the morning car not starting when the key turns. In school, it is always Ciru number one, blue and red and yellow stars on every page. It is always Ciru in a white dress giving flowers to the guest of honor—Mr. Ben Methu—on Parents' Day. If I am washing with her, we are splashing and laughing and fighting and soon we are in a fever of tears or giggles.

She twists past Jimmy, the ball ahead of her feet, heading for me. I am ready. I am sharp, and springy. I am waiting for the ball. Jimmy runs to intercept her; they tangle and pant. A few moments ago the sun was one single white beam. Now it has fallen into the trees. All over the garden there are a thousand tiny suns, poking through gaps, all of them spherical, all of them shooting thousands of beams. The beams fall onto branches and leaves and splinter into thousands of smaller perfect suns.

I laugh when Ciru laughs and I find myself inside her laugh, and we fall down holding each other. I can feel her laughter swelling, even before it comes out, and it swells in me too.

I know how to move with her patterns, and to move with Jimmy's patterns. My patterns are always tripping on each other in public. They are only safe when I am alone, or when I am daydreaming.

Ciru laughs loud, her mouth wide and red. The sound jumps toward me, flapping sheets of sound, but I am lost. Arms and legs and ball are forgotten. The thousand suns are breathing. They inhale, dim and cool into the leaves, and I let myself breathe with them; then they puff light forward and exhale, warming my body. I am about to let myself soak inside this completely when I am captured by an idea.

The sun does not break up into pieces.

It does not break up into disembodied parts when it falls into trees and things. Each piece of the sun is always a complete little sun.

I am coming back into my arms and legs and the goalmouth, ready to explain the thousand suns to Jimmy and Ciru. I am excited. They will believe me this time. It won't seem stupid when I speak it, like it often does, and then they look at me, rolling their eyes and telling me that my marbles are lost. That I cansaythatagain. They are coming close. Jimmy is shouting. Before I fully return to myself, a hole in my ear rips open. The football hits the center of my face. I fall.

Goaaaaal. A thousand suns erupt with wet laughter; even the radio is laughing. I look up and see them both leaning over me, dripping sweat, arms akimbo.

Jimmy rolls his eyes and says, "You've lost your marbles."

"I'm thirsty," says Ciru.

"Me too," says Jim, and they run, and I want to stand and run with them. My face hurts. Juma, our dog, is licking my face. I lean into his stomach; my nose pushes into his fur. The sun is below the trees, the sky is clear, and I am no longer broken up and distributed. I scramble and jump to my feet. Juma whines, like a car winding down. I pump my feet forward, pulling my voice out and throwing it forward to grab hold of their Thirst Resolution.

"Hey!" I shrill. "Even me I am thirsty!"

They don't hear me.

They are headed away from the kitchen, and I follow them into the long clumps of uncut grass at the top of the garden, Juma at my heels, as they weave in and out of Baba's tractors, swerve to avoid dog shit, run through shade and fading sun, past little eruptions of termites in Kikuyu grass, and forgotten heaps of farm spare parts piled behind the hedge that separates the main house from the servants' quarters. Then they turn, shouting hi to Zablon, the cook who is washing dishes outside in his white vest and blue trousers and Lifebuoy soap and charcoal smell. I shout hi too, now flowing well into their movements. They stop, then turn to our regular racetrack down the path from the servants' quarters to the kitchen.

I find them there, Juma's nose nudging Jim's leg, and I watch them pour the cool liquid down their throats, from glasses, see it spill off the sides of their cheeks. Jimmy has learned to pull the whole glass of water down in one move. It streams down the pipe, marble-bubbles running down a soft translucent tube of sound, like a frog.

He slams his glass on the countertop, burps, and turns to look at me.

What is thirst? The word splits up into a hundred small suns. I lift my glass and look up. Ciru is looking at me, her glass already empty as she wipes her lips on her forearm.

···

I am in my bedroom, alone. I have a glass of water. I want to try to gulp it down, like Jimmy does. This word, *thirst, thirsty*. It is a word full of resolution. It drives a person to quick action. Words, I think, must be concrete things. Surely they cannot be suggestions of things, vague pictures: scattered, shifting sensations?

Sometimes we like to steal Baba's old golf balls and throw them into a fire. First they curl, in a kind of ecstasy, like a cat being stroked, then they arch, start to bubble and bounce, then they shoot out of the fire like bullets, skinned and free. Below the skin are tight wraps of rubber band, and we can now unroll them and watch the balls getting smaller and smaller, and the rubber bands unfold so long it does not seem possible they came out of the small hard ball.

I want to be certainly thirsty, like Jimmy and Ciru.

Water has more shape and presence than air, but it is still colorless. Once you have the shape of water in your mouth, you discover your body. Because water is clear. It lets you taste your mouth, feel the pipe shape of your throat and the growing ball of your stomach as you drink.

I burp. And rub my stomach, which growls. I fiddle with the tap, and notice that when water runs fast from a tap, it becomes white. Water, moving at speed, rushing from a tap, has shape and form and direction. I put my hand under the tap, and feel it solid.

The shape of an idea starts to form. There is air, there is water, there is glass. Wind moving fast gives form to air; water moving fast gives it form. Maybe . . . maybe glass is water moving at superspeed, like on television, when a superhero moves so fast, faster than blurring, he comes back to himself a thousand times before you see him move.

No. No. Thirst is . . . is . . . a sucking absence, a little mouthing fish out of the water. It moves you from the everywhere nowhereness of air, your breathing person; you are now a stream, a fixed flowing address, a drinking person. It is a step below hungering, which comes from a solid body, one that can smell, taste, see, and need colors. Yes!

But—I still can't answer why the word leaves me so uncertain and speculative. I can't make the water stream down my throat effortlessly. It spills into my nostrils and chokes me. Other people have a word world, and in their word world, words like *thirsty* have length, breadth, and height, a firm texture, an unthinking belonging, like hands and toes and balls and doors. When they say their word, their body moves into action, sure and true.

I am always standing and watching people acting boldly to the call of words. I can only follow them. They don't seem to trip and fall through holes their conviction does not see. So their certainty must be the right world. I put the glass down. Something is wrong with me.

···

We are on our way home, after a family day in Molo. We are eating House of Manji biscuits.

Beatrice, who is in my class, broke her leg last week. They covered her leg with white plaster. The water heater in our home is covered with white plaster. Beatrice's toes are fat gray ticks. The water heater is a squat cylinder, covered in white stickyhard, like Beatrice's new leg. She has crutches.

Crunch is breaking to release crackly sweetness. Crunch! Eclairs. *Crutches* are falling down and breaking. Crutch!

Biscuits.

Uganda, my mum's country, fell down and broke. Crutch!

Field Marshal Amin Dada, the president of Uganda, ate his minister for supper. He kept the minister's head in the fridge. His son wears a uniform just like his. They stand together on television news, in front of a parade.

I am sleepy. Ciru is fast asleep. Jimmy asks Baba to stop the car so he can pee.

I immediately find I want to pee.

We park on the shoulder of a valley that spreads down into a jigsaw puzzle of market gardens before us. For a long time, I have wanted to walk between the fault lines of this puzzle. Out there, always in the distance, the world is vague and blurred and pretty.

I want to slide through the seams and go to the other side.

After pissing, I simply walk on: down the valley, past astonished-looking mamas who are weeding, over a little creek, through a ripe cattle *boma* that is covered with dung.

Look, look at the fever tree!

Her canopy is frizzy, her gold and green bark shines. It is like she was scribbled sideways with a sharp pencil, so she can cut her sharp edges into the soul of whoever looks at her from a distance. You do not climb her; she has thorns. Acacia.

She is designed for dreams.

I am disappointed that all the distant scenery, blue and misty, becomes more and more real as I come closer: there is no vague place, where clarity blurs, where certainty has no force, and dreams are real.

After a while, I see my brother, Jim, coming after me; the new thrill is to keep him far away, to run faster and faster.

I stretch into a rubber-band giant, a superhero made long by cartoon speed. I am as long as the distance between me and him. The world of light and wind and sound slaps against my face as I move faster and faster.

If I focus, I can let it into me, let in the whole wide whoosh of the world. I grit my teeth, harden my stomach.

It is coming, the moment is coming.

If I get that moment right, I can let my mind burst out of me and fold into the world, pulling it behind me like a cart. Like a golf ball bursting out of the fire. No! No! Not a golf ball! The world will flap uselessly behind me, like, like a superhero cape.

I will be free of awkwardness, of Ciru, of Jimmy, of Idi Amin dreams. The world is streaks of blinding light. My body tearing away, like Velcro, from the patterns of others.

Later, I wake up in the backseat of the car. "Here we are," Mum likes to say whenever we come home. My skin is hot, and Mum's soft knuckles nibble my forehead. I can feel ten thousand hot prickling crickets chorusing outside. I want to tear my clothes off and let my skin be naked in the crackling night. "Shhh," she whispers, "shhh, shhh," and a pink-tasting syrup rolls down my tongue, and Baba's strong arms are under my knees. I am pushed into the ironed sheets that are folded back over the blanket like a flap. Mum pulls them over my head. I am a letter, I think, a hot burning letter, and I can see a big stickysyrup-dripping tongue, about to lick and seal me in.

In a few minutes, I get up and make my way across to Jimmy's bed.

Chapter Two

Sophia Mwela lives next door to us. Sophia is in my class. She is the class prefect. I sit next to her in class, but she rarely speaks to me. Like Ciru, she is also always number one in class. Their family is posh and rich. The Mwelas talk through their noses; we call it wreng wreng, like television people, like people from England or America. Their house has an upstairs, and they have a butler and a uniformed driver. They take piano lessons.

Their father works for Union Carbide. He is the boss and has even white people working for him. Ciru and I are going to show them. We are going to dress up like Americans. It is my idea.

Ciru and I invade Mum's wardrobe. I put on one of her Afro wigs, some lipstick, high-heeled shoes stuffed with toilet paper. I ask Ciru to dress up too. No, she says. We agree to pretend I am her cousin from America. I put on some face powder, and we are sneezing. A shiny midi dress. A maxi on me. I chew lots and lots of peeled pink cubes of Big G chewing gum. We climb the tree, Ciru and I, the tree that separates our hedge from theirs.

We call Sophia.

"Sophiaaaa," says Ciru. We giggle.

"Sophiaaanh," I say, Americanly. "Sow-phiaaanh."

Sophia arrives, solemn, head turned to the side, face frowning, like a serious person, like a person who knows something we do not know.

"This is my cousin Sherry from America. She is a Negro," says Ciru.

"Haaangi. Wreng wreng," I say Americanly, whinnying through my nose, and make a little bubble of gum pop out of my mouth. My high heels are about to fall off.

"I arrived fram Ohi-o-w. Laas Angelis. Airrrprrrt. Baarston. Wreng wreng . . ."

I fan my face and let my lips rub against each other like the woman of Lux. I release them forward, to pop. *Mpah!*

Sophia says, "How is Ohio?"

"Oh, groovy. It is so wreng wreng wreng."

I say, "I came on Pan Am. On a sevenfordiseven . . ."

She turns her head and nods. Look at her! She believes!

I shrug, "I just gat on a jet plane, donno when I'll be back again."

She turns away.

"Call me. My number is five-five-five . . ."

The next day, Sophia tells everybody in class that I dressed in my mum's clothes and pretended to be an American.

They laugh and laugh.

...

Jimmy likes to roll his eyes and say groovy American things like "you've lost your marbles" and "you can say that again."

Thousands of marbles—each one tied to your mind with a rubber band—are scattered by your mind into the hard smooth world it sees.

Golfballmarbles.

The world you see undulates with many parallel troughs—a million mental alleys. Every new day, you throw your marbles out of your mind and let your feet and arms and shoulders follow, and soon some marbles nestle loudly into the grooves and run along with authority and precision, directed by you, with increasing boldness.

Each marble is a whole little round version of you. Like the suns.

In the groove.

But just when your marble is wheeling along, groovily swinging up the walls of your trough and back down again, challenging the edge, whistling and gum chewing and downhill biking and yo-yo bouncy and American—gravel pounded by rain outside your bedroom window becomes sausages frying, and sausages frying can shift and become squirming bloody intestines or an army of bristling mustachioed accordions chasing you, laughing like Idi Amin.

Your marble slips off, and it clatters into a groove that contains another marble and they knock each other, sausages and gravel and intestines and a hundred manic accordions making loud spongy noises.

And now you are moving, panicked and lost. I am afraid of accordions, of spongy sounds, of losing my marbles.

...

"This is the Voice of Kenya Television. *The Six Million Dollar Man* is brought to you by K J Office Supplies."

"It looks good at NASA One."

"Roger. BCS arm switch is on."

"Okay, Victor."

"Lining rocket arm switch is on."

"Here comes the throttle. Circuit breakers in."

"We have separation."

"Roger."

"Inboard and outboards are on."

"I'm comin' a-port with the sideslip."

"Looks good."

"Ah, Roger."

"I've got a blowout—damper three!"

"Get your pitch to zero."

"Pitch is out! I can't hold altitude!"

"Correction, Alpha Hold is off, turn selectors—emergency!"

"Flight Com! I can't hold it! She's breaking up, she's break—"

...

It is Saturday.

I fake a nosebleed, and Mum lets me go to work with her.

I don't want to see Sophia Mwela. I know she will come to the hedge between our houses and call out for Ciru and ask her where her American cousin is.

She will be laughing.

I am not talking to Ciru. Nobody is laughing at her. I don't want to stay at home today. Jimmy does not know what happened. I am sure Ciru will tell him.

Mum has a hair salon, the only proper hair salon in Nakuru, which is the fourth-largest town in Kenya. It is called Green Art. Mum also sells paintings and wooden carvings.

I sit on the floor, at the foot of a huge hunched spaceman, in Mum's hair salon. I can smell coffee brewing, from Kenya Coffeehouse next door.

. . .

The hair-dryer spaceman has a gray plastic head. His face is a huge hole gaping at me, and the hole is a flat round net for him to blow hot air. I stick my own head into his helmet and play Six Million Dollar Man.

Mary is chatting with Mum about Idi Amin. They always talk about Idi Amin in Mary's language, Luganda, which Mum speaks even though it is not her language. Museveni's rebel army is gathering force in Tanzania. They chew roast maize slowly as they talk. Mum speaks Kinyarwanda (Bufumbira), Luganda, English, and Kiswahili. Baba speaks Gikuyu, Kiswahili, and English. We, the children, speak only English and Kiswahili. Baba and Mum speak English to each other.

I am going to be a quiet superhero today. Whooshing to the sky, with my invisible cape. With my bionic muscles.

I will show them.

"Steve. Austin. A me-aan brrely alive," I wreng wreng Americanly. "Gennlemen, we can rebuild him. We have the tek-nalagee. We can build the world's frrrrst bi-anic man . . . I can't hold her; she's brrreaking up! She's brrreaking—"

The plastic helmet of the hair dryer has steamed up from my breath. I start to write on it with my finger.

. . .

Mary has big soft eyes, and she rolls her hips when she walks, which always makes me and Ciru laugh.

Idi Amin is killing people and throwing them to the crocodiles. The Nile is blocked with dead bodies. We have many aunties and uncles in Uganda. My grandparents, my mum's parents, are in Uganda.

Baba's friend disappeared at the border, and all they found was his broken glasses in a mass grave.

Mary is from Buganda. She ran away to Kenya from Amin. Many people are running to Kenya from Amin. Mum is Bufumbira. But Mum speaks Mary's language because she went to a girls' school in Buganda, Uganda's best girls' school, Mt. St. Mary's Namagunga.

Mum's stomach has started to swell with a new baby. She wants another girl.

Mum met Baba when she was a student at Kianda College in Nairobi. He was very groovy. He had a motorbike and a car and had been to England. We are Kenyans. We live in Nakuru. Mum was born in Uganda, but she is now a Kenyan. Baba is a Kenyan. He is Gikuyu. He is the managing director of Pyrethrum Board of Kenya.

I like how Mary's fingers are able to do things even when her eyes are looking away. She moves customers' heads up and down, side to side, and her fingers click fast, like knitting needles, and the big bush of messed-up hair becomes lines, and towers, like our new roads, railways, and bridges.

Kenyatta is our president. He is the father of our nation.

Kenya is a peace-loving nation.

We are all pulling together, and in school we sing, *harambee*, which means we are pulling together, like a choir, or tug-of-war. Standing on the podium of the choir, waving a fly whisk, is a conductor, President Kenyatta, who has red scary eyes and a beard. One day, we are told, Kenyatta's Mercedes was stuck in the mud, and he shouted *harambee*, so that people would come and push and push his long Mercedes-Benz out of the mud, so we all push and pull together; we will get the Mercedes out of the mud.

Every so often Mary dips her finger into grease and runs lubrication down the corridors and grid streets, so they gleam like America on television. Sometimes she eats while she is doing this. Every few weeks a new hairstyle arrives, from West Africa, or AfricaAmerica, or Miriam Makeba, or *Drum* magazine and the Jackson Five: uzi, afro, raffia, or pineapple, and Mary immediately knows how to make it.

Kenyatta is the father of our nation. I wonder whether Kenya was named after Kenyatta, or Kenyatta was named after Kenya.

Television people say Keenya. We say Ke-nya. Kenya is fifteen years old. It is even older than Jimmy.

Kenya is not Uganda.

Rain rattles the corrugated iron roof of Green Art Hair Salon. Hot Uplands pork sausages are spitting in a frying pan. It is a storm now, and the sound of the rain swells loud like the crowd after a goal in a stadium.

The door opens with a whoosh and droplets of water hit my face from the outside.

Tingtingtingting.

There is an ache in my chest today, sweet, searching, and painful, like a tongue that is cut and tingles with sweetness and pain after eating a strong pineapple.

"I found you!"

Sophia will say, if she bursts into this salon right now.

I miss Ciru.

I am already full of things to tell her. If she were here, she would pull me out of inside myself. I would wobble for a moment, then run or tumble fast and firm behind her.

A group of women rush in. They are dressed for a wedding. They are hysterical. Their hot-combed hair shrunk in the rain. They had spent the whole night preparing at home. They are late for the wedding.

The bride is crying.

"Gennlemen, we can rebuild him. We have the tek-nalagee."

Mum issues instructions. Sharp voices explode: clunking and whooshing and foaming like hands shaking up cutlery in the sink. They bubble like water when it is starting to make glass. If you stack up all the layers of bubbles, you can make a window. It will be round and soft at first, so you can put a big book on it, and jump on it and jump on it and make it flat and hard and sure.

Maybe Liza's mother came with the wedding women? She will see me; everybody will know I dressed up like a girl yesterday.

Mum will find out I wore her clothes and wig.

Everybody is against me. The ache of my pineapple situation strums against my chest, and I let it yo-yo around. It feels good.

I hear feet clumping toward me. I jump off the seat under the hair dryer and lie on the floor, under the chair. I cover my face with my hands. A body thumps onto a chair; a head eases into the helmet. The dryer starts to wheeze, and I can feels bits of hot air on my head.

It is the bride! I peep up at her, through my raw yellow ache. Through the hands covering my face. She looks beastly with her eyes upside down and her pink-lipsticked mouth inverted. I am quickly tender and pineapple pink. Butterfly belly. Barefoot on hot gravel. Her lips are a pink baboon bum, which must really hurt. I harden my eyes, my heart.

I focus on the lips. They are a safer texture: pink-lipsticked toyland, the color of happy candy, and bubblegum balloons and hard, committed happiness.

I am quickly sharp and bright and happy. I take my hands away from my face, and stand up. She grimaces and shrieks.

"Oooooooh, whooo is that? Why are you hiding?"

My face falls.

"Don't cry! Oh, don't cry!"

Now I want to cry. Her face blurs, and everything is tangled and jagged. She leans toward me, this wedding woman with shrunken hair. Her mouth is now pink earthworms and snails and teeth. Her face swells down toward me, tearing out of the traffic jam of patterns, to present itself as whole and inevitable.

I gasp. And look. The beast is gone. She is a whole person, bland and indivisible again. I am in doubt about my own recent doubts. How could she have been anything other than the thing she is now?

"Mama Jimmy. Is this one your firstborn? Is this Jimmy?"

She has opened the closed cramped world. I have been trying to keep my lips tuckedtogethershut. Forever. Quiet. Opening two lips is tearing cobwebs. A silent superhero. Cool.

"Hello, auntie," I say, drawing pictures on the floor with my foot. The pineapple rises in my chest. Maybe she will give me some wedding cake? The squeaky painful taste of perfect white sweetness. Icing tastes in your mouth like Styrofoam sounds when it is rubbed against itself.

Almost too much.

I let my eyes rise slow and cute. This game I know. I tingle and let my eyes touch hers briefly, then I look down again.

She coos.

My mother turns toward us and looks sharply at me.

Does Mum know? Did Liza's mother call her?

Mum's voice is like shards of water and streams of glass. It rises up her throat like warm suds. She has a small double chin where this noise is made, a nasal accent, but not American, or English. Her nose is long and thin.

I have discovered that nasal accents come from people with long thin noses. Wreng wreng. My nose is thin, but not as thin as my mum's. Sometimes I try to hear myself, cupping my hand over my ear and twisting my mouth to the side, but I can't hear myself being nasal. Mum reaches out her hand and takes mine. She licks her finger and smooths my eyebrow. Her fingers reach around and pull me to her chest. My back recoils from the hard bump on her stomach. I don't want to crunch the baby. Mum smells good, like powder and perfume and burning hair oil.

"KenKen"—this is Mum's embarrassing nickname for me—"what are you doing there?" She laughs, and my heart purrs.

"He is my second-born. The shy one."

One bee does not sound like a swarm of bees. The world is divided into the sounds of onethings and the sounds of manythings. Water from the showerhead streaming onto a shampooed head is manything splinters of falling glass, ting ting ting.

All together, they are: shhhhhhhhhhh.

Shhhhh is made up of many many tinny tiny ting ting tings, so small that clanking glass sounds become soft whispers; like when everybody at the school parade is talking all at once, it is different from when one person is talking. Frying sausages sound like rain on a tin roof, which sounds like a crowd.

The rain is soft now. The wedding women are in rollers. The hair dryers are all blowing, red eyes. Mum pats the bride's hair and murmurs to her in Kiswahili, which Mum speaks in an accent full of coughing Ugandan *gh*'s and Rwandese *kh*'s. Her voice is soft, and tingly, and people get tingly with her and do what she says. She never shouts.

From outside, there is a sound of thudding metal. Mary rushes outside. Then Mary is shouting at somebody in her funny Kiswahili. Then there are screams. The wedding women stand up. We all rush to the door. The bride starts to cry again.

It is Mrs. Karanja. Mrs. Karanja owns Kenya Coffeehouse, next door to Mum's salon. She does not like it when we leave our municipal council garbage cans near her café. But that is where we are supposed to leave them. The council refuses to come into our courtyard to collect them.

There is sweat on her face. Her eyebrows are clean, perfectly drawn ovals, and her eyes and lashes are sticky with brown smudges. Brown paint leaks out of the outline, down her cheeks, and her ruby-painted mouth is lifted to one side, into a sneer. One of her teeth has a smudge of fluoride brown I have not seen before. She is pulling a giant tin garbage can, and Mary, who is dark and hard and thin, is pulling our garbage can back. There is garbage strewn all over the concrete.

Mrs. Karanja's manservant stands behind her, a Pokot man, a warrior dressed in cheap military khaki and sandals made from car tires. Jonas. He usually gives me tropical sweets when he sees me. I like to sit on his knee on his little stool. He has parallel lines cut into his face and torn ears that have been rolled up into themselves.

Mrs. Karanja has rich, buttery skin. When you draw the hair of ordinary people you can draw just random dots on the head for short hair, or wildly scribble around, with a crayon or pencil, for long hair. President Kenyatta calls ordinary people *wananchi.*

With overseas white people, and international music stars, like Diana Ross, or the Jackson Five, you draw the outline carefully and color or paint in yellow, or black, or brown inside, filling in all the gaps until the picture is one clear color and you cannot see lines or scratches, just yellow, brown, or black. When Ciru and I draw overseas people, we are careful to make them look like they do in the coloring books and on television.

Mrs. Karanja has penciled eyebrows, twin black unbroken lines that belong to people who have no gaps in them. But she is breaking. She is shouting, "Why do you put your garbage can next to mine? I am tired of this. Tired! You Ugandans spoiled your country—why do you want to come here and spoil ours?"

The rain has stopped, the sun is high, and the pavement is filling with pools of growing, shaking crowds. Bell-bottom trousers flap, and some bare feet are spread open like a fan from never wearing shoes. Groups of feet pound toward us: the curio dealers on Kenyatta Avenue, the brokers who hover outside the coffeehouse, the newspaper sellers, the people who are just there and bored and getting wet from the rain.

Mrs. Karanja shoves Mary, who falls to the ground. They are hitting each other now. Bodies shuffle uncertainly in the crowd, fingers rubbing thighs up and down, hands curled into themselves.

Mrs. Karanja screams, shoves Mary away, and stands and screams, and points at Mum. Mum grabs hard at my shoulder and pulls me to her chest. Her hand reaches for mine. I try to slip away, but she is faster than me.

The guard has let Mary go, but he stands behind her. She is breathing hard, her eyes wide, teary and wild, and they are fixed on Mrs. Karanja, who swivels from side to side.

No one speaks. The wedding women are silent. My ears heat up. It is as if Kenya is over there, with the crowd, and behind us are the wedding women—who have sided with Uganda. All of Kenya is pulled together by Mrs. Karanja. And the wedding women have been shamed to silence.

Crowd legs now shuffle toward each other, whispering and frowning and smirking, nostrils open and twitching. Even the municipal council *askari* does nothing. His truncheon sits helpless; his neck stretches forward toward Mrs. Karanja, his eyes wide.

Mum's hand is tight on mine. Bodies start to rub against each other. Mum will not let go of my hand. If I was a golf ball, I would roll fast and forward and hit that tin garbage can and let us tumble. I want to howl and put my head up Mrs. Karanja's skirt and make loud spitting snotty noises, or hit the concrete wall hard with my head, bounce back, satisfied that I am not rubber. People stream out of Barclays Bank, to join the crowd across the street. I am still trying to pull my fingers out of Mum's grip, so I can pinch her hard.

Mrs. Karanja walks to the corner and picks up another garbage can. This one is full. She kicks it over and stares at us.

There is a pile now, on the ground: old hair, thousands of tiny oily coils of black string from undone hair, wet grains of old tea, KCC milk packets, shampoo bottles, digestive biscuit packets, gray lumps of wet old newspapers, one Lyons Maid ice cream packet, several Elliot's Bread packets, a tin of Mua Hills plum jam, bottle tops, maize cobs that look like bared teeth, one Trufru orange squash bottle, one Lucozade bottle for when Ciru was sick, yellowing maize skins tangled with maize hair that looks like white people's hair, empty jars of Dax pomade, raffia packets, string, banana peels and maize cobs, ants.

"Go back inside the salon." She pushes my back.

I want to say no, but I move. I slam the door behind me. The gas flames are still heating the combs and the salon is hot and smells of burning hair and Idi Amin.

I stand on a chair and watch from the window.

Mum starts to pick up the garbage. Mary helps. Mrs. Karanja stands in front of the crowd and watches. When the first can is full, they leave it and head toward Mrs. Karanja's shop. They put it on the ground, between the two shops, where all the cans from the street are supposed to be.

Mrs. Karanja follows them.

"You will see. You will see."

The crowd is still. She summons the guard and tells him to spill the garbage outside Mum's door. He shrugs at the crowd, his eyes wary and afraid. He picks up the can, walks past Mum and Mary, avoiding their eyes, and then overturns it outside the door. He walks back, his shoulders sloping, following her back to the coffeehouse. A woman jumps out of the crowd and starts to help gather the garbage; soon there is a small group helping Mum and Mary. The wedding women jump forward and start collecting. Even the bride joins in.

Mum turns back to the salon, and Mary follows. The wedding women come back in. Everybody is quiet for a moment, and then the gasping chatter begins as the hair dryers start to roar.

Chapter Three

It is school break time, and cold. July. I am standing by the new school's new weather station watching aluminum cones fly in the wind and I see my father coming toward me.

I run to him and jump: uGhh! "You have heavy bones," he says. His hands are hard against my armpits and my nose burns from the cold air as I swing, like the wind cones.

It is not my birthday. Why is he here?

He says, "Go and call your sister."

Ciru comes. Jimmy is already in the car.

"You have a baby sister, at War Memorial Hospital."

Chiqy, my new sister, looks just like I did when I was a baby, says Mum.

I am triumphant.

Because she is also the second girl, she will have a first name of Bufumbira origin, like my name, Binyavanga. In my birth certificate, I am Kenneth Binyavanga Wainaina. She is named Kamanzi. Melissa Kamanzi Wainaina. We nickname her Chiqy. In our family, as in most Gikuyu families, the first boy and first girl are named after the paternal grandparents. The second boy and second girl are named after the maternal grandparents. Jimmy is called James Muigai Wainaina. Ciru is June Wanjiru Wainaina after my father's mother, Wanjiru. I am Binyavanga, after my mother's father, and so on. So Binyavanga becomes a Gikuyu name.

We are mixed-up people. We have mixed-up ways of naming too: the Anglo-colonial way, the old Gikuyu way, then the distant names from my mother's land, a place we do not know. When my father's brothers and sisters first went to colonial schools, they had to produce a surname. They also had to show they were good Christians by adopting a Western name. They adopted my grandfather's name as a surname. Wainaina.

Baba says, in the old days, everybody had many names, for many reasons, a name only for your age-mates, a name as the son of your mother, a new name after you became a man. These days, most times, your name is what is on your birth certificate.

...

We are afraid to be inside the house. Shapeless accordion forces have attacked the universe. Kenyatta, the father of Kenya, is dead. Mum is always tired, always talking to our new sister.

Last month the pope died, and this month the new pope died, the smiling pope. All day today, they showed on television grainy old reels of traditional Gikuyu dancers singing for Kenyatta. A man and a woman do a Gikuyu waltz, another man plays shapeless sounds from an accordion as they dance, and Kenyatta, large and hairy, sits on a podium. The mourning for Kenyatta seems to last forever. There is no school.

Georgie and Antonina are our new neighbors. We like to sneak through the hedge into their garden. A whole quarter acre of ripe maize fills the back of their garden.

One warmer-than-usual day, during this never-ending holiday, we run—happymanic with uncertainty, fallen leaves crackling and breaking—and play, sun hot and sure. Soft feathers and grass in an abandoned bird's nest smell good, rotting and feathery. We find rats' nests and mongrel puppies as we run with yellow and brown beetle kites. We tie the legs of the beetles with string and let them fly behind us. Hot syrup sweat drips into eyes and stings, and I am lost in this wheat-colored world of flapping leaves and bare feet digging into hot soil.

We forget to sneak back in time, and as we squeeze through the hole in the kei apple hedge, there is Mum, a belt in hand, carrying baby Chiqy. Chiqy is crying, Mum's face stony and silent. When she gets angry she does not talk.

At the corner of this fence there is a dead log, an old eucalyptus tree, and an abandoned car we mutilate every day. As we follow Mum, pleading, I stop for a moment to perform the ritual of this place. Every time we knock on the old log, ants come streaming out. They don't stop.

Sometimes so many come out they swarm into our clothes. You hit it and hit them, and they keep swarming out of the dead log. They have patterns I can't see, but they keep perfect rhythm and time. You knock, they stream, there are endless streams hidden below safe logs, speaking not your language, arranged not like you have been taught to know.

···

It is dark and I don't know where Ciru and Jimmy are. When the afternoon shadows strike, I knock on Mum's door. She does not open. I walk to the sitting room, rubbing my back against the wall the whole way, to feel the world.

I am hungry, but do not want to go to the kitchen. The giant portrait of Kenyatta is in the dining room. His eyes watch you, red and real. I turn on the television. Cartoons. I call out, loud, for Jimmy and Ciru to join me. They don't come. I can hear them playing outside. I sit on the big green velvet sofa.

Every day, all day, we see Kenyatta lying flat and dead on television, and people come to see his body. His body is gray and covered with death-snot.

I want to explode like frying Uplands pork sausages.

The pouting tip of my cock hurts, swells, and tickles against my trousers. Then jazz trumpets burst the pressure open, and wonderful warmth seeps into my underwear, flutes down my thigh, into the spongy green velvet under my bum, a smooth steady stream of sound and liquid.

I run outside to find Ciru and Jim, before Mum finds out what I have done. My eyes are shut when I streak past the dining room.

···

Mum makes us supper, and that is nice. Baby Chiqy is sleeping. Then Mum goes away to feed Chiqy, and Baba is not yet home. If goat tripe could sing, this is what it would sound like, boiling goat tripe singing on television, singing for Kenyatta. Jimmy is in his room listening to *Top of the Pops* on BBC Radio. He is in a groovy mood, which means he wants nothing to do with us. Ciru and I are jumping on the sofas, trying to fill the strange silence with action.

An old man grins on the black-and-white screen. His beard shifts. Teeth flash. He pushes a stick across a wooden bow and string, tripe and beans boiling and spreading into the house on a hot day. My bright yellow mouth organ is stuck in my mouth and shaped like a maize cob. I am talking all muffled and letting the sounds of my words hum out of the organ. The music sounds like, like chaos.

Television voice: "This delegation from Nyanza Province is playing a *nyatiti*. They have come to sing for the late President Kenyatta. A *nyatiti* is a traditional Luo musical instrument."

Matiti. Ciru giggles. I giggle. Titi. Titties.

We like to play Maasai sometimes. This means taking off our clothes and thrusting our necks forward and making guttural sounds. We move faster and faster, making our bodies perfect anarchy. Soon we are timeless beasts, carried by dizziness and adrenalin, no thoughts or plans or ideas, no past or pattern.

The old man has a colobus monkey–skin crown. He makes belly sounds—shaking, shapeless sounds. He rubs the stick up and down, up and down against the string; the tail of each upward movement accordions dangerously against my chest. I roll across the carpet on my stomach and put my eyes next to the screen. I have done this before. Close to the screen, my panic fades. It is clear that their faces are fully owned by the television screen: they have been broken into thousands of small dots; the television has counted every piece that makes them up and they have no mystery. But when I back away from the screen, the man's shapeless sounds grab me again.

Ciru and I are jumping up and down on the springs of the sofa, and laughing and pointing at the man. We find a strong rhythm and can't stop laughing. We hug each other, and roll, Ciru and I, laughing. Our bellies hurt. I lie down and face the ceiling, which is clear and white, and my stomach settles, and I can hear the *nyatiti* rubbing away.

In my mouth is the plastic yellow grin world of the toy maize cob harmonica: fixed, English speaking, Taiwan made, safe, imported un-blemished plastic, an Americangrinning mouth organ, each hole a clear separate sound. In school we were taught that all music comes from eight sounds: do, re, mi, fa, sol, la, ti, do—but what those people are singing and playing cannot fit those sounds. Gibberish. Kenyatta is dead. Those red blowtorch eyes in the dining room pulling together all those gathered *harambee* sounds of people in the many costumes of Kenya, singing and dancing in no choir, many unrelated sounds and languages and styles and costumes, and facial expressions.

They have nothing to do with each other.

Ki-may.

This is my new word, my secret. *Ki. Maay.* I let my jaw fall slack, with the second syllable, like a cartoon man with a cash register jaw. *Ki-maaay.* It calls at the most unexpected moment. Certainty loses its spine, and starts to accordion. My jaw moves side to side, like a mouth organ. Once the word lives, *kima-aay*, it makes its own reality. I rub the word against the roof of my mouth, which is ridged like the ribs of some musical instrument. I swing my jaw slackly from side to side, let small marbles of yodel clamber up my throat, from my chest, let the breaking waves of yodel run on my tongue and leap into the shape of the word, *kie-mae-ae-ae-y . . . eay . . .*

Kimay is the talking jazz trumpet: sneering skewing sounds, squeaks and strains, heavy sweat, and giant puffed-up cheeks, hot and sweating; bursting to say something, and then not saying anything at all; the hemming and hawing clarinet. *Kimay* is yodeling Gikuyu women, Scottish square dancing to the accordion-playing man who wears a hat with a feather. It is a neon man called Jimmy, who has a screaming guitar and a giant Afro. It is ululating Gikuyu women crying around Kenyatta's body on television. Gurgling Maasai men jumping up and down. Luo men in feathers and Kenyatta beards, nyatittying. Congo men singing like women.

I can speak English. I can speak Kiswahili. *Ki-may* is any language that I cannot speak, but I hear every day in Nakuru: Ki-kuyu, Ki-Kamba,

Ki-Ganda, Ki-sii, Gujarati, Ki-Nyarwanda, (Ki) Ru-fumbira. *Ki-May.* There are so many, I get dizzy. *Ki-may* is the accordion, the fiddle, the bagpipe, the trumpet. All those spongy sounds.

I fear slides and bagpipes, swings and dizziness, Idi Amin, and traditional dancers yodeling around the dead president on television. Most of all I fear accordions.

Chapter Four

It is a Sunday. I am nine. We are sitting on a patch of some tough nylon grass next to the veranda. Mum has brought out her Ugandan mats. I am reading a new book. I am reading a new book every day now. This book is about a flamingo woman; she is a secretary, her sticklike legs improbable in cloggy high heels, her handbag in her beak.

Flying away.

The flamingo book came with a carton of books my mum bought from American missionary neighbors who were going back home. The sun is hot. I close my eyes and let the sun shine on my eyelids. Red tongues and beasts flutter, aureoles of red and burning blue. If I turn back to my book, the letters jumble for a moment, then they disappear into my head, and word-made flamingos are talking and wearing high heels, and I can run barefoot across China, and no beast can suck me in, for I can run and jump farther than they can.

On my trampoline of letters and words.

Mum is shelling peas and humming, and our bodies all hum smoothly with her. Chiqy is peeling petals off flowers; Ciru is running around with a yo-yo from the same American carton of goodies. When Ciru laughs, everybody laughs, and when she is running and laughing, everybody is warm and smiling.

Yellow dahlias hang their heads and start to shed their petals. I think about making a kite, like Jimmy showed us. Take a newspaper. Baba will beat you if you use the Sunday *Nation*. Cut one page off its twin. Use a knife to split a stick of old bamboo from the fence. Tape sticks, diagonally, with cellotape. Three holes in a triangle, in the right place. Make a long long newspaper tail. Run. Run run.

There are two old kites stuck on the electrical wire. We got into trouble for that.

Standing here, we can see my whole hometown—stretched springs of smoke and the silos, one a clump of four tall, glued-together concrete cylinders, Unga (flour) Ltd, and the other two separate metallic blue and silver tubes, silos, where Baba works, Pyrethrum Board of Kenya. We call it Pie Board. He is the managing director. It is a farmers' marketing cooperative. There is a factory. Labs and research scientists. Processing. Pyrethrins are a key ingredient for international insecticides. Like Johnson's It.

Behind us is Menengai Crater; to the west, sitting under Nakuru Golf Club, is Lena Moi Primary, where we all go to school. At the bottom, near the lake, are thousands of tiny rusty-metal-roofed houses. When school bells ring, tens of thousands of people come streaming out of those homes.

Ciru has been number one in her class every term since she was five. Last term I surprised everybody, including myself, and beat Ekya Shah and was number one in my class. I like the new things we do, like English composition, and geography especially. You don't lose marks for handwriting, and my handwriting is terrible. I do not concrentrate in class, but I read everything I can touch.

Daniel Toroitich arap Moi is our new president. He is young, awkward, and fumbling, but clean, tall, and sharp in a suit. He is on television, moving like an accordion, apologizing in his uncertain voice for just being here. He has found himself at the center of things and does not know what to do now that he is no longer Kenyatta's vice president.

Like Mary, in our class, who is large and hulking and always bent over scribbling. She pretends she can read, but sometimes we catch the book upside down, her body locked into a fierce bow, her eyes glaring at the book.

My neck and ears burn when I see a teacher turn to her and say, "Mary, what is the answer?"

Sometimes we like Moi because he fumbles, like all of us. He isn't booming like Kenyatta, or polished and slick like Charles Njonjo. His English stumbles; his Kiswahili is broken and sincere. We have no idea what man and mind he is in his home language, Tugen. That is a closed world to the rest of the country outside his people. We are not curious about that world. We make a lot of jokes about him.

It is almost lunchtime, and boiled cauliflower looms. We live on top of the hill. We look down on the town. From here, looking down on Nakuru, everywhere there are purple, puffed-up cabbages of blooming jacaranda heads. Cauliflowering, I think. I shudder and look away.

I look past the silos, to the edge of town: the symmetrical fields of green maize. Kellogg's Corn Flakes. Then wheat. Weetabix is unbeatabix. All around, in the distance, are mountains.

Nakuru is a high-altitude town at the bottom of the Rift Valley. This geography-class contradiction confuses me. Ciru and I like to call Kenya's tallest building Kenyatta Cornflakes Center.

Brown is near. Green far. Blue farthest. The hills in the distance are dark. Maasailand.

From here you can see Kenya's main highway—the Mombasa-Kisumu Road, where there are often long, long lines of army tanks and trucks going to the Lanet barracks. Uganda is still falling. Idi Amin ran away. They killed all the prisoners and left blood and guts in the prison. Some bodies had no heads. Tanzania and Museveni attacked Amin. Mum is on the phone a lot with uncles and aunties. Most of them are now all over the world.

President Moi says Kenya is an Island of Peace. President Moi says Somali Shifta bandits are trying to destabilize Kenya. Somali Shiftas don't tuck in their shirts. The king of Rwanda is nearly seven feet tall and is always standing outside Nairobi Cinema, where women come and kneel in front of him. He is not allowed into Rwanda. He is a refugee. He used to flirt with Mum before she met and fell in love with Baba.

Kings are in trouble. From presidents. The Buganda king is a waiter in London. Uganda is a picture on a map, shaped like the back of the bumpy head of somebody facing giant Congo stubbornly, his long *kimay* jaw swaying as it cuts into Rwanda. His face is full of lakes and rivers.

Presidents are also in trouble from generals. Like Uganda, and Sudan to the north. Everybody is in trouble from communists. Like

Mengistu Haile Mariam, whose hand I shook when he visited Baba's factory with President Moi and our school choir sang for him. He was very short and had size five Bata shoes, exactly my size. Lord Baden-Powell was also a size five. He left his footprint at Rowallan campsite in Nairobi.

In every classroom there is a map with a photo of the president's head in the center of each African country. Kenya is an island of peace, it says on TV all the time. People should stop politicking, Moi says.

Mum's home in Uganda is near the border with Rwanda, near Congo. She can't go to visit; the border is closed.

I look up from my book, from the surety of flying flamingo secretaries, look up first at the sky, then at pink and blue Lake Nakuru below us. A first word and picture book, my own book, snaps into place in my mind. In it, clouds are the hair of God. He is old and balding. The radiant blue light leaks out of his head. We sit inside him, receiving rain and sun, thunder and lightning.

I look up to watch the flamingos rise up from the lake, like leaves in the wind. Our dog, Juma, is grinning, mouth open and panting and harmless, and I have this feeling. It is a pink and blue feeling, as sharp as the clear highland sky. Goose bumps are thousands of feathers, a swarm of possible people waiting to be called out from the skin of the world, by faith, by the right words, the right breeze.

The wind swoops down, God breathes, and across the lake a million flamingos rise, the edges of Lake Nakuru lift, like pink skirts swollen by petticoats, now showing bits of blue panties, and God gasps, the skirts blow higher, the whole lake is blue and the sky is full of circling flamingos.

Chapter Five

Ciru and I are still in Lena Moi Primary School. Jimmy is now in form three in a boarding school called St. Patrick's Iten. Chiqy is four, and looks a lot like me. I am eleven.

Last night we had a storm, the biggest one anybody can remember. Two windows broke, and this morning we found a giant eucalyptus tree lying flat on the ground, its roots muddy and shivering with dew and earth. There are flat clouds where sky meets earth. Flat and clean and gray, like old suds. The light of the sun falls in soft shafts and everything gleams with God behind it. The air is fresh, and we are all quiet in the car on our way to school: fences, trees, and garbage are piled on every elbow of road and land.

We drive into school but can't see anybody. My father is irritated with me. He makes me tie my shoelaces. He redoes my tie. For years I will hide from him my inability to tie a tie, to tie my shoelaces, to tell the time, and, later on, my inability to do long multiplication. Friends will tie my tie for me, and I will keep it tied for a whole term.

But today seems special. The soft mouth of God is blowing moist air at us; we run through dots and dashes of shadow into soft peeping light. We run onto the pavements; long bungalows of classrooms stretch. We run zigzag, swing off one pole and vault to the next. We break out to the back, past the drinking-water tap, past the long line of caterpillar trees, which nobody will stand under for fear that the hairy green caterpillars will fall on their heads, to the field, where everybody is playing. The caterpillars cover the tree, like leaves.

In one week, all of Nakuru will be covered by a million white butterflies with pink nostrils. The grass is still damp, still long from the rain, and we watch for knots. When the grass is long we all like to tie clumps into knots that people can trip on. People are spread out all over the field, and we have no idea what they are doing. It is drizzling softly.

Then we see them. All over the field. Brought down from the sky, by the storm. Furry balls of gray. Other clumps of pink and gray. And just pink. Many of them are dead. Others have been eaten by dogs, others flutter about weakly. There are pink feathers everywhere; entrails and bone and soft, beautiful pink and string and jelly flesh. Feathers everywhere. There are clumps of ant sculptures, rolling and reshaping like clouds. Bubbles of blood. Crunched bone. For the whole morning, we pick up the baby flamingos that are still alive, and hand them to Kenya Wildlife Service people.

Lena Moi Primary School used to be Lugard School, a whites-only school until the 1960s. Now it is named after Lena Moi, the abandoned wife of our president, Daniel Toroitich arap Moi. When Moi was vice president, she slapped him during a Madaraka Day dance, in front of President Kenyatta, who laughed at him, and that made him angry and now we hear she cannot leave her farm. She comes from an important Kalenjin family, the Bommets, a big farming family, one of the first in the Rift Valley to become Christians and go to mission school. Some of them go to my school. Many Nakuru people like Lena Moi, because it used to be the white school in Nakuru. There are no whites left. There is one Japanese student.

President Moi doesn't come from an important family. He was only a primary school teacher before entering politics. He is always being shamed. When Moi was vice president, Kenyatta's friends treated him like a child. One policemen, a Gikuyu, would stop and search his car whenever he was going home. The policeman's name is Mr. Mungai, and two of his sons are in our school. He is very short, and he keeps horses. Once Mr. Mungai slapped Moi. Now that Moi is president, Mr. Mungai has left the country. President Moi wants to detain him. The school hedge runs along the road where this happened, the road to Kabarak, his wife's home, now Moi's home. Past the road to Eldoret and finally to Uganda. President Moi likes primary school choirs and gives choirmasters big promotions.

One Sunday afternoon we go to town, Mum, Ciru, and I, to buy chicken and chips for supper. Kukuden. The streets of Nakuru are empty. People are at home. Even from here, two miles away, I can hear the Salvation Army band at the bottom of town, near Lake Nakuru. There is a lorry parking lot across the road from Kukuden. And from one of the lorries a cassette tape is playing.

Congo music, with wayward voices as thick as hot honey. This sound is dangerous; it promises to lift you from where you are and drop you into a hot upside-down place twenty thousand leagues under the sea. *Kimay.* Guitar and trumpet, parched like before the rains, dive into the honey and out again. A group of men unload sacks of potatoes, and they are singing to the music. The song bursts out with the odd Kiswahili phrase, then forgets itself and starts on its gibberish again.

The voices plead in a strange jangling language, Lingala, which sounds familiar—it has Kiswahili patterns and words—but I can't understand it. It stirs something green and creamy in my belly, and I am nauseous. Men are sending their voices higher than voices should travel, letting their voices flow, slow and thick. The song's structure is . . . different, not like the easy melodies of school, the tamed do-re-mi-fa Kiswahili songs we sing for choir.

I am starting to read storybooks. If words, in English, arranged on the page have the power to control my body in the world, this sound and language can close its folds, like a fan, and I will slide into its world, where things are arranged differently, where people like Jonas, the Pokot guard, live, and in that place anything can happen to you.

I like choir. The school lets choir members off class twice a week in the afternoons to meet kids from other schools and practice for a giant group called Massed Choir that has kids from all twenty-two municipal schools. We go to the stadium and practice, over a thousand of us, to sing praise songs composed by our teachers for the president on Madaraka Day on June 1. It is fun. The music teachers of several schools compose the praise songs, and the best ones get to become headmasters or even go to work at the Presidential Music Commission near State House in Nairobi.

English is Kenya's official language. All documents that are legal and official must be in English. Kiswahili is not compulsory in school; it is our national language. That is what our constitution says. So, we have news in English and Kiswahili. Most Kenyans speak some Kiswahili. Our constitution does not name our other languages. I think it is because we want to eradicate tribalism. We are not allowed to speak "mother tongue" in school. In school, Mrs. Gichiri, our headmistress, reacts strongly to girls who are prrr-oud, who show vanity, who prrr-een themselves. Naughty boys get four on the buttocks; proud girls get four on their palm.

Prrr, said the whistle. A warning not to exceed yourself. The world in English has sharp edges. *Pr* words in English promise good futures to people who stick to brittle boundaries; *prrr* words promise breaking to those who dare to dance to *kimay*. Kenyan English places have stainless steel whistles, which tell you to march this way; they shrill sharply when you cross a line. There are bells and parades and posted rules and glasses and cups, which are all breakable. People who do not speak Kiswahili use enamel cups.

Prrr-oud. I like those sharp shrill controlling words that sound like they come from an officer's whistle. Prim. Prude. Proper. Price. Probe. Prance. Preen. Prrr-een. Baba says the pound is growing rich against the shilling. More white people are leaving Kenya, more Indians. The shops that supplied us with books and toys and British comics like *Beezer*, *Beano*, and *Topper* are becoming expensive.

If I visit you in your home and your mother starts to speak to you in your language while I am there, you will roll your eyes at me, and reply to her in English or in Kiswahili, because we have agreed that parents are ridiculous that way. More than anything, we laugh at and dislike those kids who seem unable to escape their tribe.

Sometimes we practice traditional songs for the interschool music festival. We try to make sure we do not shake our bodies too much so that we step out of the lines and lose our place. It is important that we move our limbs together, and keep in tune, and follow the conductor.

At practice, the conductor, our music teacher Mr. Dondo, keeps us in do-re-mi-fa key with his mouth organ before we start. Don't move like a villager, he likes to say. We often do not know the meaning of the traditional song we are singing, but we learn the words well. Mr. Dondo has been promoted. He is now the deputy headmaster.

When two boys come to school one day sunburned and smelling of the village, where they had gone for a funeral, their hair was gone, shaved clear with a razor blade, scalps shining from animal fat.

They are toxic. They do not turn up for choir practice.

As money gets tighter, middle-class parents prefer to have their kids walking to school, and don't mind the shortcuts. Soon kids are buying lunch in little illegal kiosks outside the school. Soon we cross into the other world, to buy handmade wire cars and trade homing pigeons from kids who speak strange languages, who laugh if you speak English to them—they understand it, but find it pretentious; kids who wear no shoes, kids who miss school a lot, and have babies very early and smell of smoke from charcoal cooking, who go hunting with dogs and catapults for antelopes and rabbits and pigeons, in the forest above our home, for fun.

Outside the once neat school hedge, through its holes, zigzag paths make their way through every part of town. Andazi, the school gardener, is getting old; he has been in this school since white people were here, and he says we have spoiled it.

I grew two inches this term, and my voice just broke, and I got kicked out of the choir because I squeak a lot. There are informal kiosks sprouting everywhere, selling everything from batteries to fresh vegetables, between the thorny hedges that are starting to grow wild in English-speaking Nakuru. There are a lot of things coming from Tawian, and fewer things coming from Britain. Baba says the British make good things but never learned how to market them, because the colonials had to buy what they made. There are hawkers now, walking the streets selling Tawian things, and more shops are closing.

Look! Look at Michael Jackson move, as if he cannot break. We try to dance like him.

Baba wakes us up this morning and tells us that there has been a coup d'état led by junior soldiers in the air force. There is shooting all over Kenya. We stay home the whole day. The government was taken over by an air force private. There is shooting in Nairobi all day, and rumors that the streets are piled high with bodies. Indian shops are looted. Many women are raped. There are curfews, for months, and arrests. Some of the Gujarati-speaking kids from school have left for London and Toronto. Nobody really can keep the holes in the hedges sealed.

Kenya is not Uganda. Kenya has big roads and railways and tall buildings, science and technology, research and big planes and thousands of troops and machine guns and missiles. With only a few guns and some ragtag soldiers, air force Private Ochuka is, for six hours, the president of Kenya. In the afternoon, the coup is put down, and thousands are killed. Nairobi has corpses everywhere.

Chapter Six

Cleophas works at home for us, as a gardener and cook. He used to be a caddy and dreams of becoming a pro golfer. He is cool and has a big Afro. Once he took me to watch *ABBA: The Movie*. During Kenyatta's time, he was always getting arrested because he looks like a Ugandan. He comes from Kakamega, in Western Province.

One day, after school, I am bored and do not have anything to read. I am twelve. Mum won't let me go to the library because they found out that I had managed to spend the whole year avoiding math homework and reading novels in class. We are writing national exams this year, Ciru and I, and Mum and Baba are being strict. Ciru is getting all girly girly lately and does not like to play or talk. She locks her room a lot and says things like "But Michael Jackson is so sensitive."

I go to visit Cleophas in the servants' quarters, hoping he has time to talk, or play music, or maybe he will take me to the kiosk to buy sweets. The door is only partly closed. There is somebody else in his room. A woman.

Their voices are floating on wet parachutes. Sometimes a sharp squeal or a groan breaks out of the breath-coated chat. She giggles, and he says something gruffly back. My neck is hot. Their laughter steams, puffs. She cries out. The metal safari bed keeps banging against the wall. I can't move. This room was once a stable for horses, during colonial days. It is dark and hot and has a green wooden window. They put in a cement floor after it was converted into rooms for servants in the sixties, before we moved here. I want to leave but can't. The lumps wriggle under the blankets. Cleophas moans, loudly; his head leans up and back. I jump up and shout something incoherent. She screams and sits up, her face ripe and wild. "Get out," he shouts. "Out!" Cleophas leaps out of the bed, covers his crotch with a thin gray blanket, still shouting, and slams the door.

One day Mum fires Cleophas. She refuses to say why.

Jimmy is home on half term, and I have found science. It is round and perfect, like a circle. One day I am reading Erich von Däniken in our bedroom. Jimmy lies on his bed next to me.

"Jim," I say, "if Atlantis was in the Mediterranean?"

"Hmmm . . ." says Jim.

"And the Mediterranean is where there are dolphins?"

"Yeah," he says.

"And dolphins are the most intelligent animals?"

"Yes," he says.

"And they like people, they are the only wild animals that like people?"

"Yeah," says Jim. He is not really listening.

"And . . . and Atlantis drowned in the sea? And the people disappeared, and there are no skeletons to be found?"

"A-huh? So?"

"So I know what happened! They evolved! The dolphins are the people from Atlantis!"

He looks across lazily at me. He is listening to *Top of the Pops* on BBC shortwave. Boomtown Grunts and Stray Cats. "That is silly," he says.

"Why?" I ask.

"When you drown, you drown."

I am quiet for a while, then I say, "But, but . . . they were an advanced civilization; they used science."

Wambui is fifteen, and she is our new nanny. She is round and hard, with round hard breasts. She comes from Dundori, where her parents got land after Independence and they grow potatoes. She likes killing chickens. She cuts their heads off and lets them run around and around and around. She laughs, and we laugh with her. We love her. She can carry all we throw at her, and she is much more than we have known. We are afraid of her.

One of her front teeth is cracked, and is stained brown. Too much fluoride in Dundori water. We have a teacher we call Fluorosis, because all his teeth are brown. Wambui's face is so angled and certain, her smile so crooked and mischievous, that she is the first nanny we have had whom we cannot control. It is clear she can go further than any of us, in any direction, good or bad, violent or funny. Her smile is a sharp lopsided V against a smooth black face—no brown or red in her skin at all. She has two shocking interruptions: sharp conical bones on each cheek, pushing her face forward and sliding down to her jaw. These and the patches of darker skin that ring her wide round eyes sometimes give her face a feverish look. She likes to read Longman Pacesetter novelettes.

One day, a few months ago, I was sitting on the veranda and I overheard Wambui on the phone. She was laughing breathily, and saying, "Ohhhh. I am mashure. I am not young. Ohhhh. I am very mashure." Her voice sounded funny and nasal, and she kept laughing hah hah hah hah . . . laughing fake, like a woman on *Love Boat* or *Hart to Hart*. "Ohhhh," her voice high and shrill like a TV and fake, "I am verry prrretty," she said, in English. Her feet were drawing maps on the ground and she was looking uncommonly shy. I burst out laughing.

She put down the phone and shouted, "Nitakuchinja kama jogoo."

I will slaughter you like a cockerel.

One day President Moi drives past our school in his motorcade. He stops. He donates a whole small truck of Orbit chewing gum. We giggle at his accent.

The morning after Moi's visit, the whole school is repainted. We are still chewing his gum. Orbit chewing gum. Gum is banned in school, but Mrs. Gichiri says nothing. Andazi, the gardener, sulks the whole day, saying this sort of thing never happened when white people were in charge. We are told that the president owns the company.

Starting today, our school is no longer Lena Moi Primary School; it is a newly painted Moi Primary School. All the old rubber stamps and exercise books are collected, all stationery, anything with the word *Lena* disappears.

Many new kids start arriving in the school. Kalenjin kids, at every level, every class. Some of the richer families, the Kenyan Asian families, move their kids to the private schools abandoned by many of the white settler families ten years ago. Greensteds. St. Andrews Turi. They want to do British system exams, are worried.

My father does not believe in private schools for Kenyan citizens. He believes it is up to us to make things work. I would not mind going to do GCEs. The local British-curriculum school has a swimming pool and horse riding, and is called Greensteds. Life there sounds very much like an Enid Blyton novel. Ekya Shah, who was briefly my best friend, went there, but hasn't spoken to me since he left. He hiccups his consonants now, like a proper Brit.

Wambui takes us to visit Railway quarters one day. The good thing about Wambui is that she takes us to places our parents or school would not approve of. She has friends there, who live in a row of one-room houses with green doors. Clothes flap on the line directly above them, and other clothes are being washed at a tap by young girls and wives.

The buildings are very old, some of the oldest in the country outside the coast, as old as the railway, the origin and spine of what we now call Kenya. Built by the British in 1901, it opened up East Africa for proper conquest. Today, the railway is collapsing. In the 1970s, some tycoons close to Kenyatta wanted to make money from trucking, to break the grip the Luo had over railway jobs. They let the railway collapse. Fungi spread on the open pipes, and green tears stream down peeling walls. A toy safari-rally car leans against a wall streaked with the charcoal scribbles of children.

It is made from wire shaped into the frame of a car and held together with thin strips cut from the inner tube of a tire. The car is complete with a long steering wheel for a child to grip and run in any direction, making hooting and growling sounds. Railway children make the best wire cars—crouched and grimacing, with steering that makes the wheels turn; with paper mudguards, number plates, and springy aerials thrust from the back of the car. When the railway was being built, in the first few years of the twentieth century, the British fought a war with the Nandi, who were stealing copper wire.

In between some of the ceilings, under the old corrugated iron roof, young men keep carrier pigeons, and their feathers are clustered in the roof drains. Jimmy comes here a lot. He likes carrier pigeons, and dogs, and has friends here.

One woman is sprawled on the grass, elbow crossed over her eyes, sleeping, her whole body receiving the sun. The smell of fish, dry fish, cooking fish, and boiling, bitter green vegetables is everywhere. It smells like a foreign country—a hot and languid place. Dried fish from Lake Victoria. Many railway employees come from all over East Africa. The railway was once the East African Railways, but Idi Amin became the Ugandan president, and Mwalimu Julius Nyerere is a communist, so the East African community collapsed. To re-create Kampala and Kisumu heat in these highlands, these women keep food boiling on stoves, and sit inside steaming courtyards and small rooms.

Two women's heads are held at the knee by their hairdressers, legs wide open. There is a pile of discarded pea pods, *sukuma-wiki* stems, and potato peels next to the tap, covered with a large web of slime. Brackish, soapy water glides into an open drain where ducklings swim. Ducks with mossy, muddy bellies wander about. One of the women, in a blue and white *kikomi* outfit, starts to talk to Wambui in Dholuo.

"Who is Engine?" asks Wambui.

"Ai? You speak Luo?" Ciru asks Wambui.

"I used to speak it well, but I forgot much of it."

Ciru and I look at each other. When Wambui speaks Luo, her body language changes. Her face becomes more animated, does more moving than her arms; her mouth pouts, her arms rest akimbo. Wambui is awkward in English, crude and ungrammatical in Kiswahili.

"He! Engine ni mwingine," says the woman in Kiswahili. Engine is something else.

"Kwani?" Wambui asks.

"I have never seen someone like that one. Chu chu chuuu all the time. He—huyo, he has no brakes when he is with a woman."

A child runs past roaring like a rally car as he steers his wire Datsun 160J. We laugh.

"He is an engineer—his mother was a Goan, from India. His father was a rich Maasai. He has women all over the railway line."

All the women start laughing. The sleeping woman wakes up suddenly and stands slowly, her *lesso* falling off. She reties it, and I see twin strings of beads running around her waist. Wambui told me beads are for making men happy in bed. I am not sure how. Wambui is winking at Ciru. Those two have secrets, and I don't like it. I miss Cleophas.

The woman stands. She is not young. In her sixties maybe. Straight and lean with sharp buttocks outlined against her *lesso*, and very short gray hair, cut like a boy's.

Time stops for a moment as she walks toward the communal kitchen. Her head is a pot gently placed on a long, straight neck, where it rocks gently from side to side; giant metal loop earrings dance with the sway; hips and buttocks are a pendulum of tight flesh. Her back is perfectly straight.

Wambui turns to Ciru and whispers sharply, "You see, I told you. The best way is to practice by carrying pots on your head."

To practice what? I have no idea, but I nod hard at them both to pretend I understand. Wambui catches my eye, mid-nod, and winks. I blush. I cannot wink well. I have practiced a cool wink many times in front of the mirror but can't get one eye to shut confidently on its own.

I have learned to lift one eyebrow really high, and keep my lips straight, which I like to do in school if somebody says something I think is too stupid for words. I call it my supercilious manner. I have tried to cultivate a sneer, but it is not very good. Wambui has an epic sneer.

There is a guy in my school, called Moses, who can keep one eye low and cool, like Steve Austin in *The Six Million Dollar Man*. Moses's father owns a nightclub. Girls like him. My nose sweats a lot these days, and my armpits smell, and I wake up at a lot at night all wriggly and hot, like Congo rumba music. I send Wambui my most supercilious eyebrow. She does not even see it—she is huddled with Ciru, and they are giggling at something.

...

It is dark. Mum and Baba are out. They have gone to State House for a Madaraka Day dance. Baba hates going. Mum likes it, because she can dress up. People from school went for choir at the stadium this morning. They will show the Massed Choir on TV tonight on *Yaliotokea*.

Sometimes Wambui talks about going to Amigos Disco. Amigos is famous in Nakuru, and I have a picture of it in my head, gray and silver, full of orange and green polyester shirts and orange bell-bottoms, bouncing Afros and sweat. Boogie down. Wambui rubs soap on her legs every day after washing us. She tells us stories about about the village, cows, digging with a hoe, maize and beans, hard hands, hunting for pigeons with the barefoot boys, and Mau Mau days. Her grandmother was in the Mau Mau. She knows how to play soccer; she can make and shoot a catapult.

She likes to talk about the corrugated iron township, Boney M., Sister Sledge, Tabu Ley, and Maroon Commandos. When she speaks English, her *r*'s and *l*'s get tangled up, like my hair if I comb it dry. All her *d*'s become merged with *n*'s. All her *b*'s merge with *m*'s. Maloon Commados. M'boney M. She makes us laugh. Idepedence Nday.

It is dark. Chiqy, my baby sister, is asleep. Wambui is plaiting Ciru's hair in Mum's chair in the sitting room. I am not happy. I am used to moving from Ciru's bold girlness to a boyishness that stands behind Jimmy. I don't have anybody to follow.

I move to the back of the sofas by the windows, which are cool from the night outside. The curtains of the television room are green on white: thick, stately, teeming with life, an ecosystem of snarling flower heads, ecstatic stems and leaves bent forward, like italics.

Now they are putting on Mum's lipstick and makeup. *Mmmm-pah.*

They keep smacking in front of a small mirror. *Mmmm-pah*. Sometimes they try on Mum's shoes and clothes.

The news is over, and now there is a full hour of Independence Day ceremonies on television. Wambui likes *Yaliotokea*.

Mp-ah. M*h. They still kiss the mirror, and now they are putting on face powder.

Trumpets are blaring on television and groups start to march. *Mp* and *mpr* words. You have to inhale and push enough air down your mouth to make sure that you make a promising *mpr*. Permanent bonds. On headstrong things. Boys. Paper. Stubborn girls. Citizens. Two solid things meet, and one is, or both are, left changed forever.

Imprint. Impress.

Trains and trains of people swarm the screen. Schoolchildren; Salvation Army bands, the navy, the army, teachers' choirs, traditional singers from all over Kenya, religious groups all marching to the stadium in Nakuru, to sing for the president. It is Madaraka Day, when we got *uhuru*, so every year we sing for the president.

The camera swings, and we see a massive group of people sitting on the soccer pitch in the stadium, waiting for the president. All around are piles of celebrating accessories. Some gleam in the hot sun, like iron roofs: trumpets and drums and shiny uniforms and belt buckles. Different tribes in different nationalizing uniforms that we call traditional. The military people are crisp and beautiful—there are no straighter lines in Kenya, no whiter whites.

There are also feathered ankle rattles, women in dyed-grass skirts, groups of men wandering around aimlessly drinking sodas, ankle bells rattling and clanking, enormous drums.

There are many whistles. Troops of Scouts called to order by whistles. I am in Kingfisher Patrol. Every year we go and march past Baden-Powell's grave in Nyeri. He founded the Boy Scouts and could skin a rabbit with his fingernails. He was buried in Kenya. *Mprr*. Traditional bandleaders with feather and skin hats, and fly whisks sing *mprrrrr* every few minutes to push the song forward. Army and police bands are called to order. Impound. Stamp. Impede. Sta-mpede.

All around, choirs are practicing. The groups are spread on the grass, arranged in three or four lines, according to height—the tallest at the back, their eyes open in complete earnestness, their eyebrows jostling up and down, men's chins forced down into their throats to sound bass. "Fuata Nyayo, fuata Nyayo. Tawala, Moi, tawala."

Rule, Moi, rule.

The women are dressed in *kitenge* print dresses that reach their ankles, with freshly plaited or hot-combed hair. All the choirs sing with a cartoonish expression, and Wambui mimics them, her newly lipsticked mouth adding some exaggeration to the effect: eyebrows up, cheeks sucked in, mouth open as round as the letter O. Mr. Dondo, our choirmaster, tells us that the eyebrows create a feeling of happiness, when the mouth is making an O. When the mouth is released, the choirs bare their teeth, polite hotel slices of breakfast pawpaw, to look extremely happy. Proud. Pretty. Prim. Promising. Eyebrows subside.

My lips close down firmly on each other. Imp. Imprison. Implode. Implant. Impede. After each *mp*, there is a little explosion of air outward because your lips purse as if prepared to rein in the words after each *p*. Improve. Impress.

My groin is hot with friction. I can hear the night outside; crickets are the sound of a vacuum. I am careful to make sure every slit in the curtains is sealed. The man is dancing with the woman in his arms, like white people, or square dancers, but this is a Gikuyu traditional dance. It also looks like a Scottish dance. One man has a feather in his hat. Another man plays an accordion. The old dances were banned by the missionaries, and now many dances happen in rows and columns. Impede. Imperil. Improve.

Baba is Gikuyu, but I can only understand one or two words. Ciru is laughing and squealing, and the world is so big. Wambui will laugh and laugh like Dracula. Accordionland stretches like a giant trampoline forever. I will be unbearably butterflying, turning in circles like the dancers, dizzy without respite. The choirs are back singing, and Wambui is singing with them, some Moi praise song.

I lie back and watch the ceiling. Juma sleeps on my thigh, and I let my mouth shape a perfect O. I start to mouth the song, mimicking Wambui's accent silently in my head and letting silver pictures flow, of my Amigos Disco, Afraha Stadium, *uhuru* world.

Wambui has a lot of stories about lost women, about Ugandan women who steal Kenyan men, about women poisoned and cursed, about women who give birth to beasts because their neighbors cursed them. Wambui once told us about a Ugandan woman with big buttocks who lives in Ronda and sells red mercury, which is more expensive than gold, because it is nuclear, and America is buying it. It comes from Congo. And it makes women give birth to rotting vegetables. The women are very beautiful and like to trap men.

Wambui told me that in the old days, before the arrival of colonial missionary *mprrs*, young Gikuyu couples would take off all their clothes and dance the whole night. Women would have their private parts tied up so they would not misbehave. Otherwise, they would dance and dance and play with each other's bodies, would forget themselves, she said.

Baba has a book called *The Mind Possessed*, which has wonderful pictures: in a voodoo possession ceremony, a group of people roll on the floor, having jumped out of their rows and columns, the whites of their eyes disappeared; a white woman is having an orgasm, as buttocks thrust into her.

Imperil. Baden-Powell, who invented Scouts, made King Prempreh of the Ashanti kneel before his quickly assembled throne, made of boxes of biscuits. Gikuyus are complaining that Kalenjins are sitting on them.

The president's convoy arrives, and large rusted gates swing open on the television screen as the commentator starts to boom. The mass of people queue up behind the convoy to enter and circle the athletic track.

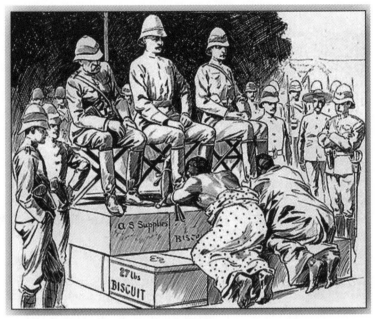

The downfall of King Prempreh of Ghana, from *Diary of Life with the Native Levy in Ashanti* by Major R. S. S. Baden-Powell

They all go around the track, gleaming and shining. President Moi and his cabinet mount the VIP section. People stand in lines in the field and listen to the national anthem, mouthing loyally, the president's ivory and gold stick lifted for all to see.

There is a group of ministers' wives expressionless from makeup. There are the lines of soldiers spread all over the rusty stadium—their shoes and instruments and garters and buttons and trumpets fine and sharp and true. In front of the president, a line of long-distance runners in blazers wait for awards.

Wambui says, "Ah, this is boring." She turns down the volume, and we watch the parade in silence. She puts on the giant Sanyo radio behind the sofas. It stands on four legs, and it is covered in brown vinyl.

Wambui's favorite radio show is on. DJ Fred Obachi Machoka is the Blackest Man in Black Africa.

Salaams come from Francis Kadenge Omwana wa Leah, with greetings from Zambia. Zachariah Demfo of Lake Babati. Robbie Reuben-Robbie from Kitale Salaams Club, who says, "Keep on keeping on."

Boney M.'s "Rivers of Babylon" is playing. Jimmy said the song is taken from Psalms in the Bible. I don't believe him. It is too cool. Wambui starts to dance, arms flying.

"Oh, I rove Boney M.!" she says. She starts to sing. The letter *r* climbs into her Gikuyu tongue intact, slaps against the roof of her mouth, and is broken into a thousand letter *l*'s. Only one of them can survive. It runs down her tongue, an accent jet plane, and leaps forward into the air, "By the livers of mBabylon . . ."

Ciru and I look at each other and start to laugh.

The president stands on the now silent TV screen, behind him a row of provincial commissioners in khaki and pith helmets; in front of him are rows and columns of human order: tribal dancers, soldiers, Scouts. Two lean Kalenjin long-distance runners climb up to the podium to receive medals from the president, who is from their tribe.

I close my eyes. Gikuyu letter *m* breaks free of his place in the stadium and runs around manically, looking for the Gikuyu *b*. They stand together and hug, bonded by fear into a new single letter, a tribe. *Mbi.* Sometimes you try, but your tongue can't wrap right around the rules. *A, mbi, ci.*

Policemen circle them; the president pauses. *N* starts to agitate, standing there in straight colonial stadium lines. In National Stadium lines. *D* shakes like an accordion and wriggles across to *n*; they start to do a waltz. Kanu Khartoon Khaki wants them to behave, be what you are supposed to be, stay still and do what Kenya Khaki says. KANU, our one party, is father and mother, says President, and Khaki people salute. *A. mBi. Ci. nDi, E, F, nGi.*

Wambui dances across the carpet, mouth open, singing her M'Boney M. song, mangled in her Subukia accent.

"M'by the livers of m'bambyl-oon, where we sat n'down, yeeah we

wept, when we lemeber Zion. Kitanda Whisking, blabbin' us away cap-
tivtee, inquire-ling for us a song, but how can we play the Rord's song in
a stlaaange rand . . ."

We roll on the floor, laughing at Wambui. She glares at us. Face
hot, lips red. I will *mpah* you, she seems to say, lips pouting and eyes
feral. But she stops singing. "Send your salaams," screams Fred Obachi
Machokaaa. Roby Reuben Rrrrrrrrbobie is asking for Habel Kifoto and
the Marrr-oon Commandos.

Wambui squeals and jumps, her breasts bouncing, "Ohhhh. Haiya.
Chalonye ni Wasi? I rove this song."

I lie back on the carpet. I close my eyes, my back prickling, and let
her limbs climb into my mind's living room—where the turgid disco
ball throws a thousand nipples of light on me and skirts twirl and glitter with silver. Her full fiction world comes surging like current, and
happiness bursts out of me like a trumpet.

Mprrrrr . . .

Wambui, my Wambui is a trumpet, a Gikuyu Scottish strumpet, a
woman in long skirts from a Barbara Cartland book cover, from Mum's
secret cupboard, *We Danced All Night*. Wambui is broken English,
slangy Kiswahili, Gikuyu inflections. She is Millie Jackson. A Malloon
Commaddo. She is a market woman. A (L)Rift Varrey girl. Third generation. Her aunt is half Nandi, her grandmother a Ngong Maasai.
Wambui is Gikuyu by fear, or Kenyatta-issued title deed, or school
registration or because her maternal Gikuyu uncle paid her father's fees,
or because they chose a Gikuyu name to get into a cooperative scheme
in the seventies. Maybe her grandmother, born in a Maasai home, married in the mixed-up Rift Valley, was a feared Gikuyu general during the
Mau Mau. It could have been different. Blink.

My fiction Wambui will upend the fate of her mother; she has no
fear of starting new, in a new place. All of her clothes glint with sequins
and disco, in black and white, on television. They all became Gikuyu
after Independence, for the president was Gikuyu, and so the river of
independence gold spoke Gikuyu and wore pith helmets on podiums.

Wambui is hoisting up a naked leg like the Solid Gold Dancers with Andy Gibb and Dionne Warwick. Her brown tooth gleams wickedly. Pubaf!

But she is mproud. And those with more than her can impede.

Twin military trumpets tear the track open. Charonye ni Wasi. Maroon Commandos is a jazz rumba band originally from the army. Kenyan Olympic distance runners, in blue Kenya blazers, flowing out into bell-bottom trousers, like mermen, waiting for the Independence Day medal ceremony. If they stand upside down next to the president, the trousers sink to their ankles. Tall, lean, shiny legs and polished thighs, thin where they meet the mpresident's fattening cheeks. President leans back, and blows hard, para raraa rara rara rara raa ra, his cheeks swollen with national fat. They swell, his cheeks, rising Kalenjin balloons, now floating above Kenya, a new tribe, lifted over frail Kenya like helium. Their tall, burly president rules, and rows and columns of pressed khaki protect him. He is no longer awkward.

If there is a Nandi Wambui, a Kalenjin hidden inside Wambui's bloodstream, it is not strong enough to break away, pure and clean, and jump on the podium. She could have become a Luo, if they stayed there long enough, and she married there; she is dark skinned enough to get away with it.

Below the heroes of Kenya are rows and columns of citizens, in clear straight lines, in crisp uniforms, Boy Scouts and policemen, the navy, the army, and ten thousand schoolchildren in new uniforms. Then there are the tribes—each one in a costume, here to tell the president we sing and dance for you.

Strumpet Wambui stands to attention and lifts her leg Hollywood high, then puts it down. The disco ball turns. Little droplets of disco light are spinning gently around Wambui as she turns. Her buttocks wiggle. The song gentles. Enter the chorus of men's voices singing, "People of Taita eeeeh, people of Taita we greet you. How are you? We are here, we are fine, we don't know about you back home . . ."

These short lyrics are a call home that I don't know, that Ciru does not know. We do not know how to be from two nations: home home

(home squared, we call it, your clan, your home, the nation of your origin),
and the home away from home—the home of the future, a notyet place
called Kenya. We are Milimani kids, speaking English and Kiswahili.

Trumpet carries the first part of the song, sharp and spread outward.
Standing trumpets bracket the song with controlled rhythm beats, the
loudest part of the song. *Mprrahh.* No drums. No traditional drums.
This is national music, taken from folk songs, and brought into rows
and columns, by Imperial British Biscuit podiums, marching crews of
barefoot porters, dutiful missionary boys, soldiers in Burma, colonial
village headmen with military whistles, guitar and military trumpet and
other sounds from labor lines and colonial ghettos, English universities
and their local satellites, and the promises of the grandsons and granddaughters of the first ones to be so violently formatted.

Us. Me.

The sound stampedes out of its rows, *mpah,* and is never cutouts
and offcuts; the song is a whole new full thing. When they soften, the
Taita lyrics come again, a magnetic missive from the faraway city. Lone-
liness. Wambui's hips spin softly as she mouths the lyrics, looking sad.

> We are in the city eeeh, we are in the city so do not forget us!
> What is important is good health.
> This world journey is full of hardship.
> *Everything* costs money
> If you want maize meal, costs money
> If you want vegetables, costs money
> If you want drinking water, costs money
> Mpraaaraaa rara . . .
> We will write you a letter.

The song comes to a full stop. A full three seconds of silence as
rumba momentum builds. The choral voices are now a sheet of frenzied rubber, Kenya streeeetches and bleats, held together by the military
trumpets and cash crop exports, the future, only the future, laboring
bodies, a railway, a mpresident.

The song has very few words. Five or six sentences repeated over and over. What is . . . more, are all the speaking mouth organs, the things you have no words for, the groaning sax, the military trumpets, the low growl of a clarinet, speaking home to your ear, a new kind of home, Cuban sounds that came from radio broadcasts from the Congo in the 1940s; Taita poems; Congo sounds; marching soldiers in Burma, high plaintive male voices—men sound girly in industrial metal lives. Music makes whole worlds, out of unwhole lives. Like crying and pissing and laughter, it promises to carry all of you, even the parts of you that cannot work together.

I open my eyes. Juma is still whining. Wambui is sweating and panting and laughing. I close my eyes. My new word *bureaucrat* is running around my mind in a panic, stamping and coding and reminding me to never forget that one day, one day I will arrange the words right for this strange night.

Last year, before the coup, this same Madaraka Day, I am in the stadium with the school when the crowd attacks the mountains of crates of bread and Fanta surrounded by military *mprrs*.

Police chase people around the stadium. Schoolkids from the richer schools, us, are hit and pickpocketed by the poorer barefoot kids in torn uniforms. Parents parked outside the stadium are crying from the tear gas. The main gate is shut. We are stuck inside Afraha Stadium.

Riot police unload behind the main gate. When the gate is opened we surge forward, looking for our parents and running away from riot police batons. Crowds attack the kiosks of biscuits and sodas. Mpreeeh mpreeh, shrill whistles everywhere. High school students are stoning buses. Sirens sing as the road clears for the president, his ministers, and a huge convoy of giant black Benzes.

I duck into the car. Mum's face is set. "Next year you are staying home," she says. Tears are streaming down my face as we drive away. The song fades, and in my mind rotting voodoo vegetables gather, and screaming night crickets, and radiation-reddened Ugandan women from Wambui's stories fall and burst, splat, seep into my nostrils. They join the grimacing faces from *The Mind Possessed*.

"Your Excellency," said the sycophant on the podium, "I impress upon you . . ."

I scramble from the claws and shadows and stand next to Wambui. They are laughing and breathing hard, Wambui and Ciru. Then we are all laughing.

"One day," says Wambui, licking her red lips, "I am going to be rich."

Science is smaller than music, than the patterns of the body; the large confident world of sound and body gathers. If my mind and body are quickening, lagging behind is a rising anxiety of words.

I do not have enough words for all this.

Jimmy and Ciru are already learning to play the piano, letting sound be its own truth. I have no such facility. Words must surround experience, like Mum's new vacuum cleaner, sucking all this up and making it real.

Whooosh.

There she is, back on the roof of my head, clear as anything. Wambui, all of thirteen or so, barefoot in a torn red dress, legs chalky and dusty, a ringworm on her head, with a Huckleberry grin, eyes darting from side to side, in a Dundori public *baraza*, a day before another Madaraka Day, whispering some snarky comment in Bawdy Gikuyu, or Rude Kiswahili, right in the middle of prayer for the president. A sharp trumpet flares again, the village subchief doubling back after a public meeting, and wagging his finger, in a pith helmet and khaki uniform. The hearts of the villagers clench for a moment in fear, and he growls: "Who said that?"

The subchief—I shall call him Carey Francis Michuki—is fat and stubby, and pleased to see all eyes staring at the ground; the villagers are suitably obedient, in rows and columns. Yesterday three women who sell illegal liquor spent the day whitewashing the stones that mark his little compound, around the flag. He hurrumps and ghurrumps, an Independence Day cockerel, chest swollen, *Jogoo, mimi ni jogoo.* Imposing. He grabs hold of his lapels, his colonial buttons shine, he is the most ironed man here. Tonight the Kenya Breweries rep and the British American Tobacco rep and the Imperial Biscuit reps will get him and the district commissioner drunk, with their entertainment allowance, so the convoys of goods can move unimpeded. Anybody who threatens the convoys of biscuits and tobacco will spend the day kneeling outside the tin hut with a Kenyan flag blowing outside. Impudent. Pumbaf. The subchief turns and waddles back to his station, two hungover administration policemen walking unsteadily behind him, whistles in pockets, as Wambui's mother shoots a warning to her with a wagging finger, as I decide that one day I will write books.

Chapter Seven

It is 1983, the year of national exams. I am still reading novels everywhere, and I am always in trouble with Mum. Our school is for future doctors, lawyers, engineers, and scientists is what we are told by all our parents; this is what we believe.

The school is run by the town. Some parents are poor, some are rich, the fee is low. Our headmistress has raised much money together with parent volunteers to build a library, classrooms, a weather center; to maintain the pianos; for seedbeds, a home-science workshop, a dining hall, and a workshop to study carpentry. We bought a tractor, new lawn mowers. We have a swimming pool fund. We bought two minibuses for school trips to national parks and other places. Our school is always first or second in the district in national exams. There are the army kids, the kids from Egerton Agricultural College. Nakuru is an agricultural town. There are some farmers' kids, kids whose parents work for the wheat board or are senior civil servants in the municipal council or the district and provincial administration. There are kids from railways, train drivers' kids, and foremen's kids. There are doctors' kids, lawyers' kids. Nurses' kids. Engineers' kids.

Something has shifted. In the world.

The Swedes made the first announcement that things are no longer the same. One day they come and set up right next to the flag, where no pupil is allowed to play. It is here that we gather every day for parade. The whole school stands on the grass watching. Mrs. Gichiri stands too, watching. There are two giant drums of cow shit standing next to our proud national flag; there are pipes and meters and things connecting to other things. The Swedes fiddle with the cow-shit machine earnestly. We hear some burping sounds, and behold, there is light. This is biogas, the Swedes tell us. A fecal martyr. It looks like shit—it *is* shit—but it has given up its gas for you. With this new fuel you can light your bulbs and cook your food. You will become balancedieted; if you are industrious perhaps you can run a small biogas-powered food mill and engage in income-generating activities.

This way, they said kindly, eyes as blue as Jesus's, looking at us through steel glasses, you can avoid malnutrition. This is called development, they said, and we are here to raise your awareness. Biogas rose up the pipes and gurgled happily. We went back to class very excited and making farting noises. Heretofore our teachers had threatened us with straightforward visions of failure. Boys would end up shining shoes; girls would end up pregnant.

Now there was a worse thing to be: a user of biogas.

...

Even though Mum is complaining, Ciru and I are doing well. Sometimes she is first in school. Sometimes I am first in school. She is the youngest in the class, but her confidence gives me confidence. I do well enough in math, even though I pay no attention to it.

To me every new thing is always splintering into many possibilities. These can still spin and spin around and leave me defeated. I stand and abandon my homework, retreat to the toilet and read a novel. Sometimes when I start to spin, I simply let myself be Ciru, and look on the page, and start to write and answers arrive, and after a while I realize I have followed a straight line, and I am done. I lied to one teacher that we are twins. I dream that we will always be together, like twins. I love to read books about twins, identical twins who can read each other's minds. If she does something that is her own, if she won't let me join in, I am okay only if at the end of it she pulls me in, so we can laugh at it together. If she looks away, shuts me out, I lash out, or hide away. She locks the door to her room a lot these days.

Chiqy, now five and everybody's darling, likes to knock on my door, and I often don't open it. I watch her disappear to the Bishops Lodge, across the road, and return with a group of kids. She is the boss, and they follow.

Whenever grown-ups talk politics, we whisper. Baba plays golf every weekend this year. Come Sunday morning, we tear up roads up to make his tee-off time. As usual, our plan is to launch ourselves into a frenzy of splashing and swinging and sliding with fellow golf children and lick tomato sauce and molten Cadbury chocolate off hot fingers and generally squirm and bliss around. Eldoret has a great golf club. Uplands pork sausages.

Mum has been going to church more. Sometimes Mum sleeps the whole afternoon. She is diabetic. All our uncles and aunts on Mum's side are now diabetics. Today, she insists we find a church service. We drive around for a while and end up in some corrugated iron church, with no windows. We don't want to go in, but Mum's face is set, so we don't argue. The heat and light are blinding, and people are jumping up and down and singing what sounds to me like voices from an accordion. It smells of sweat and goats.

We sit. All hot and in Sunday sweaters and collars and Vaseline under the hot iron roof, and people spit and start and this is because we are frying, not because God is here. In the front, there is a line of young women dressed in long gowns: bright red and green, with a stiff cone rising outward up their chins. They are jumping up and down. Up and down. And some of them have rattles, and some have tambourines and they are singing loud and sweating in that gritty dusty Kenyan way—not smooth and happy like American gospel on television.

And the man in the front stands on the pulpit, sweating and shouting. The Catholic Church I know is all about having to kneel and stand when everybody else kneels and stands, and crossing and singing with eyebrows up to show earnestness before God, and open-mouth dignity to receive the bread. Some women will not open their tongues for the priest—this is too suggestive. They will cup their hands and receive bread, and put the bread demurely into their hands and move back and bend one knee briefly before fading back to their seats and adjusting headscarves before sitting, kneeling, standing. Kneel. Stand. Massage rosary. Service ends in fifty-seven minutes. Then announcements, when the priest says whoever wants to donate money for the parish fund should do so, and nobody ever does.

This service goes on and on. Mum is shushing us a lot. Why does she come here? What is she looking for? Jimmy is quiet and looks pained. Mum, dressed in a simple, elegant dress, her hair professionally done, with her angular Kinyarwanda face looks out of place here. She does not seem involved; her face is set.

People are dressed in wild robes: orange Peter Pan collars, neon blues and golds and yellows. People reach into bras and pockets and purses and take out notes and envelopes and throw them in the moving dancing collection baskets. A crescendo is reached, after we have given money, and people are writhing and shouting in the heat. Words are flowing from their lips, like porridge, in no language I know, but in a clear coherent pitch. Each person has her or his own tongue.

In the Catholic Church, we all recite the same prayer and make a chorus out of it. Here, a chorus is made out of each person's received tongue. The drums in the front set the tempo, and the pastor leads with his own languageless tongues, on a microphone.

The church I am used to uses stories, parables, little priestly essays, and short written lyrical prayers. Some people just hiccup for twenty minutes. The pastor is saying, "RECEIVE, RECEIVE your own TONGUE." And eyes are closed, and each person lets go of something, like me pissing in the sofa. The whole crowd has a group sound, and the instruments make this all one sound, and this sound carries us all, but each individual lives inside his or her own sound. One woman, all sharp angles and awkward shapes, is just hiccupping, as if her secret language is all starts and stops, and her elbows keep hitting the man next to her, who doesn't even notice. In the front, eyes are closed, tears are flowing, and handmade bottle-top tambourines rattle at full slapslapslap, the tin roof church is so hot. Our hot wet breath is now dripping back down on us from the roof. Some faint. I want to drink.

Why is Mum here?

Ciru and I are both certain we will get into the best schools in the country. I apply to Alliance High School, Ciru to Alliance Girls. In the district mock exams, I am third in the district, and first in our school; Ciru is second.

Mrs. Gichiri calls me in to her office one day. She is my English teacher. Mrs. Gichiri. She is worried that my compositions are too wild. She says I should concentrate, keep them simple. She is sure I will do well. Like your sister, she says, beaming for the first time I can remember.

A few years ago, President Moi announced that he was going to re-structure the education system. The kids who are a year behind me will abandon the British-style 7-4-6 system and do a new one, called 8-4-4, that is supposed to introduce more practical education.

CPE is our national high school entrance exam. All papers ex-cept English composition are graded by a computer. You only use your computer-issued number. You do not write your name on the exam sheet. Your school is only a number. This way, it is unbiased.

It is scientific.

When the results come out, Ciru is the top student in our school. I am fifth. I am not happy. I expected better. But—we are both among the top twenty students in our province, Kenya's biggest province. Relatives call from all over the world to congratulate us.

One day a friend of my father who works in the ministry of educa-tion calls him and tells him that he has not seen our names on the list for any schools. After the test results are out, head teachers from high schools across the country meet and select students, strictly based on merit. National schools, usually the best schools, pick the best students from each province. This way the whole country is represented in the student body. Then there are provincial schools, and district schools, day schools, and, at the bottom, there are what we call *harambee* schools, schools built through community contributions.

The terrible curse of the past is that it always starts right now. Hind-sight will pull facts to its present demand; it is the dental brace that will reshape your jaw, your resolve. When hindsight desires enough, it oblit-erates uncertainty. All the selected past becomes an argument for action.

And the tribe was made flesh, and dwelt among us.

Neither Ciru nor I is called to any school. No school at all. Rumors are spreading everywhere. We hear that lists of selections, long reams from a science computer, were taken away; that names are matched to numbers, and scrutinized, word by word, line by scientific line, for Gikuyu names in a secret office by Special Branch people.

Kenneth B. Wainaina. June Wanjiru Wainaina—Ciru's full name. Unfortunately, I do not use Binyavanga—maybe that would have caused some epistemological confusion.

Gentlemen, we can rebuild tribe. We have the technology.

These names were crossed off lists.

In Rift Valley Province, Kalenjins get places in the best state schools. Baba and Mum argue. She is trying to get us into private schools. Baba says no. For the first time in my life, I call somebody because he is a Gikuyu, as I am properly discovering I am. Peter. An old friend and classmate. We call each other, whispering about other friends, walking through each person's grade, his tribe, the school she is going to.

Measuring. Networks light up all over the Rift Valley. This is happening! Let's stand together. Phone calls, small meetings. Quiet lunches. Promises. Soon, Peter and I are in the same school.

I have never heard of Njoro High School. Most state high schools in Kenya are boarding schools. It is eighteen miles away, and I never knew it existed. It is a district school. I never thought I would end up in a third-rate school, a low, low idea. Ciru has never heard of Kapropita Girls Secondary School, where she has been called. She is told the school has no tap water. Girls fetch water from the river. When people ask which school I am going to, I keep quiet.

There are some new high schools now, with the best facilities, the best teachers taken out of other schools. For Moi's people. Moi Forces Academy, and Kabarak High School, and Sacho High School. After one term, a stroke of luck. Ciru gets a place in Kenya High School, a posh old national school that Moi wanted to turn into a teachers' college. He changed his mind, and Mum heard, from the new secret networks, they were doing a recall. Rumor has it Moi has a schoolteacher girlfriend there. He likes to date schoolteachers, we hear. He gives their husbands diplomatic postings.

It is January, 1984. I am thirteen. I was circumcised in December.

I am a man.

Chapter Eight

The lights are off in my dorm in Njoro High School. I have one huge pimple on my forehead. I have decided to run away from school tonight. I am worried because our head boy is a homosexual. It is broadcast on every toilet wall in the school. I am not sure what a homosexual is.

It is midnight. Before I went to bed, at around eleven, I made tea for our house prefect and collected water for the second former who sleeps in the bunk bed below me. This is the first full day here that I have avoided being beaten.

I usually get a slap every morning when I try to jump from my top bunk to the ground without touching the marked section of floor immediately below me. Johnson's territory has been marked with white chalk. He is short and looks like a rodent, with sharp pointy teeth and jerky movements. He is stronger than he looks, and his slaps leave an imprint on my face. This morning I woke up before he did, jumped as far as I could, and managed to land past the line of chalk, tearing a bit of flesh from my waist on my metal suitcase, which sits on top of a locker at the side of the bed, well inside his chalk line. To access my suitcase I had to lean in from the back of the locker on tiptoe, and I felt for my towel and soap and toothbrush with my fingers. I told Peter the whole story. I told him I planned to run away from school tonight.

I have set my alarm for 2:00 a.m. I am packed. I am sleeping when my bedding is torn off the bed. They stand around my bed, a group of seniors in blazers, carrying mugs of cocoa and torches. One of them carries a cane. They tell me to get out of bed. Peter is standing with them. He winks at me, to say everything will be fine. I get up, in my pajamas. The grass outside is wet with dew and I am in my rubber *patipatis*. I follow, afraid. It is cold. Njoro is eight thousand feet above sea level.

We are in Mobair and Kibet's small cubicle. They are our dorm prefects. They have become my protectors. In return, I provide biscuits, jam, and peanut butter, goodies from a home that is richer than most of the students'. I make tea. The room is full of people, some in pajamas like me, and some in full uniform. Those in uniform are all senior prefects. I join the juniors in pajamas. There are seven or eight of us.

All of us sit on one bed, heads hanging. One tiny boy is crying.

George, a third former, is testifying, "He took me to the volleyball court. Every Sunday night."

"He promised he would make me a prefect."

"He sexed me."

"He told me to kneel down and suck his Jomo."

"After prep. He told me not to wear underwear."

"Before prep."

"Inside the food store. He gave me free margarine afterward."

Jomo is Njoro High School slang for *cock*. Named after our dearly departed president, Mzee Jomo Kenyatta. For their sexual Jomo efforts, some boys got a special diet in the dining hall, a few extra precious potatoes. An extra slice of bread in the morning. Tea with milk.

Jomo Kenyatta, assisted by Israel, built the tallest building in Kenya, Kenyatta Conference Centre, round and ribbed, like Rough Rider condoms. At the top of the building, where the flared crown sits, there is a revolving restaurant, a podium, where you can sit and spy on the whole city. Two cooperating boys became school prefects. The young guy who was crying was taken to Nakuru town for sausages and marsala chips at Tipsy Restaurant after a long sexing session on the volleyball court one night.

Soon it is my turn to speak.

I met him the first day of school. I wanted to go to my new school by public transport, but Mum would not hear of it. So we stood in the parking lot, she and I, by her smart big town car, and her in lipstick.

He made a beeline for us. He had an Afro, strange for 1984. Big and shiny. He was tall, well ironed, and wore a blazer.

"George Sigalla," he said. "I am the head boy."

Soon Mum and I waved good-bye to each other. George's arm was around my shoulder. He got me a reasonably new mattress, got me registered, and accompanied me to the dorm, which fell silent when he entered. He helped make my bed. Told me to come to his study before prep for some cocoa. Within five minutes of his leaving, my bunkmate Johnson had slapped me and dared me to go and report him to the head boy. Lionel Richie was crooning some love thing on his radio when I knocked.

"Do you want coffee? Or are you afraid of stimulants?" He giggled. He was sweaty and awkward and I was not comfortable. He showed me his certificates, from the National Music Festival. On the table was a bottle of Limara perfume and a jar of Hair-Glo (Africa, it's good to know, with great new Hair-Glo, you gat style).

He leaned in and sat next to me on the bed. He started to reach up my thigh. I froze. The hand moved higher. I gulped down the coffee and stood to leave. He caught me at the door. "Don't tell anybody. If you tell anybody . . . !"

...

I find out, from Peter, that the Boy Scouts are going to Nairobi International Agricultural Show. He helps me bribe my way into Boy Scout—hood. It costs me three loaves of bread. I was a Scout years ago, but lapsed for cooler things. This is cooler. We are going to take the train to Nairobi. Mobair and Kibet are Scout leaders.

We are at the train station and it is 2:00 a.m. The train reels in and is packed. Packed. The windows are portraits of tangled beasts—mashed mouths wrapped in glass and steam, and snarls and noses and bits of clothing, limbs—steam in, steam out.

This is funny. Until we discover that we are traveling third class; later we find out our teacher was cutting corners with our money. So we squeeze into this train from Kisumu. For an hour I can't find a place to put one foot down. As this train is from Kisumu, the land of freshwater fish, everybody is carrying dried or smoked fish to the city. It is hot.

People sing and pray and sing and pray.

We spill out of the train seven hours later and march, legs wobbly, uniforms crumpled, in a Boy Scout line to Rowallan camp.

The camp is beautiful, rich red Nairobi soil and giant trees and parkland and cool and forest. But there are not enough tents for every-body; some of us have to find somewhere else to sleep. The rest set up tents and tramp around happily. We end up with our teacher, booking a small room in a long row of one-room tin-roofed houses that face each other, dripping thick green tears of age and smelling of old drains. We set our sleeping bags down.

Later, we sleep. And then we are woken. First it is a rattle, then a din. Screaming. Clanging. Banging. Shouting. Singing. Churching. God. Strange languages. The whole night, they dance and sing and scream and bang.

In the morning, people are whistling happily and gently and head-ing to work, secular people in uniforms. Some women are washing clothes at the tap between the line of houses, singing softly and chat-ting. Children frolic.

•••

George Sigalla, the head boy, is demoted. The prefects all went to the headmaster. He spends the rest of the year alone. People spit at him when he walks past. I often want to wave, say something. I never do. I try hard to stay close to the line, keep myself inside myself, and be some public person who fits in. Sigalla is always among the top students in his year. The school falls silent when his name is read out at assembly after exams. He stands straight, never bowed, walks through crowds and queues without looking sideways, always immaculate, his face con-temptuous and fearless.

It's hard not to be impressed.

The whole school whispers about the new headmaster—suspiciously young, visibly Kalenjin. Mr. Kipsang. We mimic his accent and laugh at him when he is not looking. The previous headmaster, a Gikuyu, is gone. I wonder if they found out about me and Peter and our Gikuyu conspiracy to get here.

Chapter Nine

School is closed for Christmas and Ray Parker Junior is the coolest man in the world. "Who you gonna call? Ghostbusters."

We all want his hair. Ray Miaw Miaw, we call it.

Mum has driven to Eldoret with Chiqy to pick up Jimmy. Ciru arrives tomorrow. I am already at home. I take a long bath.

I let my body sink into the water, to let myself see the thick colors of things outside. Soon my eyes are numb, and hot snails of thick feeling climb up from my stomach to my chest. I marvel at the beauty of limbs moving under the water, and soon I am lost and I panic.

I am always afraid of being hijacked by patterns. I rise and turn the page of my novel. Then I spend an hour with sugar and soap and a hard brush trying to push back my hair into a Ray Miaw Miaw. I keep getting it perfect, but then when it dries a little, it starts to crack. Black America has a lot to account for. First it was bloody Afros. What East African can grow a bloody Afro? It would take forty years.

In the 1970s Mum made a good living selling Afro wigs. For the natural look. I find I can maintain the style if I keep my neck still and make sure I don't frown or grin too widely.

In August Mum announced that she has abandoned our polite middle-class Catholic church, fifty minutes of kneel, stand, kneel, stand, then go swimming.

She has joined a church we have never heard of, Deliverance Church. She says she is cured of diabetes. She was driving from Nairobi, a trip to see her doctor, and she found she could not stop crying. She stopped by the side of the road, and finally gave in to what had been calling her, she said.

She told God to heal her. I put on pleated maroon pants and my maroon moccasins with white socks. Deliverance Church is three hours of guttural noises in Nakuru Town Hall. Screams and tongues, bad microphones and bad American accents. Hell or sweaty ecstasy. Bible study three times a week. Conventions and crusades, bad English, parallel translations of every shouted sweaty sentence, from English to Kiswahili, sometimes from Kiswahili to Gikuyu too. People carry giant zippered King James Bibles. Attention necessary, no dreaming, no escape. No R&B. No Ray Miaw Miaw. It is rapture or dread.

Jimmy is the head boy at St. Patrick's Iten, which is a very famous school. Mum says he also got saved. Ciru seems to be teetering. Her new school is posh. Kenya High School. But even there the fever of God is spreading. Last term girls went hysterical when one girl was possessed by demons. A very handsome preacher, who had a Ray Miaw Miaw and looks like Jermaine Jackson, came and cast them out. Much of the school got saved. Chiqy, my baby sister, is too young to be threatened by all this. All over Kenya, as politics sour, there is a fever of rapture-seeking.

When I hear Mum's car at the gate, I get dressed quickly. I walk to the kitchen. Mum's Peugeot is parked outside. Jimmy is carrying a giant metal suitcase.

There is somebody else in the car. The first crutch peeps out of the car door and an arm knocks against the frame. Jimmy grunts hello; his eyes catch mine and swing toward the car, a quiet command. I look away, trying to resist. But I have none of that where Jim is concerned. I move to help.

The legs are not straight; they are thin twisted sticks. There is a sharp smell of sweat, and the crutches are cheap wooden things. These four muscleless limbs seem unbearably brittle, as if they are about to break. I catch the eye of the cripple. His school uniform shirt is soaked. His face is square and dark and full of naked agitations, hot rivulets of veins; cars are hooting and traders are shouting outside the market on a hot day, and his jaw is that guy, that uncomfortable village guy, stranded in urban panic, his jaw muscles clenching. You cannot moon-glide out of the fate of that face. You cannot smooth your hand over your head and feel the hard transforming Ray Miaw Miaw. He is my age, but he has the immobility of an adult. I mumble hello. His eyes are large and fearful when they catch mine. The door yawns and swings, the crutches bang against metal, and he lifts his legs with his big hands and throws them out. They wobble, and he tumbles to the ground, and I help him up, my stomach accordioning.

...

After tea, we all drive down the hill. Here, where we live, used to be Europeans-only Nakuru. We drive past the town center, heading down, past the old Indian and Goan areas, down toward the lake, where tens of thousands are crammed in one-room homes, the former colonial labor lines, where "Africans lived."

We park at a primary school, which smells of urine. Jim and I help the cripple out. People are staring at our car. Sometimes Mum is just a Ugandan. A woman of cooked bananas and old kings and queens and hills far away, good education, and a language that makes us giggle when she is on the phone. Sometimes she is an elegant woman of no easy placing, who allows us to think we are different in a small provincial town. Glamour. Here, she seems . . . wrong, and I know we will spend this Bible study being stared at.

The pastor comes forward to give her a special greeting as we stand behind, shuffling, hands politely behind our backs. We move into the classroom, which is just rows of broken benches. All the windows, from the colonial days, are broken. We sit. The pastor is tall, and has rheumy eyes. Even here, in Deliverance Church, he is considered over-enthusiastic. The dead shall rise, the sick shall be healed here; his voice comes from the belly, harsh and hoarse, and blood rushes to his eyes.

I wait for the terrible moment when he will ask, "Who here has not received the blood of Jesus?" and I will refuse to put up my hand, and Mum's stillness will wound, and then we give money, and then songs rise, and throats open, all of them like crickets in the night; some eyes roll back, one man's chest heaves up and down and he wheezes as if demons will, right now, shoot out of his heart. He is crying.

Pastor John asks them to leap, leap and be healed, leap right into heaven, leap over the burning fires. All this time, all these hours, the cripple has said nothing. He said nothing at home, as he fumbled with his tea and saucer. He said nothing when I greeted him. All his sounds are only metal braces hitting wooden crutches, squeaks of wood on the floor, formless trousers whispering as they rub the floor. His loudest sound is a giant silence, every time he moves. I wait for it, the crack, and the break, the collision of metal, wood, and bone.

Then he speaks.

A wail. Thin and rusty, it cuts through the pounding waves of God noise. The sound he promised arrives; he clutters to the floor, moaning and crying. His crutches all over the place. Benches scream as we clear out; his arms flail on the floor. I want to leave this place and sink into the hot bath again. Mum kneels over him, the pastor looms, his arms reach forward, and he urges the cripple's moan forward—release it, the poison, the demon, the sickness. Yesss. Yesss. Everybody hisses. The moan rises, and rises.

Then I see them, those thin dead legs jerking to life inside the metal braces.

...

The crutches and braces have been abandoned. The cripple crawls all over our home, his spaghetti legs twitching. He sings, low chesty God songs.

Jimmy is always off on his long runs; he has timetables. Jimmy's day has a plan. He has made his home life into a vocation: bike, gym, run, basketball, arranging music collection, girls, books about fast cars and planes and guitars. There is no room for negotiation. The world must submit to his timetable.

The vague get hijacked. If I am sharing Jimmy's room, I will wake up a few minutes before he does, and I will busy myself as he does, grunt as he grunts, move with male resolution as he does, and I can do this without thinking about it. When he is gone, I can escape to other places, where people with certainty shoot up elevators; they rise to the roof on New York escalators; they reach in and kiss, ride words to the sunset.

Some of them flounder and flail, then on page 187, as they are about to break apart from the unbearable pressure of being themselves, of being vulnerable to the insistence of others, they find a power. Oh! Here they were, thinking they were made all wrong, but everybody has a moment when the world stops, pauses, turns, approves, and says, it was you all along, it was you who held us all up, and we never noticed . . . oh, Da-yana, Daai-ana, it was always you I truly loved.

I often have the house to myself. Now he is here. He shuffles around, praying loudly, asking for nothing, saying nothing. If this moment continues, it becomes inescapable. I no longer fear that the cripple will clutter and break. I fear that he will crawl, and kneel, and stand.

Those who come from the most painful awkwardness have the most triumphant stand-ups; they have seen a failing world and can fully appreciate a working one. The charisma of his new patterns will occupy this whole house. I will be colonized by them. With every step, he is killing the once-a-year Jesus who smiles beatifically and says nothing, really.

Nonono. My deal is simple. Keep loose and float. Follow easy patterns, and schedules. Commit only to a present tense that lets your legs move behind others, and keeps your head in the clouds. Being cool is never stepping beyond your comfortable patterns.

Too many things are calling, suddenly asking for heres and nows, for all of me here and now. Sex has started whispering in my ear, demanding a plan of action. What need do I have for these things? For to be what I am, as promised by fictions, by fantasy and the future, is to fly, from dorm bed to Motown, from the household of the king of Siam to running Huckleberryfree on the field, from my bedroom directly into the Walton household, to *Star Wars*, to stardust. To be, one day, a Television Nairobi professional with a car. An escalator guy in a suit. Every evening cool with jeans and a beer on a good sunset balcony, listening to R&B.

To succumb is to let them all in, to see the confusion; to succumb is to be a porridge-spouting Godguy, sealed shut by some hot Pentecostal spirit. The spirit crawls all over the floor, legs starting to waken, threatening to stand.

I pray, one day. I watch the cripple scraping the floor with his knees, and I promise God silently that I will get saved. I will, I say. When I am twenty. Let me stay loose, I ask, and the cripple's legs buckle and he tumbles.

Crutch! God!

God! Let me have sex first.

His name is Julius. He leaves one day, asks to be taken to the bus station. He crawls properly now. We never see or hear from him again. I am sure he knew how much I wanted him gone.

···

It is third term. I have adapted to boarding school. I feel okay, as though I have been here forever. I don't know what comes over me. I am sort of fooling around in the field one Saturday, a novel in hand, as usual, and I get an old urge.

I stand, then walk, past the dorms, and the staff room, past the gate, in full school uniform, past the consequences, the cane, the suspension letter, the ruined record. I do not use one of the usual tricks to sneak out, the holes in the fence, the bribed security guards. I walk into Njoro town, eat chips and drink a cold Fanta, and take a *matatu* home, to Nakuru.

There is nobody home. I climb into the house through the window and run a hot bath. Mum finds me asleep in my bed. She sits there, runs her hand across my forehead. I can hear her there, quiet, and I am not afraid; I just want her to keep her hand right there. She runs it through my hair. Her hand. I keep my eyes closed for the longest time and listen to her breathing.

We have tea and cake. I gulp it all down.

"I have to take you back to school, you know."

I nod.

"Do you want to go back?"

I nod.

She takes my hand and turns it. I try to pull it back.

"What happened to your thumb?"

My thumbnail is mushy and bleeding, with pus. Over the past few months, I have been peeling my nails with a razor blade during night prep. Short, tight bursts of quiet peeling, nibbling, and scraping, only stopping to turn the page of my novel. Sometimes I stay up late at night and peel at my nails under the bedcovers. Always hungry. When all the unfeeling casing is gone, I can sleep well.

I don't know what she says to the headmaster. I am not punished.

After a few weeks, Mum comes to visit me at school.

"Pack your things," she says. "You are going to a new school."

Chapter Ten

We drove to Nairobi today, my father and I, to the city. I have five pimples. The capital city, for me, is the opportunity to spend time on soft teenage hydraulics—bookshops and burgers and *Right On* magazine and soft-cheeked girls who say "That's fantabulous!"

We drove here, to Nairobi, my father and I, to get some complicated tractor or combine harvester machinery fixed. We do these things from time to time these days. My father throws the request casually—my mother must have suggested it in forceful whispers: get him out of his room.

They are both being nicer than usual and I am being spoiled. I put my book in my bag and head off to the car. My father is like warm bread: he smells good and radiates good biology, and my enzymes growl and glow around him. The car's bonnet is open. So. I want to know about clanging metals and growling engines, and I stand there on the side, after you suck the oil out of a tube, in a manly way, and spit it on the ground and say, "They are not aligned."

Nods. We stand, all of us, looking at the car's entrails, in meditation. "No. No."

"This car is injection."

And, feet apart, we shall consider this—and jump into action, heaving and arranging and pulling and revving, and soon things will purr, and exhausted men will come home sweaty and eat hearty, and sleep the sleep of the dead. *Jua kali*, is the name we have for this enterprise. Hot sun. They live and work outside khaki Kenya; here they are free to make themselves what they want.

Hot sun city. There is a large industrial park—a slum—surrounding us, a flat plain of corrugated iron sheeting.

Take the sun—give it ten thousand corrugated iron roofs—ask it, just for the sake of asking, to give the roofs all it can give the roofs and the roofs start to blur; they snap and crackle in agitation.

Corrugated iron roofs are cantankerous creatures: they groan and squeak the whole day; as they are lacerated by sunlight, their bodies swollen with heat and light, they threaten to shatter into shards of metal light. They fail, held back by the crucifixion of nails. Corrugated iron roof people do not go to the grassy leafy part of the city without a clear purpose. The police will get them. City council *askaris* will get them. The hotter it gets, the more it seems that some heat and light will burst out of this place.

We are in a large patch of earth in the middle of this glorious and terrible light. There are mountains of twisted scrap metal and spare parts all around us, baked by the sun, red from rust, black from oil, and brown from dust, throwing crumbs of defeated iron to the ground: cars, parts of cars, the innards of air conditioners; dead exhaust pipes, no longer coughing or snoring or spitting illness.

One guy runs past me, waving some spare part and rattling loudly in Gikuyu, and another man runs after him. They are partners, dancing, arm in arm, shoulder to shoulder, one laughing, the other growling.

One is bent over, the other reaching for the end of his arms. His hands, which are holding the rattling part. Then, one laughing, the other not. And it is a game and a dance.

Then it is a fight.

A crowd gathers. Men cheering. My father frowns and his huddle of freelance consultants break away to witness and bay.

And.

The fight is over. They are separated.

I invent a word. *Hughagh*: (a) a sound that is at once the belly under a fist's assault and what issues from the mouth when the chest is banged; (b) a mid-chorus reminder of one's reservoir of strength: commonly used in jingles and sports shows, by army tug-of-war teams, and by female tennis players.

Immortalized by Billy Ocean: Hugh agha ha! When the going gets tough, the tough get going, yeah! Hugh agha ha! Yeah yeah yeah.

Hughagh rules football matches in City Stadium; the city comes to a standstill as Gor Mahia football club fans make their way back home. *Hughagh* is a policeman. Is a member of Parliament on a podium with his hidden little groups of paid thugs in the audience. Sometimes *hughagh* is a fist in your woman's face; sometimes *hughagcgh-hic* is lubricated by a tin or two of fine *kumi-kumi* liquor, mellowed in rusty ten-gallon drums that once stored diesel. Three tins and you will sleep on the open drain outside the drinking shack and wake up blind for life, or paralyzed.

Hughagh can be fun, too: *hagh hagh,* you laugh at those who are poorer than you, laugh from the bottom of your belly at Kirinyaga people if you are from Kiambu, at Tugens if you are Nandi, at Punjabis if you are Gujarati, at the small tribes if you are from a big one.

Somebody taps my shoulder, a thin Somali man, handsome, in giant white-rimmed opaque sunglasses, a maroon shirt with little gleaming snowflakes all over it. The shirt is not tucked in, Somali style. He flashes his eyebrows up and down for me, our little conspiracy. And out of his hands a crackling magic mat unrolls.

Sunglasses, wrapped in noisy plastic paper.

"Ferrari," he whispers, his voice carrying Yemeni monsoons and bolts of cloth. I consider, briefly, and decide not to risk it. Ferrari is a very cool thing. It roars forward, streamlined and low, lipstick red; it slinks and gleams and smells of fresh glossy magazines and cool. But if he is selling them, he is multiplied by ten thousand and so it must be that everybody in Nairobi has Ferrari.

I shake my head. He thrusts them closer to me. Surely I have not seen them well. I move away and turn. He comes around to me with a new grin and thrusts a watch in front of me. A muscle in his jaw curls into sharp knuckles, stems of khat peeping out of the side of his mouth. His left cheek is swollen, his eyes red and bleary.

Khat is salesjuice. Supercaffeine.

"SayKo!" I point at my watch and shrug.

His finger jabs agitatedly at his watch.

SayKoSayKo! Let us get excited, my friend. Listen.

The South Africans sing "SayKunjalo—the time is now." Sekunjalo. SayKo. He puts the watch to my ear, and I establish, beyond any doubt, that SayKo is ticking. Nownownow. And now I know—that he will jab and poke at me until I am in a frenzy and will lash out or buy.

SayKoSayKo! SayKoSayKo! SayKoSayKo!

Because when it gets too hot, we melt. Or break. My pimples are glowing. I can feel them. I push his hand and move away, close to the huddle of Sokasoba men and my father, who will not appreciate being interrupted.

"Heeeeey!"

They shout. My father frowns.

"Waria!" Derogatory term used in Kenya for Somalis.

"Toroka!" Run. Leave. Depart from here.

One of them shouts at him, "Waria!" And Waria grins and walks away, and I feel like shit. He makes his way to somebody else and somebody else, grabbing, gesticulating, jawing, jabbing. Tick. Tock. SayKo. SayKo. SayKo. And steam rises. Growl, Ferrari.

They say, in my new school, that electrogalvanizing deposits the layer of zinc from an aqueous electrolyte by electroplating, forming a thinner and much stronger bond. These multiple layers are responsible for the amazing property of the metal to withstand corrosion-inducing circumstances, such as saltwater or moisture. Besides being inexpensive and effective, galvanized metal is popular because it can be recycled and reused multiple times. We call it *mabati*. Or corrugated iron.

Take: ten thousand hammers, ten thousand languages all shouting, ten thousand specialists of ten thousand metals arranged into ten thousand loud permutations to fix cars, tractors, plows, pots, pans, woks, mills, chairs.

Sell: sunglasses, pirated cassette tapes, Swiss knives, spanners, boiled eggs in blue bowls, sausages in sweaty glass-and-wood cases strapped to a thin torso, key chains, plastic ducks or bunnies wound and yapping frenziedly in MadeinTaiwanish.

It is hot and yellow and dry in 1984. Many of these people have certificates. Marketing. Carpentry. Power mechanics. Electrical technology. This is the dump site for certificates that did not send you anywhere.

I am standing and nodding, and huddled men confer around my
father.

"Sokasoba?"

"Nooo. The shock absorbers are okay."

"These old pinjots are very good. Three-oh-five. Ni injection?"

I nod.

I know nothing about old Peugeots. There are things men are supposed to know, and I do not want to know those things, but I want to
belong and the members need to know about crankshafts and points
and frogs and holy manly grails and puppy dog tails. Secular things to
hang on to.

At the edge of the field of fixers, there is an old gentleman with a
fresh old school haircut, complete with a trimmed line above his left
temple, what white people call a part, an appropriately biblical word for
African hair engineered with great will to separate in this way. He is
wearing a tweed jacket, a hat and feather, and his old leather shoes are
gleaming with all the dust. He is selling old tins and cans and drums
and all other manner of containers.

One guy is cutting tubes from tires and selling the strips: those
strips, called *blada*—for children's catapults; to tie your goods to your
bicycle or on the roof of a *matatu*; to make a hosepipe fit a tap and not
leak at the point of contact. For intricate toy wire-cars, for the boot of
your car in case of any one of thirty thousand things that can go wrong
that a *blada* can sort out. Who does not have a use for *blada*?

There are piles and piles of corrugated iron sheets. *Mabati*. For recycled roofing, for millions of one-room Nairobi people. I rub my hand
along my jacket's shoulder pads, thrilled at its padded promises in this
clanging world. I am different. I am different.

I am bored with Baba's mechanics and walk around. It is lunchtime,
and women are gathered around huge pots cut out of old oil drums;
beans and maize are boiling, men queuing for a two-shilling lunch.

Screaming, shouting, ladles clashing hard onto enamel plates. Now it is the smell of boiling suds of beans.

The grass has been beaten down to nothing by feet over many years in this large patch of ground of banging. Somewhere, not far from here, an open-air church service is taking place: loudspeaker and shouts and screams.

You would not believe that not five hundred meters from here are roads and shops, and skyscrapers and cool restaurants that are playing the music of noiseless elevators, and serving the food of quiet electric mixers and plastic fridge containers. Burgers and Coke. Pizza.

I love the music of noiseless elevators: the whoosh of hydraulics, a promise of soft landings. I love easy pop, Michael Jackson, and the Gap Band. People are standing next to big, cheap speakers from Taiwan, which I am sure are bouncing up and down on the cheap wood mounts, making their own drumming sound to add to their cheap crackle.

Thin men, with corrugated brown teeth from *miraa*, and muscular jaw muscles, and glazed, wild eyes, focused on one repetitive task. And from them, from their speakers comes the sound of Congo—and this sound is exactly the sound of all the clang, the rang-tang-tang, tinny clamor of agitated building, selling, and the multilingual clash of mouth cymbals, lifting up and down, jaws working, eating, trading, laughing. And people singing are the sound of melting metal. In that urban Congolese music that sounds like it clangs: Lingala, that jangling language of Kinshasa. But around them, electric guitars twang hard, things bang.

Why don't we listen to crooning and soft drums and strumming pools of water and acoustic guitar meadows? Why not listen to plaintive old folk songs, leather string and goatskin box? The wooden sounds of long ago?

Wood rots. Wood will not bend in heat. Wood burns and crumbles. Early this century. The searing heat of Belgium's lust in the Congo insists on new metallic people. We, in Kenya, don't understand the lyrics—we don't speak Lingala—but this music, this style, this metallic sound has become the sound of our times.

Work your metal to the frenzy of your plan and let the heat around grow and grow and soon something gives, your future—on the softer side of town, in the soft melt and grass of your new square stone house in the village. After a day beating metal, you go home and sleep under your galvanized metal roof, and it rains, and no sleep in the world is better than the sleep under the roar of rain on a naked *mabati* roof. Something gives: of the body and its limits, and you're in a zone, a stream of molten creative metal. Your labor can beat, bend, melt, harden, shape, aggregate, galvanize. Labor that can defeat tiredness, because dance and song is labor that leaves you exhilarated. This is rumba. *Mabati* music. Metal music.

Baba is done. "Let's go," he says.

"Baba . . ."

"Hmm . . ."

"Can we go to Wimpy?"

"Sure." He smiles.

Chapter Eleven

Forty Kenya shillings at Ndirangu's.

Opposite Matatu Stage, Thika (near Josphat Bar and Butchery). Always in stock: Mills and Boon, Silhouette Romance, Robert Ludlum, Robert Ruark, Frederick Forsyth, Danielle Steel, Wilbur Smith, and James Hadley Chase.

All form four and six textbooks available.

Ask for Malkiat Singh notes and form four marking schemes.

Ndirangu provides an endless supply of books to middle-class Thika girls, working secretaries, bank clerks, schoolgirls on holiday, and housewives every day. I sneak out of my new school to trade with him. Each new book I read has to be more, bigger, more melodramatic to keep me interested. I gobble them like candy. I read two or three of them a day. I can write one, I am sure, a big saga and make lots of money, and eat pizza every day.

Will he kiss her? The Argentinean polo player has melting eyes and thick eyelashes. One moment they are glowering like a demonic Inquisition chimney, the next they are looking at her and saying caara, cara mia. Or the Argentinean version—something caramia-rish, and then because of her beauty they heat up blacker and shinier, blacker and velvetier, blacker and blacker, until they can't heat up any more and black Latin tenderness drips from his eyeballs like hot oil, it purses itself up like a kiss, and grabs her and . . . and . . .

...

Mang'u, originally Kabaa High School, is the second-oldest school for Africans in the country. Because it is in Gikuyuland, in Central Province, it was easier to get me a place here. Mang'u was founded by the Holy Ghost brothers in 1939. In the 1960s they decided to offer aviation as a subject for Mang'u students. They bought a glider, were given land by President Kenyatta in this dry, snake-ridden bush, and, together with the government, started to build a new school.

But the money ran out, and only the first phase of the school was completed. When it rains we are overwhelmed with mud. Our toilets block and spill over every week. The showers have collapsed. There are strange animals breeding in unfinished dorms. Many classrooms have no windows.

All those shining alumni, like Vice President Kibaki, do not come back here. Their money supports schools like St. Mary's, private Nairobi schools where their children now go to do British GCEs and international baccalaureate. Mang'u is a national school, and it attracts the brightest students from all corners of the country. Some rich, some very poor. Some come having never seen a faucet.

There is a guy in my class from one of the villages in Taveta, where the Kenyatta family owns land as big as a whole district. Many of the Taveta people there are casual workers for the Kenyatta plantation. He works as a casual laborer on farms during the holidays to earn money for fees. He walks from Thika town and arrives with his uniform torn and faded. He is all giant forearms and huge digging calves, and he sits through the night, every night, with his books.

He rarely talks, is always in a good mood, always dazed from books.

Mang'u High School, every year, supplies a third of the students to Kenya's medical school. We top every science subject in the country. We hover near the top of everything else.

We are believers. More than any other school in this country, we believe in raw and bloody hard work, in impossible academic standards. No teacher sets the bar—the old culture of our school does.

Food is boiled. Boiled maize and beans with thick chunks of soupy cabbage. Boiled in giant steel steamers. Our school caterer tells us a growing boy needs one piece of meat the size of a matchbox a week for good health. Boiled beans are good. She says. Sometimes fights break out over potatoes.

On Thursday nights, it is rice and beans—top layer that dark brown cap of liquid beans dripping down a hard fist of rice. Top layer, *topi*, is our favorite. We queue up at the dining hall half an hour before the supper bell, plates and spoons in hand, salivating. Topi. Topi. Topi. If the bell is ten minutes late, there are scuffles and fights for the door.

Our headmaster, Karaba, whom we love, has bought pigs. He wants to improve our diet. He tells us every week. Ohhhh, one day we will have a proper pork-o mearo. We dream about pork-o.

Roasting porko, frying porko.

Porko Mi-ro.

Two plump pink and yellow students land in Mang'u one day. Brothers. Their plump and pink parents have a fat old Mercedes. Their mother is plump and pink and yellow. Their father is plump and yellow. They look like an American sitcom about rich Kenyans. They come to Old Boys dorm, carrying boxes and boxes of food and big sweaty smiles. Roast chickens arrive from their driver every Sunday. Fresh bakery breads. Pizza.

We call our two new benefactors Pig and Piglet.

At assembly one morning, Karaba announces that by December we will have our first Pork-o Miro.

Our stomachs growl.

A proper porko meal-o.

My thumbnails have healed and have character. They are bumpy and black. I still use a razor blade, gently now, to try to shape them to my will. I have a callus at the base of my right thumb, from licking my thumb and forefinger and rubbing them together to maintain that perfect friction for turning pages. Reading is a fever these days. These two fingers remain perpetually ready. I lick them and rub them together every few minutes. Each time I chew the callus off it grows back, not to its original thinness.

It is 1984, and there are strange things happening.

The drought is the worst since 1870, some say, when the Maasai were broken by rinderpest and civil war. No. The famine is the worst since

1930, when thousands starved after the British had "consolidated" the diversified lands of Gikuyu families.

Breakdance: The Movie breaks every record; people queue for hours for morning shows, cut class, and spin and robot. They are screaming all over campus. There is also a new season of demons. This we are told by the God people, who are growing louder every day. They are everywhere. The posher parts of Nairobi are flooded with cattle as nomads descend on watered lawns from the plains, wearing blankets and being chased about by police. In the news we see the acres of dead cattle carcasses. Some Maasai land at people's gates half starving and offer to be security guards for food.

Teenage Nairobi girls decide that Maasai braids are the new fashion, and we see venerable warriors in red *shukas*, sitting in suburban gates. Teenage girls are sitting on the grass in front of their stools, heads leaning back and singing the latest Lionel Richie, as the Maasai warriors delicately braid hair for food money. Maasai braids are cool. Ndirangu, my bookstall guy in Thika town, tells me that people in Muranga no longer go out at night.

They fear ghosts.

Karaba, our much-loved headmaster, is gone. Moi transferred him. Our new headmaster, Jos (very very) fat Kimani, is a caricature of greed, with thin legs and a massive belly. Some strange-looking creatures arrive a few months after he comes. Some are long and thin and wiry and they chew gum and play basketball. Headmaster JosFat swaggers at parade, swinging his belly from side to side, his jowls shaking as he says we will make this the best sports school in the country, and we watch these long students bouncing basketballs, all of them looking quite quite old. Bathroom sinks are now covered with stubble and discarded razor blades. In class they sit, all lanky, looking confused about prefixes and suffixes, division and multiplication. Ati nini?

Soon JosFat is in the papers. He is now part of the country's Olympic Committee.

He is Jos fatter than ever.

...

One day we gather in a small smelly study in Old Boys. The school video player sits in the cramped room—and Fat Freddie, who has contacts in America, produces a new videotape.

For a year and more, there has been no rain in Kenya. Lush temperate forests are glowing red. The skin has peeled off all of eastern Africa, and the earth is naked and burns the feet. From under the earth dark melting things creep up through the cracks of the soil.

All over Kenya, there are stories about packs of rabid wild dogs. We call them T9. Some say their eyes glow in the dark. Some say they are bionic and can leap over thorny hedges. They like to sneak up on drunks at night and bite off their ankles. Everybody returns from the holidays with T9 stories. We hear rumors about a place called Nyati House. In Nairobi. There is a giant bronze buffalo head in front of Nyati House, and it is there that people are taken after disappearing from homes at night, to spend days being beaten on the testicles by Special Branch people.

There are ten of us in the room. It smells of socks and bread and cheap margarine and cocoa.

Freddie puts the tape on, and we watch it, hear the heartbeat, see the gravestone: SMOOTH CRIMINAL; the dead silence; the neo-ancient Egyptian woman turns her head; fingers crack, a cat purrs, hats poised leaning over one eye like the past about to come to life, clothes rustle. Then Michael Jackson appears in a white suit, shining. He tosses a coin. For the longest moment, it falls into place in the jukebox.

The whole beat of the song is taken away from the instruments and given to his body—it jerks, slows time, wheels; it jerks when sounds swing; it marks time and seems to move not with time and beat, but in relationship with it. He has detached his body from those restraints. He is teasing time and space. His body is a needle, ducking headfirst into the stiff fabric of the world we know, the whole sepia-colored past world tucked into his trousers. Now he scrambles history with his bod, makes it all a game for the body to enjoy; he is more flexible than physics. He is a plastic man, and he cannot fail.

...

One day, one slow hot day, we look out of our windows and see the sun is red and glowing. In the flat grassland distance, Kilimambogo mountain is dripping red liquid embers. The fire spreads toward us; the sky is dark with smoke. In the afternoon, the stampede begins. Teachers drone and drone, and from our classroom windows we watch giraffes speed past, chasing hyenas, zebras, small antelope. In the news, we hear that a lion escaped from Nairobi National Park and was terrorizing Langata residents.

That night Wahinya finds a puff adder in his locker. He is reaching his hand in to get some bread and margarine, and something wriggles in his hand, and he screams. The next morning we find two adders stranded on the cold pavement outside our classroom. It is so hot, every day, so dry, we wet our shirts for Double History in the afternoons, and in half an hour they are dry.

Moi and his cronies are on the radio daily. It is in the papers every day. These are dark days, we are told. There are dissidents everywhere. We have to all unite and silence the dissidents. From the radio, we know that foreign influenzes are invecting us, secret foreign influenzes are infringing us, invincing us, perferting our gildren, preaking our gultural moralities, our ancient filosofies, the dissidents are bushing and bulling, pringing segret Kurly Marxes, and Michael Jagsons, making us backliding robots, and our land is becoming moonar handscapes. They took the rain away, the Maxists, the Ugandans, wearing Western mini sguirts, and makeup, they are importing them, inserting them inside invected people, these dissidents, like Ngũgĩ wa Thiong'o, and that man called Raila Oginga Odinga.

Luvisia Wamalwa was born again. He came back after one holiday, looking sheepish, and said that he had backslid. Our world is born-again or breakdance.

...

Wahinya, of the puff adder in the locker, starts to vibrate one day, in the recreation hall. His whole body vibrates, his head nodding up and down, each separate segment of limbs jerking like a robot every evening after supper, music thumping from illegal radio cassette players. Soon many of us are breakdancing.

Meanwhile, groups of students disappear at night to the vast acreage of bush behind the dorms, and we hear them at night screaming Cheezuz, Loord God, and moaning, throats vibrating, drums even. Murage, the breakdancer, who has rings of smudged dark cirrus clouds around his big eyes, spins on the smooth floor, falls to the ground, and spins on his back; his back arcs, like it is about to snap, then his head is a spinning top, whirring like a dervish, his legs turning like cake-mixer beaters. He stands, tongue hanging, his eyes bursting with red veins, "Chaka Khan, Ch-Cha-Chaka Khan . . . baby baby when I think of you . . ."

A crowd has gathered around, clapping, and Ondiek, the oldest student in school, and in my class, stretches his arms toward Murage and starts to pray in tongues: be defeated, breakdance devil, be defeated.

As the madness grows, the fever of studying grows. We Mang'u boys are engineers by sensibility, and we believe there is a formula to fix any bump. Wayward nature and coincidence can be managed by design. Not ideology or revolution. We discuss new ways to contort, rearrange, redesign ourselves to fit in. We study through the night, sneak away to drink on weekends. Others go to mass gatherings of hundreds of thousands of Pentecostals in Uhuru Park.

Ondiek and his Christian Union crew bring the preachers, who land, from Bible courses in Texas and Nigeria, wearing white blazers, maroon shirts, and gray shoes and say Gaaaaaard a lot, and Cheezuz, and all over our school campus there are crusades, and group screams and seizures. With equal abandon, all over Kenya, streets line up with kids now called Boogalo Shrimp and Shaba Doo. *Breakdance* is the biggest movie in Kenya's history. Our largest stadia hold giant Pentecostal crusades with hundreds of thousands attending. Me, I watch, and read more novels, read and throw them away like chewing gum. I know there is no end to them—whenever I finish one library's fiction section, a new library, a new section, a new friend introduces me to a new thing. I am reading a lot of sci-fi.

On the coffee plantations in the hills behind our school, on the giant Del Monte pineapple plantations in the plains to the east, bodies are being found without genitals. *Makende* cutters, we are told. Rumor has it the genitals are going to India. On television, a dirty pale man who has wild eyes and sings for a band called Boomtown Rats is crowned the king of Ethiopia. He is everywhere. Every news broadcast, every song in the whole world. Bob Geldof.

Wherever he is people fall, twist, writhe, lose language skills, accumulate insects around their eyes, and then die on BBC. Food pours.

They feed us yellow American maize in the dining hall. Donated from America. We have a huge *ugali* fight, throwing balls of yellow *ugali* at each other and laughing. We hear rumors that maize flour has chemicals in it, for birth control. It tastes of chemicals, we are sure. We hear it is only fed to animals in America, yes, yes, it smells bestial. It is yellow, a wrong, wrong color for our national staple.

One hungry day, we find ourselves surrounding JosFat's office. An all-school riot.

The whole school is singing South African liberation songs. JosFat is sweating. "You want money? You want money?" he says. "I can give you money." He rushes into his office. Then sneaks out of it hurriedly, through another door in the administration building, and jumps into his car. We throw stones at it and run around the school, breakdancing and shouting and singing South African songs.

We head for the farm. Boomtown rats. We light night fires and roast maize; soon we are pounding out porko miro! Porko miro! We invade the sty, grab the pigs, all of them, and soon pieces of roast pig, some half raw, some burned, some still hairy, are being chewed by us all. We are burping, drunk and happy when the police come. Even the born-agains eat pork this day.

National exams come; results are hung up. We have the best results in our history. The best in the country. The mythology grows: when the pressure rises, when things get worse, we improve our results. We are special. People like us, engineers and doctors, should rule the world.

...

In 1987 we write our fourth form exams. I fail in all the sciences and do well in all the arts. I am one of the top students in English in Kenya, and probably at the bottom in physics. I move to a new school to do my A-levels, which takes two years. Lenana School. I pick French, literature, and history as my subjects. Mang'u does not accept arts students for A-levels.

I spend all useful time in my advanced-level years making plays and novels, or reading and looking for scholarships in America with my best friend, Peter Karanja, who loves novels as much as I do. I do not study much.

Our most successful play is a courtroom drama called *The Verdict*. I play a prostitute with a heart of gold called Desirée who falls in love with a repressed boy who murders his mother. The stage is beautiful. We have raided the chapel for fine Anglican velvets and old wood tables with gravitas. Everything is in the school colors, maroon and white, with the white rose embroidered everywhere.

Lenana is an old settler boarding school. Once it was a cadet high school, the Duke of York, for the children of British settlers threatened by the Mau Mau. It is a whole world away from Mang'u.

At the climax of *The Verdict*, the defense lawyer, played by Peter, jumps off the stage and releases a volcano of rhetoric that leaves the audience gasping. We steal much of that from the courtroom scenes in Richard Wright's *Native Son*. It does not occur to us what Richard Wright would think of us dressed up as if we lived in the colonial White Highlands, in Nairobi, using his words.

We win all sorts of prizes. On a high, five of us start a theater company, the Changes Pycers, and put on a play at the French cultural center with our pocket money. We make our posters and rehearse all over town in secret. Lenana is a boarding school—and strict.

The school principal is furious when he reads the reviews in the newspapers.

We can't believe that we have pulled this off.

After school, I spend a term at Kenyatta University, doing an education degree and majoring in French and literature in English. I am terrified I will end up becoming a schoolteacher. A fate worse than country music. Ngũgĩ wa Thiong'o is a writer and playwright, a Kenyan playwright, and people say he says that women should not perm their hair or wear lipstick. I have permed my hair. I like it. Ngũgĩ wa Thiong'o is Kenya's most famous writer, and was arrested by Moi in the early 1980s and imprisoned. He is in exile now, and he is trying to bring down the government. His books are banned in Kenya. He is a communist and says that to decolonize we have to write our literature in our languages. I don't like Moi—but if those people take over the government, what music will we listen to? *Nyatiti?* I love writing. I love the theater. I fear writers; they want to go too deep and mess up the clear stepladders to success. I cannot see myself being this sort of person. I dream of studying advertising. Anyway, the toilets at the National Theatre smell. I can make plays in my extra time. Musicals.

Chapter Twelve

We are sitting in a cheap bar in Westlands, Nairobi, Peter and I, getting drunk and celebrating. It is 1990. Peter is off to America on a scholarship. I am leaving too, to study for a bachelor of commerce degree at a small university in one of South Africa's black homelands, Transkei. My parents are worried—the government, pressed by the IMF, is about to stop subsidizing university education. I am already a student at Kenyatta University, doing a degree in education. Because courses are very competitive, I failed to get the course I chose, law. Education would have been fine with the subsidy, but after one semester, for the first time since Independence, Moi announces that we have to pay our own fees; our parents have to support our university education. Baba and Mum were not keen on letting us leave the country so young at first, but the university system is in some chaos, and now that they are being forced to pay, we may as well pay for courses we can choose.

Uncle Kamazi, Mum's younger brother, who teaches mathematics and statistics at the University of Transkei, helps us through the application process. South Africa is opening up, he says; there is opportunity there. It is cheaper than America or Europe. We have family there. Baba likes the idea. Mum is all for it. I want to leave, Ciru wants to leave.

A woman stands and walks toward our table.

She is older, and glamorous, in a short blue shimmery dress. She sits next to us without asking and flicks her fingers at a waiter, her skin Hollywood yellow and matte, lips shiny pink, eyes lazy and smoky.

Mpah!

"A Black Russian," she says to the waiter, who bows, and our eyes widen. We have no idea what a Black Russian is. We know things are very black indeed in Russia. That walls and countries are falling all over the place.

Her accent has something in it, German maybe, mixed into her

Kenyan accent. Her hair is long and shaggy, the color of caramel chocolate, like Tina Turner's.

"I am on holiday," she says, in an air stewardess voice. "My husband
is from Austria. We are divorced."

We order Black Russians. We get drunk and dance. She plays the
big sister, the naughty older cousin, the dangerous young aunt—flirting
with us, laughing at our youth, shocking us by saying the things her
husband liked to do in bed.

"He did not like me to perm my hair," she says, tossing her mane.
"He wanted me to grow dreadlocks. He did not like me in makeup. He
liked to see me eating with my hands. He would make me sit on his lap,
and if I put my hands in the food and mopped the soup with bread and
put it in my mouth, I could feel his *mkwajo* rising under me. Sometimes
he would play a video of a woman being fucked from behind by a big
black man, and shouting in her language. I think she was a West African.
She was shaking her buttocks, big fat buttocks, like those dancers from
Congo. He got very excited. I got a lot of money when we divorced."

Our schooling machine, nationwide, merit-based, proud, and competitive—Kenya's single biggest investment—is falling apart, and the
new season sounds like Band Aid. It's all over CNN. Open mouths,
and music, thousands and thousands of white people throwing food
and tears and happiness to naked, writhing Africans who can't speak,
don't have dreams, and share leftovers with vultures.

My friend Peter and I spent much of our A-level years in Lenana
School mastering the language of American scholarships and avoiding
actual study. If our fields and labs and classrooms look the same as they
did ten years ago, we don't notice.

Since the 1950s, all the Kenyans who did well in exams have not
had to worry about money. The idea was that this was the way to make
new people. The children of dirt-poor peasants could become doctors.
This is where my parents came from. Now, the IMF has insisted that we
stop spending so much government money on education. It is truly the
only thing that works in Kenya. There is a national network of schools,
and every year tens of thousands find their way into skills and futures.
Now the Berlin Wall has fallen, and our great universities, where the

rich and those who came fom poverty were finally equal—that is gone. Even those with money cannot afford much. They were not prepared for this. There is suddenness to things. Big big things around the world are changing overnight, and there is a sense of panic. It is possible to believe what Geldof is promising, that we will fall down a big Africa hole. The project to make people like us is ending. Now those who have, grow, and those who don't stay behind. Those who have can leave. Some parents sell their most precious assets to send their kids away.

Peter got a scholarship.

I didn't—I enjoyed the fantasy, but not the applications.

We are drunk. The woman throws her head back to clear the gleaming hair from her forehead, laughing loudly, dripping gel. Bel Biv DeVoe shakes thick, dark, and low in the bluish light of the bar. She is model lean, not Congo dancer round. She smells of hair oil and Poison. Sometimes she retouches her lipstick, and all the time her shoulders pop unconsciously, her chin dances gently, as Janet Jackson, Neneh Cherry, and Babyface thump in the background.

The college manuals that arrived in the post from America have photos of international students of many colors sitting on stairs and looking very relaxed and international. Like Model UN club kids, but after they have had polite sex. Some wore jeans, some wore saris, some slouched, some stood straight. They were clean. No ribs sticking out. No moans.

At the bottom of every photo, they gave their opinion, like, What's really cool about Brandeis is its diversiddy. They looked like pictures on television from the seventies, the early eighties. UNESCO concerts on the children of the world—a possible world full of many kinds of normal people: all doctors and bankers and lawyers, and all these things are possible, for any shape of anybody. All those kids we used to watch on television were now in Massachusetts doing diversiddy.

I want to do diversiddy.

We order tequila shots. She shows us how to drink tequila properly. Salt and lemon, and she tosses them down expertly, and licks her lips and pouts.

After a while, her accent loses its German. She shouts something loud in Gikuyu to one of the waiters. She knows his name. He smirks and shrugs and arrives with a tray of more drinks, no longer a man in a bow tie and white shirt performing an international Westlands service, now he is a Gikuyu man swaggering.

I read *Decolonising the Mind* by Ngũgĩ wa Thiong'o a few week ago. It is illegal and it was thrilling, and I had vowed to go back to my own language. English is the language of the colonizer.

I will take Gikuyu classes, when I am done with diversiddy and advertising, when I am driving a good car. I will go to the village and make plays in Gikuyu, in my good new car. I will make very good decolonized advertisements for Coca-Cola.

I will be cool and decolonized. An international guy. Like, like Youssou N'Dour. Even Ngũgĩ is in America.

The waiter drops the tray hard on the table; drinks spill off the top. She shoots him a sharp look, and he laughs.

I am now very drunk. The nightclub's lights are caterwauling above me, like a frenzied child with crayon lights, scrawling and squealing with delight. Then we are dancing, close, she and I. She whispers things in my ear. She smells of chewing gum and liquor.

Michael Jackson is squealing "Earth Song," and his softer tones whir in the spools of her breath, like a winged termite after the rains. The termite heads straight for the tubes of fluorescent lights on our veranda—it crashes and falls, its paper wings crumple and break.

I must hold myself together. I break away and go to freshen up in the bathroom.

She is sitting, her hair askew. Her legs are open now, and she bends to scratch her thighs, the stockings seamed. Gikuyu *r*'s and *l*'s tangle and snarl into her English, like a comb on untreated dry hair. Her head still nods to the music, now a little too vigorously. The soft international jungle on her head parts every so often, and we glimpse the roads she used to arrive here, the stitches from the grafted pieces of hair, the patches of bald, the little spurts of darker, kinkier hair pulled brutally into the weave, so brutally that there are little eruptions and scars on her scalp.

Illusions are peculiar creatures. We assume whole things, when a stranger's movements show a pattern that seems consistent but a single sharp contradiction arrives and a person becomes not whole but a series of mistakes: bits and parts.

A whole system falls apart—if no faith or vision carries it.

Her hands are no longer red-tipped tools made for lifting Black Russians to her Hollywood lips. They exist only to be measured against the wrong-looking Hollywood powder now visible on her face. It is not for her complexion, so her skin color must peel under chemicals so she can look right. But rightness, coolness cannot be faked. Once this is apparent, calluses spring up on her palms.

I look at her sharply. The curtain of face powder has opened, and there they are: three small dark tribal marks on each side of her nose, not from the weather, not from work, or an accident, three deliberate, immovable lines on her face.

"Where are you from?" I ask.

Her eyes still. They are beautiful, clear and light brown and velvety, large with long lashes, slanting down as they meet at the top of her nose.

"Subukia." She knows. Her body slackens. A lock of weave falls over her nose, but she does not notice it. She hunches forward.

Wambui, all those years ago. She reminds me of Amigos Disco Wambui dancing on Independence Day, so easy to believe in the person she wanted to be, so impossible for me to accept that person has come to be. The waiter stands behind me, hands me the bill, still grinning; his eyes run down her breasts and to the middle of her now slack legs.

I pay the bill. More money than I have ever paid for anything. I am ill. Her eyes swell with tears.

Me, I want to peel it all off: the hair, the skin, the Black Russian hand gestures. I am so angry at her fake attempt to be what she is not. That she fooled me. I want to put a hoe in her hands and tell her to go home to Subukia and grow potatoes.

...

Your first adult act, at Jomo Kenyatta International Airport, after your passport has been stamped and you have crossed into NoMansland, on the way to study finance and marketing at the University of Transkei in South Africa, is to watch your parents and baby sister turn away at the airport, your second-ever kiss from your mother still tingling guiltily on your neck, like brackets, as your feet rush clumsily toward the duty-free shop.

Your sister Ciru, who is traveling with you, to study computer science, is more sensible and keeps her dollars in her pocket. You stop in front of a woman who, in that fat Ndirangu novel, is somebody who wears a thing called a chignon, which is a vague thing to you, but you know it involves hair that manages to face the sky and stay in place, and you know it smells like this: like crisply unwrapping paper and hidden machines that let you stand still and dream while they propel you to where you need to go.

This is not like Nairobi's new secondhand markets, where students now shop for imported things. Street upon street of Kenyan shops and textile factories stand disemboweled by the death of faith in a common future. The owners have left the country, or have entered shady businesses that simply find ways to steal from the treasury with the help of Moi's cronies. It's not worth making anything anymore. Mountains of Care Clothes are everywhere. They come in massive containers from Europe and America. A few days ago, I stood next to a filthy-looking man who was standing on a mountain of clothes spread on giant flat sheets of black plastic surrounded by the smell of rotting fruit, in the hot corrugated market, sweating and hot and shouting and throwing a hundred-shilling Hugo Boss jacket at my face.

Here, there are rows and columns of Marlboros in the duty-free shop that are not battered from the bumps of smuggling. They are not bought from a khat-chewing Somali trader, on Kenyatta Avenue, with strange scripts in Arabic, or wrong bottles in the wrong box, or a slightly off-kilter brand name. Porchi. Poisone. Sold by thin, thin men, from Somalia. Dominos of nations tumble around Kenya—and Somali men walk about, overstimulated, and thrust their faces into yours, dribbling chewed khat, eyes bleary, jacket open and say . . . kssss, kssss, kssss, kssss . . . Rolexxx . . . xss . . . xxxsss . . . SeyKo.

Mandela is free, and South Africa has malls.

I know now I am on a highway to everywhere. I can get on an escalator with no jostling, no moving, and let machines carry me all the way to the world I want: where there are no gaps in me. There are no background noises here, no whispers in many langauges in this airport, no *kimay*. I pull the wallet out of my back pocket, my eyes half-lidded with self-conscious indifference, hand in pocket, nose sweaty, and buy a smoky green bottle of Polo aftershave.

Fuck Kenya.

Chapter Thirteen

Brenda Fassie was brought up in one of South Africa's worst townships, Langa—in the Cape Flats—once a wetland, now just dust, where not even grass can grow. She was the youngest of nine children. Her mother played the piano. At age five, she was singing for tourists to make money for her family.

She left home at fourteen. Rumor has it that she slept with truck drivers and made her way to Johannesburg, Egoli, the City of Gold. She joined a band called Joy, and later became a part of Brenda and the Big Dudes—where she had her first hit, "Weekend Special," a song about one-night stands.

Brenda Fassie is Langa in a summer heat wave. She is streams of sunlight on rusty township roofs. She is the cramp of life close: strands of sound twist and turn into a thick rope, in her throat—*mbaqanga*, gospel, the old musicals, the choral protest songs, gangsters and money; sex for sale; liberation politics; gumboots and grannies spilling in tens of thousands into this cramped township. It is these sounds bending and melting; it is them shouting louder to be heard; it is drunk and beaten jazz saxophonists in shebeens. Roofs start to crack and squeal in the direct sun. She stands and belts—a whole township street of burning silver and rust. Whipping sounds rattle and bang in her head.

She had no teeth in her first album. This was a strange fashion at the time in South Africa, among some brassy urban black women. Several front teeth were removed, some said, to give men more pleasure. Then she got false teeth. Those who know her say she has a habit of taking out her false teeth when she is drunk at parties. I want to stop paying attention to her. I can't stop paying attention to her.

...

Transkei women know their cars.

Kofi is a Ghanaian student at the University of Transkei. His car has sixteen valves. Not fourteen. Not twelve. It is his brother's car, really. It has sixteen valves. I know this because every time we are sitting in Kofi's car, swarms of honey-colored girls come up and say:

"Ooooo . . ."

". . . sixteen valve!"

Last night we went out looking for women. A group of us students, from Ghana, Uganda, and Kenya. All of us have parents or uncles or aunts who teach at the University of Transkei, deep inside Xhosaland, near Mandela's birthplace. I have two uncles here, my mum's brothers, both university professors.

Kofi suggests St. John's College in Umtata. This high school, I am told, was once one of the best schools for blacks in South Africa. Nelson Mandela went to school here. We park outside the dorms. The dorm door is open. No security guards, no gate, no teachers. We walk right in, and Kofi is twirling his sixteen-valve keys.

Broken windows, peeling paint, and many small groups of girls in makeup and skimpy clothes. If one day, the day apartheid is dead, the day the world is fair and equal, and all of those who watch R&B videos have equal access to represent these sounds to the world, Kofi will be among the selected.

We know, he knows.

When we met, he asked me what my rap name was. I did not know. He smiled, a secret smile. He stood against a doorway, his whole body leaning to the same side as his fresh slanting haircut, his smile lopsiding in the same louche direction. He had on a long baseball top, and a bandanna around his head, full of stars and stripes.

His father is a professor, and he is applying to go to America, to Ohio to study business administration, followed by an MBA. Meanwhile, he will DJ at parties.

The girls line up in the casting audition; the girls near the door are all dressed to party. In the distance, the sullen girls are huddled, pretending not to be interested, some in school uniforms, others carrying books, one with a Bible ostentatiously open. I am wearing Polo and my jacket—the one I bought all crumpled from a pile that stood next to a public toilet in Gikomba, Nairobi. The jacket occupies South Africa well.

Everybody feels small in their localness, and everyone finds it hard to imagine that those from far away are uncertain in their localness too. Here, in this jacket, I am only from abroad. I have discovered a glossy black lining, which I have rolled back. It sits, shiny—like a Coca-Cola smile—folded over the tweedy gray jacket.

"You," Kofi says to one of the girls. His finger curls to her. I am always tempted to lean my head sideways when I am watching Kofi move. I vow to have a lopsided haircut; maybe it will make my body lean the right way. "Come here." She comes. Soon her friends join her. We don't talk really. Kofi leans forward, and walks, swinging his MC body from side to side, and we all pile into the car.

Nomarussia, one of the women, in new thick clean brown braids, like Janet Jackson, turns around on the seat and nods to her friend. "Sixteen valve."

We sit in a nightclub called Dazzle, children of the mad rush out of Africa. This is not Africa. We are told that every day by people here. Are you from Africa? South Africa is not Africa.

There are Kenyans here, Ugandans, Ghanaians. We are all united by a network of relatives, professionals from Africa outside South Africa. Most of us are studying finance or computer science—some wind from somewhere announced that it is the next big thing.

Nomarussia turns to me. "Hugo Boss!"

She smiles, wide.

"I like men from Ghana," she says, and takes in my carefully permed and gelled hair, the black polo-neck under the jacket. "You look like Luther Vandross."

Her hand touches my wrist, and goose bumps gallop across my shoulder blades.

"You Ghana men are very handsome," she says, her skin clear and yellow and gold. "But how come your women are so ugly?"

On the screen, a dark R&B American man—he could easily be Ghanaian—is standing in front of industrial pipes of MTV smoke, leaning against a doorway; his hair leans, his body leans, and he sings some luurve thing, his skin dark, and around him a harem of milky-colored women with long milky hair are grinding their bodies and pouting, surrounded by smoke and light.

...

Club Dazzle is packed now with university students and some high school students. A Brenda Fassie song is playing, and all the girls have rushed to the floor to dance. We stay behind.

Nomarussia comes back, with her friends. Their little shiny bags open and little gold penises with red, coral, and pink tongues pass across the tables, lips stretch, and contract, shared lipsticks are returned, and necks are dabbed. *Mpah!*

Kofi is dancing now. His girlfriend moves awkwardly next to him. The song changes, and now he is doing something MC Hammerish that looks like running on the spot while he is pushing his elbows up and forward and down again. The waiter is here.

I lean my eyebrow to him. "I'll have another Black Russian," I say, my arm around Nomarussia's back.

I feel her stiffen as the waiter turns to her for her order. "Savanna," she says quickly and blushes.

"Would you like to dance?" I ask. She blushes and says yes.

"So what do you want to do when you finish matric?" I ask.

"Finance or information technology," she says, with certainty. Her father, she says, was in exile in Russia fighting apartheid. Her mother called her Nomarussia. Here, in Umtata, Transkei, South Africa, the girls drink Savanna cider. Men smoke and drink beer. Women cannot smoke in public in Transkei. Everybody wants to study accounting or computers. Women cannot go to a nightclub on their own in Transkei. It is 1991. Mandela was released a year ago.

Chapter Fourteen

Victory Ngcobo, my new friend, is a long happy guy with arms and legs like the last piece of spaghetti slithering across the plate as your fork chases it. His life is set. He works weekends, driving a taxi to Butterworth, two hours away. He studies hard and does well in his exams. He is twenty-two years old. He supports himself fully, and his family and extended family. He pays school fees for four of his brothers and sisters. He pays tuition for his younger brother, who is a first-year student at the University of Transkei.

He makes most of his money selling beer and dope from his room, which is a shebeen. He smokes ganja only once a week, on Friday night.

Lulama, his girlfriend, studies at a technical college not far from us. She is quiet. She visits every weekend. During the weekend, she runs his business, cooks food for him, and hangs his laundry for the week, which she takes home with her every Sunday to wash and iron. They are going to get married as soon as Victory graduates.

Victory pays Lulama's school fees at Butterworth Teknikon. She is studying social work and business management. He writes her management assignments for her. He is doing a BCom, majoring in business management.

Victory is a demonstrative lover, full of kisses and hugs. "My wife," he says. You cannot persuade him to go to a party when she is around.

Lulama wears no makeup. Whenever Victory is busy, she comes to my room and sits on my bed, reading a magazine and asking me shy questions about Kenya. She has no fear of me, and I am uncertain around her; she looks me directly in the eye, not afraid to smile and stare at me without blinking. Whenever she speaks to Victory it is in their language, Xhosa. Mostly, she does not speak to him with others around. Sometimes, if there is a group of customers drinking with Victory, she creeps up to him and sits on his lap and whispers something in his ear. She never joins in the conversation if there are men talking in Victory's room.

In this filthy drunken residence, in this homeland university, the garbage chutes are piled high with rubbish. Students regularly shut the campus down, over one or another political issue. All over South Africa is liberation talk.

I hear the first moment of a protest march while I am lying down in bed. A thin reedy sound rising. Laughter, doors slamming, a student politician mouthing slogans, laughter, some drunken jeers, and bottles breaking on tarmac. Chants.

ANC. PAC. ANC. PAC.

Sounds slide away from the weak strings of song, doors slam somewhere, and the sound bursts out: clapping, and then thumps, loose and leisurely, feet thumping randomly, but stronger; another door slams, now there are echoes as a swarm of wings flap their way through the floors of Ntinga Female Residence next door and burst out of the door, a wind of sound, flapping and rolling like sheets, like the sea; now a group thump, tenors swoop like a swarm of swallows diving to earth, ten thousand beaks of attacking altos, ten thousand wildebeest feet stomp in Xhosa.

The train is sound flying in circles. Sometimes it glides, feet thumping as the train whoops.

I peep out of the window and see no swarm—two thousand students have gathered in a messy sprawl at the door to the residence, but every foot, every voice is doing what it is supposed to do to support the strike.

...

Victory and I are drinking in his room, with Monks, his roommate, and Sis D, who came to the university in her thirties and so drinks publicly and nobody says anything about it. It is the second day of the campus-wide strike.

We talk about Brenda Fassie's new scandals. They are fast and furious now. She was seen playing soccer with young boys on the streets of Hillbrow, Johannesburg, topless. Then she shocks the conservative country by announcing she is a lesbian.

Then she is touring in the United States, dancing at a club in Washington, D.C., when one of her breasts pops out. She grabs it and says, "This is Africa!"

Brenda is where sex and struggle politics met. She is Hillbrow, in Johannesburg, where tens of thousands of illegal immigrants find themselves selling and trading and changing and dying and making money and losing money. Where black meets white, drugs meet dreams, and music soaks it all in. Hillbrow is where she always seems to end up when she is down on her luck.

Finally, we have watched TV, and we shake our heads. Brenda is finished. Drunk and incoherent, she misses concerts. Rumor has it she is on crack cocaine, which has landed in Johannesburg and is ravaging whole suburbs.

...

The strike stretches. The faculty union, the workers' union, the students' union join. On Friday, hungover, I make my way to Victory's room. Reggae is thumping on the stereo. Ayibo! Victory is always laughing as he complains about the striking students. I am always worried that things will break, as he whirs around the room on unsteady-looking limbs. "Damn. Damn. Not enough stock," he says. "No class tomorrow and I don't have enough dope."

Once you have spent enough time with him, you see his grace: counterintuitive, not moving the way the group moves—he always looks for the gaps between things: opportunities and ideas. If so many black students live only for the utopian future, Victory is on the ground, looking out for the things nobody noticed. Many students don't approve.

Yu! A whole university student! Selling something? Ayibo. Why can't he get a scholarship and apply for store credit cards?

I met a Ghanaian man a few months ago at a baptism for Kofi's niece. He is a bitter administrator of an agricultural college in the Ciskei. His students were on strike because he had cut the maintenance staff on the farm.

"Clipboard farmers!" he shouted. "They want to become clipboard farmers!"

Victory offers me a beer. I never seem to pay for beer when I drink with him. I gave up insisting. He is excited.

"I will make a lot of money this weekend. It is month end, and students have money."

"Where is Lulama today?"

"Lulama stayed in Butterworth for the weekend," he says. "She is studying for an exam."

He jumps to his feet and is out of the room. He comes back an hour later with crates and crates of beer. We load his giant freezer together, and wait for the liberation songs to become partying songs so Victory can start counting money.

Nonracist, nonsexist South Africa. This is shouted everywhere, every day, on walls, on posters. Villages. Cities. Hills. Student residencies. It is scrawled on the walls of toilets.

...

A year passes.

We are at Club Dazzle. My new friends Trust, Kaya, Feh George, from Sierra Leone, and I. Kofi is in America. We notice something strange. There is a huge group of women on the dance floor. All of them have baby dreadlocks; they are wearing trousers and men's shirts. They are all smoking on the dance floor, laughing and looking free and happy. We are not happy.

The bouncer makes his way to them, and tries to pull one of the smoking girls off the dance floor. The group attacks him, pulls their friend back in, and continues dancing.

My friend Trust goes up to them, to ask one of them for a dance. He comes back, sweating. "What is it?" I say, laughing. His eyes are wide open. "They say they are lesbians."

Soon, they are on campus too, girls having all-girl parties, buying their own booze, and smoking in huddled groups in public. Every single one of them has dreadlocks. Liberation is coming. It is all over the radio.

Chapter Fifteen

I have a small black-and-white television in my new room off campus. It is on all day. A metal hanger thrust into the broken aerial helps me get a good picture. It is 1993. Mandela snaps and crackles onto the screen. De Klerk is whirring backward, stuttering and all *kimay* and defensive. Bodies pile up in Zululand. Chris Hani is the angry man of the left, popular among the youth. White South Africans are terrified of him. They like Mbeki—he speaks smoothly and smokes a pipe. Ramaphosa too is a contender—for the next generation after Mandela, which is aging.

Over the past year, as I fell away from everything and everybody, I moved out of the campus dorms and into a one-room outhouse in Southernwood, a suburb next to the university. I do not know what happened. All of a sudden, I was moving slower, attending class less, and now I am not leaving my room at all.

My mattress has sunk in the middle. Books, cigarettes, dirty cups, empty chocolate wrappers, and magazines are piled around my horizontal torso, on the floor, all within arm's reach. If I put my mattress back on the bunk I am too close to the light that streams in from the window, so I use the chipboard bunk as a sort of scribble pad of options: butter, a knife, peanut butter and chutney, empty tins of pilchards, bread, a small television set, many books, matches and a sprawl of candles, all in various stages of undress and disintegration.

There is a secondhand shop in Umtata that is owned by the palest man I have ever seen: he has long spindly fingers, almost gray, and wears a brown sweater. He is Greek and talks to his mother a lot on the phone. He has a book exchange section. I take my batch of books out; he values them and gives me a list of my options. I will steal a few. He never watches. I walk out with books thrust into my trousers, front and back, and head for the bus station.

Back in my room, my head aches. It always aches when I leave my room for too long. I have managed to avoid my landlord for two months. When he knocks on my door, I do not respond. My curtains are closed. The keyhole is blocked. I am not home. Notes are slipped under my door. Notes are thrown away.

Ciru is about to graduate. Computer science. She is teaching at a local college and working at the computer center on campus. Sometimes she comes and knocks and knocks. She slips money under my door, even brings food sometimes. Once in a while I find myself at her apartment. She opens the door, doesn't say anything serious. We chat. She pours me a drink, she laughs, and I find myself laughing too, like we did when we were young. Twin Salvation Army marching bands on a hot dry Sunday in my hometown, Nakuru, Kenya. They bang their way up the sides of my head and meet at some crossroads in my temple, now out of rhythm with each other. I am thirsty with the effort of them, but my body is an accordion, and can't find the resolution to stand.

I relearn finger-tatting patterns, from my childhood, unraveling my sister Ciru's new handmade poncho and getting belted for it. There are several odd shapes, little curling braids and bracelets, on the floor next to my bed, all made from my winter sweater. I can hear my landlord, a Ugandan geography professor, moving about in his room. Three Mozambicans have been thrown off a train in Johannesburg. It is in the news. Black immigrants are being beaten daily now in Johannesburg.

I stretch in bed. New books by my side. Saul Bellow, Nadine Gordimer. A matchbox sits in a saucer, Lion matches, its belly sunken and crusty with crumbs of cigarette coal. It is stuck in a hardened wallow of wax. It leaves a clean wedge as it rises, swelling ominously and blurring as I swing it away from the full glare of the bedside lamp. The candle roars to light, spluttering like late-night cats fucking near the garage outside.

...

We are children of the cold war. We came of age when it ended; we watched our countries crumple like paper. It is as if the Great Lakes are standing and rising above the map and tilting downward, and streams of Rwandese, Kenyans, and others are pouring into Congo, Tanzania, Kenya. Then Kenya shook and those stood and poured into South Africa.

Spring is coming, and I am agitated. My hair is no longer chemically treated. It has grown kinky. My fingers watch themselves on the candle-lit wall as they play with an Afro comb splitting my scalp into clean squares, section by section, pinky swung away, thumb, fore-, and middle fingers set to work, bumping each other first, soon remembering Mary's clicking fingers in Mum's salon.

On the news here, a fourteen-year-old Rwandese boy crossed the border into South Africa. On foot. Build your little tower of hair, watch it droop sideways, run your forefinger and feel the hidden orders of all that mass of kink, split and squared and built into a field of short stumps of lace. Do not look at your fingers; they will immediately seize and get confused.

Auntie Rosaria lives in Rwanda. With her three sons and husband. We haven't heard from her since the killing began. Mum is beside her-self. I should call her.

I don't call her.

Doctors from Kenya, old Mang'u boys, are flooding South African hospitals to work. Let time be each open-ended knot; time is your fingers reaching into the back of the head and grabbing the wild bunch of un-sorted hair—squeaky from just being washed and brittle from drying. Pull the bunch together, so it does not curl back into itself, and hold it like a posy of flowers; rub your fingers off the sides of your posy to keep them from becoming too slippery. In minutes you, the uninitiated, are moving across the growing chessboard of plaits, finger pads kissing each other rapidly, like Mary's—eyes glazed, and talking softly to the back of Mum's ears, nothing at all you will ever remember.

This year, Kenyans start to arrive in South Africa in significant numbers. Sometimes I leave my room, always at night, and find myself in parties with small groups of young people. They carry stories that flow down the continent: Oh, the roads in southern Tanzania? What roads? And they laugh. Some people came regularly, to buy old Peugeots in South Africa from old white women and drive them back to Kenya for sale. After a few trips, knowing how to bribe; where to hide in plain sight; how to build a bulletproof refugee story; how to pay college fees; what to say in job interviews. (I am not political. Your roads are soo good. They will kill me. The politicians. I am from Rwanda. Somalia. Liberia. I lose my papers. I am orphan. No no am not doctor, I am refugee baby of Geldof. Look, look my face looks like pity baby of Geldof. No spik English.)

You collect information about traffic police in Botswana, who cannot be bribed; about college life in Harare. It is soo clean; education is cheap and good.

Moi rigged the elections, and the economy is sinking. There have been ethnic clashes in the Rift Valley, not far from where my parents live, where I was brought up.

In 1992, thousands were displaced from Rift Valley Province in Kenya. The principal aggressors were Moi's militias. There are retaliations—and soon it is not clear who started what, where or when—and soon the violence spreads out of the Rift Valley, into Nyanza and Western. It seems clear that Moi's rule is soon coming to an end, and this serves as a sort of final solution, to rid the Rift Valley of "foreigners."

I am desperate to go home. But I do not know what I will do there without a degree, with no money. My father begs me, on the phone, to stay and find a way for myself.

I do not tell him explicitly that I am now an illegal immigrant. I do not say I haven't attended class in a year, I have failed to let myelf disappear into the patterns of a school where there is no punishment, no bell, no clear timetable, no real shame, for I am not at home, and don't much care for the approval of people here.

I switch on the television, switch off the television and watch the swollen glowing belly of the screen for a moment. The night is quiet; I sit up on my bed and light a cigarette. The matchstick belly dances, a giant trembling feather of flame tiptoes across the wall. I reach out to kill the candle. Giant baby finger shadow and thumb shadow meet awkwardly on the wall. Thumb has learned not to think as it moves across hand to make a pincer with pointing finger, but pointing finger is busy carrying Olympic torch with the Big Man, middle finger, who does nothing at all, just stands there all up yours and presidential, but claims some kind of dubious authority based on height. Finger pincer meets flame, which screams for a moment before going dark. I wriggle back into my own pillow, and my tears start falling, and they don't stop.

Brenda Fassie is back on the radio. A softer, surprising Brenda, singing the gospel song "Soon and Very Soon." We are disarmed. And sigh. We don't know if the song is so powerful because of her backstory, or because of the unusual sincerity of her delivery. She should have been called Grace, a lyrical tongue of silver light, built from shacks and gold dumps, of dust and cramps and dreams. Look, she says, what you can make of this.

There she is, an open target, taking bullets, and standing, each time more battered, but still coated in light. Why, why, Brenda, we ask, do you keep on loving and burning? Close yourself, Sis Brr. Close yourself, girl.

...

Chris Hani is dead in his driveway, he has been shot dead, and blood drips from his head and rolls down South Africa's smooth tarmac, and you stand, dizzy. You make your way to the campus for the first time in over a month.

You buy several quarts of Lion beer. Victory drinks a lot now. He has a potbelly. He is dating a forty-year-old woman, with light glowing skin, a bank job, and a sixteen-valve car. For sex, he says. I am going to make money, he says. I am going to be rich. Lulama broke up with him. She is a lesbian, he says; she drinks with her gang of friends.

I bark and bellow with my friend Trust, in Victory's little shebeen. You can hear yourself grunt, and everything you say for the first few minutes is a sort of echo, as you watch his Adam's apple bobbing.

You can hear the swarms of roars all over the campus.

The country will explode. Chris Hani, the last big barrier of the ANC's left, is dead. Umtata is burning with anger. Students, even the cheese and wine club fashionistas, are turning over bins and chanting.

Chris Hani is dead. We all saw the body on the tarmac on television, blood oozing from a broken head. Mandela, on television, begs people to be calm.

Trust's cousin has a car. We drive around town. The whole of Umtata is on the street, crying and singing, feet pounding. We park at a giant open-air shebeen called Miles, after its millionaire owner. He has recently converted it from an old warehouse. It is at once a giant whole-sale outlet for the thousands of Victorys of Umtata, and also a place where all the slinky car people can show off their music systems, and girls of the St. John's Colleges of the world can choose the most compelling thumps and valves and bass and mags. An open-air, summer-party place. You can buy meat and sausage and barbecue.

Our car is parked next to Tsietsi and his friends. Tsietsi used to stay across the corridor from me when I lived on campus. He has a gun and is a bad drunk. He claims to be a well-known gangster in Johannesburg. His friends are covered in gold and cologne, the new language of these post–Berlin Wall times.

He likes to hang with some Zulu boys from Durban. One of them is Brenda Fassie's ex-husband's brother. He looks just like his celebrity brother, Ntlantla Mbambo, but he has a clubfoot. A year or so ago, Brenda Fassie and Nhlanhla were having problems, only a few months after their wedding, which was in every magazine, every newspaper, every television program.

Tsietsi and his gangsters have a huge stereo in their room on campus. They leave the door open—this way any woman passing by may peep in and be invited for some Fish Eagle brandy. Victory has banned Tsietsi from his shebeen. He likes to pull his gun whenever he is upset. A young woman—she can't be older than sixteen—walks past his car. He grabs her arm. She resists. He is pulling her close. She is screaming.

I am hot with life and it feels good. I let the vodka jump down my throat. I can feel it running down the pipes, can feel the fumes out of my mouth, and I am so hot, I wait for them to catch fire.

Gasoline catches fire. My fist is in his mouth, and his teeth have cut into my knuckle. I pound him and pound him. Now he is crying.

It is terrible and I don't know what to do. He bawls, loud and naked.

Ndiyaku . . . ndiyaku . . . he is pumping his finger up and down like hip-hop or a cocking gun, or some obscure signal to the gangsters of the world that I am marked.

His friends just stand there, doing nothing.

Trust is streetwise. He is from Diepkloof, Soweto. Johannesburg is bigger and more violent than Nairobi. He knows I am in trouble. Me, I don't care. It's so good to feel alive again.

...

Trust grabs hold of me from behind, and he is all apology, his eyes never leaving Tsietsi and his friend, hand pumping downward gently, like hydraulics, "Ah-sorry maagents, ohh-magents, he is drunk, magents, he will sort me out, ma-gents, sorry ma-gents. He is just a drunk *Kwererekwere*, ma-gents . . . these foreigners, you know, ma-gents, they are funny like that, ma-gents, Chris Hani is dead today, ma-gents, people are just being crazy," says Trust.

Then it lands. Pang.

A quart bottle of Lion beer shatters on my head. The feeling is beautiful. Tsietsi is strutting forward, his friends holding him back, his thumbs thrusting down like the buttocks of a sixteen-valve car, his chest thrust forward, as he pushes forward, and is pulled back. I burst out laughing. I can spread this heat all over the world.

I start to move toward Tsietsi. Tires screech behind me, and Trust bundles me into the car. Ciru is in the car with us. I don't know how she got here. She is crying. I ignore her.

I feel wonderful. There are little delicious explosions in my head for days—small starbursts, spreading out around my skull, like my mother's kiss. I lie in bed for a full day afterward, my heart beating, ideas and dreams punching, biting, hissing and kissing and rolling in, as shadows move like mud on the white ceiling of my small room.

Then I fall asleep again, waiting for the next surge.

Chapter Sixteen

It is 1995. Mandela is the president. We all danced and cheered for the inauguration. And I am going home. They sent a ticket. My parents. The day after tomorrow, I will be sitting next to my mother. I will wonder why I don't do this every day. I hope to be in Kenya for nine months. I intend to travel as much as possible and finally to attend my grandparents' sixtieth wedding anniversary in Uganda this Christmas. Ciru will fly to Kampala and join us.

There are so many possibilities that could overturn this journey, yet I cannot leave without being certain that I will get to my destination. If there is a miracle in the idea of life, it is this: that we are able to exist for a time, in defiance of chaos. Later, you often forget how dicey everything was; how the tickets almost didn't materialize; how long you took, time lost and you were snarled up in your own hair for days; how the event almost got postponed; how a hangover nearly made you miss the flight . . .

Phrases swell, becoming bigger than their context, and speak to us as truth. We wield this series of events as our due, the standard for gifts of the future. We live the rest of our lives with the utter knowledge that there is something deliberate that transports everything into place, if we follow the stepping-stones of certainty.

For the first time in months, I find I can move with conviction. I pack, scrub, clean, comb, and even get to the aiport on time. I tell myself that the problem with me is simple. I am homesick. I hate my course. My body agrees.

...

I take the cheap Transtate bus in the afternoon, to save money for drinking with Trust, who has moved back to Johannesburg, where he works as a management trainee for a major insurance house.

This is the bus that black laborers take to and from Johannesburg.

It is full of miners and businesswomen who buy things in the city to take back home to sell. All sleeping and drinking and quiet. Deep gothic gospel chorals chant on the stereo. And Dobie Gray, and Percy Sledge.

If you look out of the window into the dry countryside of the rural homelands, you see not crops, not human life; you see discarded plastic, as far as your eye can see, Transkei daisies they are called, like the millions of drifting people who work and consume shiny products. In this bus are men in overalls, with scarred faces, bleary eyes, and lips burned to pink splotches, from liquor. They sit in groups, in every bus rank of every small town we stop in, drinking clear bottles of cheap liquor. At lunchtime they eat sorghum beer, which is thick and nutritious, but leaves you drunk after lunch. Work, and drink, and work, and drink.

We drive past small rural towns, where girls and young men stand outside shops: a mountain of fried chicken packets pounded into the ground by months of feet; brochures grinning at you with shiny trinkets, from the floor, from a barbed-wire fence; magazine cutouts of clothes and glamour plastered on the walls of people's rooms. On every surface there are shiny trinkets of gold plastic and blue and pink and bright yellow and green drinks being sipped out of packets that have a young beautiful person leaping in the air in rapture, a straw in her mouth. Yogi Sip!

Mandela is president. And Brenda Fassie now looks haggard and beaten. False teeth and shame. There are now new black people in suits and ties, on television, on the streets. There are black people with American accents, with white South African accents, soft breasts, six-pack abs and regular features and good straight teeth, all over the radio, on television, in magazines showing off their new homes in white suburbs, their 2.3 children gleaming with happiness and swimming pool health.

There are black people talking about the market in serious credible tones. A good chunk of my finance class is in Johannesburg, working for Arthur Andersen. Marketing people are talking about a new thing called branding. Branding is changing South Africa, somebody told me once when we were drinking somewhere. You can no longer just tell people to buy the blue dress. Marketing has decided that to sell a thing you have to take time to create the right thoughts, feelings, perceptions, images, experiences, beliefs, attitudes. So, suddenly there are jobs for people who know all cultures. White people can no longer sell things to black people. It is about money, and money has decided to become like a rainbow. Kwaito—a South African version of American hip-hop, hard, material, and cynical—is in.

Brenda appears on television railing one day: drunk, high, and incoherent. "This is not real music," she says. "Kwaito is not real music."

One day, it seems like an age ago, on a campus trip to Durban, we stopped the bus in the middle of the road to piss in the wilderness past Kokstad. The sky was huge; the air was cool and dry and smelled of tarmac fumes and daytime heat. The bus stereo system was on, and we were all drunk and somebody started to sing, and soon all drunk sixty of us were arranged in lines by the side of the road, doing the Bus Stop, laughing and singing, not one note out of place. The sky was huge—we were only a few miles from the border, and beyond the road were giant white farms—and we all knew there were guns there and threats, but in this moment we were all one woven mat of bodies singing struggle songs. I found I knew the words, but not the meaning; I knew the intent. Cars honked rudely, and we boarded the bus and sang all the way back to Umtata.

Mandela is president. We are entering the city limits of Joburg. I am going home. We find, for the first time, nothing at all to like about Brenda Fassie. We don't want casualties from the past; they remind of us of the essential cruelty of hope.

What if change comes and we find ourselves unable?

...

Trust picks me up at the Rotunda, and we head for Tandoor. It is a sea of thumping, ganga and dub, flying droplets of sweat. We whir and stomp: furry black and peroxide caterpillars spraying sweat all over the room; rasta colored hair shells and beads clicking; the thump of reggae, bass, and very sexy black people: mocha, cappuccino, frappé skins, warm moist air, open-air rooftop, minty Zam-Buk ointment and black sweat, charcoal-colored gums, and slow, blurry hugs with people you have never met.

It is 5:00 a.m. We are in a cab across the street from Tandoor.

The driver, a Zambian guy, is dressed in a white leather cowboy suit, with tassles and a leather Stetson, and lots of gold jewelry. We haggle and he tells us to get in. We try to get out of the cab, and from across the street we hear guns and screams. A car speeds off—as the crowds of Saturday-night partygoers scatter behind us. Police alarms start.

We jump into the cab.

We do a tour of Hillbrow as he picks up people and drops them off. Trust starts to complain.

"Ah, bro. No problem, bro. I will drop you. I cannot lie. If you give me time, I will drop you for free. You are my brothers. Where are you from?"

And we start to chat. He was an accountant in Ndola before the copper prices fell. Do we want to hear some music?

We say yes. Spools of light whoosh past us. We are singing along.

"Like a rhinestone cowboy . . ."

...

He picks up two women from a street corner. Both of them are drenched in perfume and powder and cheap wigs.

He swings his head back to us, grinning wide. "I cannot lie, brothers. Johannesburg, it is a crazy place. Eh?"

We are in the Zambian man's apartment, with the two women.

Three somber Malawian men are unpacking boxes of wooden carvings as brandy gurgles into our glasses. There are mattresses spread on the floor—there must be fifteen or twenty people staying in this apartment. On the table there is a pile of marketing books, correspondence college manuals. Steaming plates of *nsima* and stew arrive, from the women in fishnets, Mary and Violet. We all dig our fingers into the common tray and eat. The taxi driver–cowboy grabs Mary's buttocks as we eat. She laughs and sits on his lap.

"We have to take care of each other! Who will take care of my sister?"

He is addressing us.

"I must watch out for my sister, and she can cook for me. This country is very dangerous. They are very violent here."

"Who?"

"The blacks."

Trust turns to him, eyes flashing, finger raised to protest.

"Ah. Sorry, brother. Sorry, brother. It is apartheid."

He stands and pats Trust on the back, says, "Let's smoke some ganja."

"You *Kwererekweres*," says Trust ruefully.

We go out to the balcony. Yeoville.

It is a lovely building from the 1930s, shaped like an oval cylinder, with a thin seam running around it on each floor, large oval clear-eyed windows and oval balconies, clean lines—but this is still a building from another age, of hooting ice cream vans and round brass doorknobs. Strings of an old clown's tears run down the peeling walls. The night is dry and cool, and the air hurts the nostrils.

Evans is his name, he says. His red and black cowboy shirt is unbuttoned and he wears a gold chain. He has hair on his chest, another surprise, and large, very dark lips, charcoal and ashy like a heavy marijuana smoker's. Even his teeth, which are large and very white, have sooty edges, and there's a gap between the two front teeth. His smile warms me.

Seeds inside the joint crackle as we pass it around. Mary and Violet come, with a new guy, young, shiny, and dapper in a black suit and tie. "My young brother," says Evans. "George. I brought him here from Zambia. He has finished his BCom at Wits, and is now working at First National Bank." They used to live in Tembisa, but once Evans was beaten up in a shebeen for being a foreigner.

"They don't like us," says George. Evans's face darkens. "They don't like us because we remind them that they are still slaves."

I shoot a sharp glance at Trust. He missed that—he is looking intently at the crackling joint, his lower lip thrust forward like a cash register tray. I giggle. George grins back at me and winks, takes his jacket off. He sets up a grill, lights the coal, and brings meat from the kitchen in a bowl.

Soon, the room is spinning. Faces swell in and out; Evans's teeth move, as he laughs up and loud. He jabs Violet's waist—that's her name, Violet. She jerks her waist sideways.

"Ah, *mpslp*," she clicks and slurps, and laughs, and that sound makes me so homesick, I hurt. Mum's kiss sat there, that day, puckered up in one spot, its dainty legs pumping on the spot, as if this was the only way it had to keep itself together. Then it collapsed slowly, stretched, diluted and gentler, tingling for long minutes.

I am being attacked by sheets of dancing city lights. I close my eyes as panic rises. Saliva slices back, over, then under Evans's tongue as he talks to Trust; then a hiccup as a burp reaches the back of his throat and he coughs forward suddenly, and breaks into laughter and I turn to look at him. The sky and stars start to wriggle and streak in my mind. A tongue slips past the gap in his mouth; meat falls onto a flame and squeals.

We are eating. On the balcony, the air is soft and the sky is spinning and I am starving. We all dip into one large tray of *nsima*, then dip the balls of maize meal into the tomato gravy. I can hear teeth clicking as we strip bones of meat. Am I seeing things? I close my eyes, dizzy. A red, wet moan climbs down from the roof. Then it starts to dribble—soft wobbly carrots creep through the gaps, swollen turgid potatoes fall and splatter.

I rush to the toilet and throw up. I miss my room. It's been so long since I walked into the world without fear. Already I have been out of my room longer than I have been in a year. I am afraid I can't handle myself. I can't go and hide in my room now. I stretch my mind to my bedroom at home—I will be home tomorrow. I will be home tomorrow.

I stand on the balcony away from the rest. I look at the sky, and the giant roof of dark offers spongy, confident promises—it can take any assault and remain unchanged. Screeching giggles and screams circle faster and faster, smaller and smaller, then gurgle into a sinkhole of incoherence as early-morning traffic rises.

It is Trust's hand on my shoulder.

"Are you feeling better, bro?"

I nod.

"Are you also from Zambia?" I ask Mary, one of the fishnet women.

She shakes her head. "Malawi. He is just a friend. This is my house. He drops me home every day, and takes my daughter to school. I make food for him. He can't cook, this one."

Congo rumba music blares out of a small cassette player on the floor. Her cousin, Violet, dressed in a tight sequined dress and a cheap weave, is dancing, on her own, to the rumba. The lumps under the blankets on the floor don't move.

The sun has started to stream in, still soft and gold. People curl out of their mattresses, grunt hello. I count at least twelve people in this apartment. Giant plastic bags are packed as curio traders start to prepare for work in the flea markets of Johannesburg. Two girls, both seven or eight years old, emerge in full school uniforms, navy blue and white pleated skirts, so short, those South African skirts, neat and innocent with matching satchels and smug white South African accents. They stand, hands shyly swinging behind backs, as they greet me, heads bowed respectfully. Evans is scratching the braids of one of them as they look at our disheveled bodies without mirth or surprise. They speak their language and help their mother set the table. Their mother, Violet, is now wrapped in a sarong, hair under a scarf, skin scrubbed to reveal twin burn marks on her cheeks. Skin lighteners. She looks like a mother now. Her night face is gone. I can't see Mary anywhere.

A young man comes in, takes off his security guard jacket. He grabs the books from the table and disappears into one of the rooms.

As they eat Kellogg's cereal, the girls watch television, giggling.

There is an ad with an aerodynamic man dressed in a neon bodysuit. He is running after drinking a healthy power drink. "Your body remembers," the ad says. "Your body remembers."

"No sleep. We must work! A man should not sleep," roars Evans.

We are in the taxi again—and soon outside the gates of a prosperous-looking, mostly white school. There are a few brown kids around. The boot is full of wooden carvings, and the car groans and sways, as other cars, sleeker trophies of a credit economy, whoosh away. The girls get out, are admonished to behave by their cowboy uncle. They tumble out of the car and walk, now slouching and chatting loudly, their bodies different, English-speaking bodies. They don't look back. They merge happily with a group of mostly white, preppy-looking kids.

"The de-kaff generation," Trust says, sniffing. "They speak with, lak, white, lak, South Effican accints." We stop for some Chicken Licken (s' good s' nice) on the way back to Trust's place in Soweto. Evans refuses to charge us any money. "We are brothers," he says. "We have to help each other!"

Chapter Seventeen

My passport has a problem. It has swollen and is now a lumpy accordion—full of watermarks, corrugated pages, and slurring visa stamps. It spent a full cycle in a washing machine. The man at security looks at it, then at me and my somewhat tattered and grimy bag, and waves me past, his head shaking.

They say those streams of puff behind planes are made by the same thing that makes steam puff from your mouth on a cold day: when two air masses that are not fully saturated with water vapor mix, the air remains at the same temperature but drinks in all the vapor it can, until it saturates and forms a kind of cloud. I wonder, sometimes, whether the substance we call reality is really an organization as formless as the puffy white lines that planes leave behind as they fly.

Since I was a child, my mother has performed an act of will on me. I present myself within her reach, annoyed at something, or upset at somebody. The first thing she does is reach forward with both her thumbs on my eyebrows and push the flesh to the side, her voice flattening my frown, then her hands run down both my cheeks, and I am a lumbar guitar; my vertebrae are fret markers.

I would not have survived my season of falling if Ciru had not always been there, just there, making sure, giving me pocket money, and wisely keeping her distance.

People pull you out of yourself, and from the day I met Trust Mdia, he has done this. Each time I have come to him, drunker and dirtier, he has taken what he has seen, ignored the beast, and spoken to the friend, so I have found myself being, with him, a considerate, eloquent person, a normal person.

...

I get the window seat, and as soon as I am settled, stuff sprawled around me, my seatmate arrives. He is tanned and wiry and surfer slouchy, with shaggy blond hair that leans down his forehead, a 180-degree combination protractor and triangle: a curly and bouncy geometry that flops about and returns to its location quite exactly. I can't stop looking at it. Boing! The word jumps into my head. He unloads his bag on his chair, a laid-back nylon puzzle box with strange bulges and slits and zips all over. They look carelessly placed.

He gives me a tight, measured smile and goes to work: straps scream, zips purse thoughtfully, before he unrolls the conveyor belt of symmetrical teeth, which grins lopsided, like Tourist Info, Bondi Beach, to reveal small, billabonging netted storage compartments, where carefully rolled tattered and softened jeans sit with a rolled smaller bag of various happy unguents.

He lifts his shirt, a colorful thing wrapped around his lower belly snaps open, then a flap screeches up, then a zip grins and eats his passport.

He sits down. Snap. Then arranges himself in the seat in a sort of half-yoga position, one knee up, tourist guidebook slouching on his thigh. He pops a little capsule of chewing gum into his mouth.

The in-flight magazine describes a new thing called bungee jumping. People stand on giant cranes, on top of giant cliffs, with rubber bands around their waists, and jump and almost kiss the ground at superspeed, and are yanked back up, bouncing on the spongy world, which refuses to offer threats. The moment he is comfortable and settled into his book, I want to pee.

...

When you are lazy and locked in your room for days, fluff, in the right light, looks like thousands of starlike creatures somersaulting in the air. They swell out of nothing and somersault and burst or vanish again into nothingness, and others swell, as if something on the other side of reality is blowing the smallest bubbles in the world through holes we can't see.

There is a moment, five minutes into the air above Johannesburg, airplane nose up and back flat, where the basics are established outside my window: giant piles of earth from the gold mines that look like plasticine playground pyramids, thousands of swimming pools, and more thousands of paper and cardboard and corrugated iron shacks, and even more thousands of matchbox homes. From the air their place in a political project is clear: tiny, tiny little squares of measured and regulated space.

An Excel spreadsheet city. Each little box is the same size. Places that could spread out to the moon are folded into the physics of this universe—and you walk away from some highways and you are in a dense black hole called Alexandra, which has close to one million people in two square miles, but you look at the spreadsheet, and Alex is one little box, the size of twenty or so compounds in Sandton nearby. So millions of words and lives and economies have disappeared behind the clean lines. The residents of Sandton write bewildered letters to the newspapers, unable to understand the unstoppable epidemic of crime.

It is all strange to me still, this country, where every human economic activity has been tagged and measured and taxed. Everything is numbered. Anything you want to buy is within reach; it has been broken into many tiny pieces, and you can buy it, a piece at a time: a car, a house, a CD. Even Woolworth's lamb chops are available on credit, bought by township mamas for special meals and paid off over several months with interest.

If you click on one of those boxes, any one, a whole giant world tumbles out, a sort of apartheid hypertext of massive worlds hidden inside the boxes, brewing and growing, and emerging from the invisible to pay for Woolworth's lamb chops. Once a rare 7 Series BMW disappeared into Alexandra, from Sandton, and was found days later in Singapore.

Inside those mine dumps, over a hundred years ago, when Joburg was a rough and ready gold city, a Zulu guy called Nongoloza set up a gang of thugs called the Ninevites. They were highly organized.

"I laid them under what has since become known as Nineveh law," he said to his white captors when he was arrested. "I read in the Bible about the great state Nineveh which rebelled against the Lord and I selected that name for my gang as rebels against the government's laws."

The Ninevites became legends—it was said that they had occupied disused mine shafts, where they had a Scottish bookkeeper, white women, shops and boutiques. It was said they were immune to bullets. Around 1910, the authorities caught up with him. Nongoloza's fellow gang leaders infiltrated and organized the prison system in South Africa. To this day, gang members in South Africa's male prisons trace back their history and ideology and culture to the Ninevites. And Nongoloza remains a cult hero.

We burst through cloud. I pick up my novel and try to be airplane blasé, like Billabong next to me, who has not moved, but I want to fidget and peer down from the window.

I want to pee. We are asked to fasten our seat belts as the plane dives into clouds: they are, to us in this plane, eyes closed, hard rocks battering the fuselage.

Chapter Eighteen

I am nervous. Nairobi has burst out of itself, like a rotting fruit, and I don't think I like it. The taxi drives from the airport into the city center. Around us are *matatus*, those brash, garish public transport vehicles. *Manambas* conduct the movement of the *matatu*, hanging out of the open doors, performing all kinds of gymnastics as they call their routes, announce openings in the traffic, and communicate with the driver through a series of bangs on the roof that manage to be heard above the music. There are bangs for oncoming allies, bangs that warn of traffic jams ahead, bangs announcing an impending traffic policeman. There are also methods to deliver the bribe, without having to stop.

The taxi drops me off near the Stanley Hotel. I look abroad enough for them to let me store my bags in the lobby.

I walk. I don't know if everything looks drab and dirty because I have been somewhere cleaner, or if it has always been that way.

To look down that tunnel of buildings: lower Moi Avenue; Moi, the president who oversaw the fall of the colonial city and opened up the informal sector for growth by inadvertently breaking the grip of the politically connected Kiambu Gikuyu and Asian business mafias. Moi Avenue, the street that marks the end of Nairobi the international city and begins the undocumented sprawl of an African city.

To look down this tunnel one sees swarms—people and small stubborn constructions climbing up the skyscrapers like termite mounds on a tree. Secondhand clothes shacks, vegetables, wooden cabinets, behind which whispered watch repairs take place in Dholuo; soft cracking KTN news on a muffled radio; Dubai product exhibitions thrust out of storefronts and into the street. Shoe shiners and shoe fixers telling improbable political tales that later turn out to be true; both solicit work by keeping eyes on feet, and you start guiltily when you are summoned for repair or shine. Gospel books and tapes spread on plastic sheets on the pavement, next to secondhand international magazines—NBA! GQ! FHM! Bright bold Buru Buru *matatus*, trilling like warring species of tropical birds, jerking forward and back, revving forward, purple lights flashing urgently, to try to catch passengers in a hurry to go home, who discover too late that this urgency is fake: the *matatu* will wait until it is full, then overfull, then move only when bodies are hanging outside the door, toes barely in the vehicle, *songasonga mathe, songasonga*. Lunchtime Pentecostal God, unregulated, tax free, as attractive a business as selling on the street, Lunchtime God bludgeons the air around us, from small upstairs rooms, screeching preachers, moaning Christians, lunchtime prayers, shine or repair.

In the distance, the sheets of iron and slum, stretching beyond Machakos bus station. A *matatu* swerves past my feet, almost crashing into me. The driver winks, hoots, reverses back, a short funky beep beep; the conductor slaps the side, throws his eyebrows about in my direction, swinging his head to the door. I shake my head and laugh. The car swings past me again, teasing, nearly hits me, and zooms away, its fat buttocks bouncing suggestively on the potholes, Oriental back lights blinking suggestively, words flashing—Just Do It—above a painted snarl. Another one swerves past—this one candy-floss pink, with speed-blown wings of metallic blue on each hip. It blinks, lights cartwheel around the roof like dominoes, and a ghostly purple light shines inside.

One guy is hanging on to the roof by his fingernails, one toe in the open door, inches away from death, letting both hands go and clapping and whistling at a woman dressed in tight jeans who is walking by the side of the road.

This is Nairobi.

This is what you do to get ahead: make yourself boneless, and treat your straitjacket as if it were a game, a challenge. The city is now all on the streets, sweet talk and hustle. Our worst recession ever has just produced brighter, more creative *matatus*.

It is good to be home. There are potholes everywhere. Even the city center, once slick and international looking, is full of grime. People avoid each other's eyes. River Road is part of the main artery of movement to and from the main bus ranks. It is ruled by *manambas*, and their image is cynical, every laugh a sneer, the city a war or a game. It is a useful face to carry, here where humanity invades all the space you do not claim with conviction.

In this squeeze, people move fast and frenziedly. And behind all the frenzy there is weariness—nothing is coming. After the strikes and battles in South Africa, which involved everybody, this defeated place is hard to take. Some people look at my budding dreadlocks and hurry away. I spell trouble: too loud looking and visible. A street kid gives me a rasta salute, and I grin back at him as he disappears between people's legs, a bottle of glue in his mouth, his feet bare and bleeding.

Urban Kenya is a split personality: authority, trajectory, international citizen in English; national brother in Kiswahili; and content villager or nostalgic urbanite in our mother tongues. It seems so clear to me here and now, after South Africa, which is so different. There, there is a political battle to resolve embattled selves. Every language fights for space in all politics. In this part of town, all three Kenyas live: city people who work in English making their way home; the village and its produce and languages on the streets; and the crowds and crowds of people being gentle to each other in Kiswahili. Kiswahili is where we meet each other with brotherhood.

It is an aspect of Kenya I am always acutely aware of—and crave, because I don't have it all. My third language, Gikuyu, is nearly nonexistent; I can't speak it. It is a phantom limb, *kimay*—and this only increases my desire to observe and belong to this intelligence and its patterns. All city people inhabit several worlds in many langauges. There are people who speak six or seven languages.

So many times, you hear about somebody who was living another life in another language, and when he died, whole families came crawling out of the woodwork. Widows fighting next to the lowering coffin. Before I left, I thought of these things as exceptions, things that happened sometimes, to some people. That is not true.

Something twitches at the back of my neck, then there is a silence, for a moment a feeling of time suspended. Then I see the trucks roll in.

Khaki legs jump out. A group of women street traders, grandmothers, some great-grandmothers, stand and scatter, as *askaris* with big clubs unload from a city council truck and bear down on them. For selling. Illegally. On the street. The same city council collects tax from them every month.

I run. We all run. Dust rises; tomatoes scoot onto the road and bleed as *matatu* wheels smash them. There are plastic shopping bags everywhere, floating and flapping, Taiwan Tigritude. There is hooting, screams, and laughter, and the dull, wet thump of heavy sticks on soft bodies.

I have ducked into the doorway of a shop, and stand and watch as an old Gujarati woman looks at me suspiciously. Her eyes follow my body. I am sure she is about to scream for the police, but she will have to pay them too. I reach into my pocket, and a handful of notes comes out. I buy a *khanga*, which sits on the wall. She starts to chat as soon as I have paid.

"So, you come from America? My daughter is there."

"Doing what?" I ask.

"Computer science," she says.

I walk out. Nairobi blinks, and people slowly make their way back and set up shop, as the truck roars away. I have some dirt in my eye, and I am rattled. A man walks past me, carrying key chains for sale, bellowing in Gikuyu. He has one of those rare reddish faces that occur in some people, always with freckles, always with hair the color of Krest bitter lemon, with thick hillocks of cheekbone, and his eyes catch mine. They are pale brown and squinty, with dirty gray eyelashes. He winks. I swing my head to the side and smile. I am rattled, and there is dirt in my eye.

I make my way back to the softer city, shoulders jostling me. City buildings sway, giant baby giraffes with shaky knees, sandpaper tongues licking my dusty itching face. Everybody is rushing. A rather serious-looking man in a suit is begging an *askari* in English, and when a whip is raised, he crouches and begins to plead in Kiswahili, and the whip comes down on his neck and he is bleeding, bwana, oh, bwana, his head shaking side to side as he sidles back smiling nervously, then screams as the thump registers. If they were of the same tribe, he would probably have muttered something, in one of fortysomething first languages, mother tongues, and the *askari* would have looked from side to side quickly, and frowned in pretend annoyance, wagging a finger, go now, and don't do it again!

Three forked tongues! See how they split and twist and merge.

Light bounces off cars and glass windows, and I can see Tom Mboya Street, swollen and pushed back by batons, hooting and smelling of burning carbon, burst toilets, layers of sweat, mashed fruit, and teargas—and all of this is nothing under the weight of the rivers of surging people. It has been years since I saw my parents, my brother Jim, and my sister Chiqy. Even in Nairobi's chaos, I am strong, there is a thread, thin and as certain as silk that makes my legs move forward without doubt. If I am not certain about anything else, I am certain that the world of my family is as solid as fiction, and I can relax and move toward them without panic.

Chapter Nineteen

Nakuru.

I am home.

Mum looks tired and her eyes are sleepier than usual. She has never seemed frail, but does now. I decide that I have changed, and my attempts at maturity make her seem more human.

We sit, in the dining room, and talk from breakfast to lunch. Every so often she will grab my hand and check my nails. She will lick a spot off my forehead and smooth my eyebrows. She stands to clear the table. She is swiveling her radar, like she used to when we were children, half-asleep, shuffling softly in her caftan, and walking around, after feeling disturbed by something intangible. We wander and chat, and things gather to some invisible assessment inside her, and she turns, sharp and certain, and says, "You smoke."

I nod, eyes tap-dancing awkwardly, waiting for it to come, the full blow of power. It does not come: there is restraint.

They are worried about me and, for the first time in my life, worried enough not to bring it up. I have not spoken to them about my stalled degree in a long time. They know. I know.

After supper—*ugali!*—I make my way around the house. Mum's voice talking to my dad echoes in the corridor. None of us has her voice: it tingles. If crystal were water made solid, her voice would be the last splash of water before it set.

Light from the kitchen brings the Nandi woman to life. A painting.

I was terrified of her when I was a child. Her eyes seemed so alive and the red bits growled at me. Her broad face announced an immobility that really scared me; I was stuck there, fenced into a tribal reserve by her features. With rings on her ankles and bells on her nose, she will make music wherever she goes.

There are two sorts of people. Those on one side of the line will wear thirdhand clothing till it rots. They will eat dirt, but school fees will be paid. On the other side of the line live people we see in coffee-table books, we see in weekend trips to the village to visit family, on market days in small towns, and on television, translated back to us by a foreign man with a deep voice that has come to represent timeless days and bygone ways.

These people are like an old and lush jungle that continues to flourish its leaves and unfurl extravagant blooms, refusing to realize that somebody cut off the water.

To us, it seems that everything is mapped out and defined for them, and everybody is fluent in those definitions.

The old ones are not much impressed with our society, or manners—what catches their attention is our tools: the cars and medicines and telephones and windup dolls and guns and anthropologists and funding and international indigenous peoples' networks.

In my teens, set alight by the poems of Senghor and Okot p'Bitek, the Nandi woman became my Tigritude. I pronounced her beautiful, marveled at her cheekbones, and mourned the lost wisdom in her eyes, but I still would have preferred to sleep with Pam Ewing or Iman.

It was a source of terrible fear for me that I could never love her. I covered that betrayal with a complicated imagery that had no connection to my gut: O Nubian Princess, and other bad poetry. She moved to my bedroom for a while, next to the faux-kente wall hanging, but my mother took her back to her pulpit.

Over the years, I learned to look at her amiably. She filled me with a fake nostalgia that was exactly what I felt I should be feeling because a lot of poetry-loving black people seemed to be spontaneously feeling this. I never again attempted to look beyond her costume.

I stand under her picture; I can see trails of our pencil marks, childish scribbles still visible under new coats of paint. She is younger than me now; I can see that she has girlishness about her. Her eyes are the artist's only real success: they suggest mischief, serenity, vulnerability, and a weary wisdom. I find myself desiring her. And I am willing to admit that this could be, too, because she has started to look like it is funky to look somewhere in this new Zap Mama, Erykah Badu, Alek Wekky world.

I look up at the picture again. Then I see it. Ha!

Everything: the slight smile, the angle of her head and shoulders, the mild flirtation with the artist. I know you want me, I know something you don't.

Mona Lisa. Nothing says otherwise. The truth is that I never saw the smile. Her thick lips were such a war between my intellect and my emotion. I never noticed the smile. The artist was painting "an African Mona Lisa."

The woman's expression is odd. In Kenya, you will see such an expression only in girls who went to private schools or were brought up in the richer suburbs of the larger towns. That look, that slight toying smile, could not have happened with an actual Nandi woman. The lips too. The mouth strives too hard for symmetry, to apologize for its thickness. That mouth is meant to break open like the flesh of a clapping Sunday.

...

I wake up early, and walk out of the gate and up the hill to catch a view of the lake and the town.

I am avoiding Baba. He has been gracious so far—has said nothing, but a chat is looming. Clearly Mum has insisted on taking care of my situation. So, maybe he won't say anything. I am racked with guilt. All that money wasted on my degree. He is about to retire. Chiqy is in boarding school now—and will need to go to university.

We live in a house on the slopes of Menengai Crater. This used to be a whites-only suburb.

While I was reading all those distant English books as a child, the idea of spring made its way into my picture of my childhood environment, Milimani. We have no real spring—we are on the equator. But for me, spring was every morning, dew and soft mists, and the lake still and blue in the distance, sometimes all pink with flamingos rippling with a breeze, and rising like leaves to whirl and circle in the sky. Autumn was September, when the jacaranda trees shed all their purple flowers and the short rains began—and the idea of an autumn, of a spring, was also resident in the imagination of the English settlers who planned this leafy place, and thought of blooms and bees and White Highlands made into a new English countryside.

Old colonial homes like the one I was brought up in are the solid material matter of this town, pretending to be its complete beginning, and stubborn in our minds.

Yesterday Jimmy was dispatched—by Mum for sure—to take me for a long drive in his new banker's car, and compassionately collect information.

"Do you want to talk?" he asked.

I did not know what to say.

He bought ice cream.

After a few awkward minutes, we drove out of town, and he introduced me to the woman he plans to marry. Carol.

"Don't tell them yet," he said.

In the first past we know, there are small gaseous memories of old, old people, the Sirikwa, some who lived at Hyrax Hill a mile or so away. They built irrigation canals at the escarpment I can see from here. Ten miles above us, on this hill, is Africa's second-largest caldera, after Ngorongoro. There is a road to the summit, and from there you can see the massive saucer-shaped crater, twelve by eight kilometers, five hundred meters deep, on its sheer cliffs. It was formed eight thousand years ago, after its last major eruption.

Over a hundred and twenty years ago, one of the decisive battles of a great war is said to have taken place here. For centuries the Maa military complex—a cattle-keeping civilization—had dominated much of Kenya's hinterland. As the cattle were the currency of trade for many Kenyan societies, including my own, the Gikuyu, the Maasai's great herds made them the wealthiest society in the Rift Valley. They were our bank of protein. Because of this, most of Kenya's towns are named by the Maasai. Nakuru means *dusty place*. Menengai is said to mean *place of corpses*.

The British built their railways, roads, and satellites; then came the people and roads we built after Independence, on the same model, somewhat skewed and uncertain. Then as our parents served warm beer and oat porridge, the Jetsons arrived on television: slouching, gum chewing, marketing America.

And brewing inside this space, from fifty or so ethnic histories and angles, is Kenya—a thing still unclear, picking here, marrying across, choosing there; stealing here, and there—disemboweling that which came before, remaking it. Sometimes moving. Sometimes not. Some say all we do is turn, like rotisserie chicken, on the whims of our imperial presidents, Kenyatta and Moi. They run around the country all day, every day, to see whether we are browning well enough for supper.

I was about fourteen years old when Baba and I spent a night in a shabby old colonial hotel, the Devon, in Nairobi. I was all pimples and uncertainty. Things were awkward. Baba and I had never shared a hotel room on our own before.

He started a lecture on keeping the bathroom tidy; we talked about my maths grades, which were, as usual, abysmal.

I defended myself by saying, "If I had 10 percent in maths, and I am among the top five students, it means I did very well."

We both laugh nervously. Then he frowned, and his lips got very managing director. I was sure there would be more to talk about, but not here. Home is the place where such battles are fought with traction, Mum invisibly deciding the parameters of the battle—thrust, withdraw, attack, push all buttons.

Go nuclear.

Baba sat on his bed in his vest and read the paper for a self-conscious while, then stood. My face was, as usual, hidden behind a novel. Every movement was louder than it should have been. He then stood around awkwardly for the longest moment—surely all of one minute.

Then he a-hemed and said "I think I will go out and play the slot machines"—and I nodded, relieved, and he turned away, and this is the reason I will remember that day so clearly; his hand missed the doorknob, and he stumbled as he stepped out, this person I know never to be clumsy, and I can feel it as loud as an ocean in a shell, the way his body has always turned back to the trunk of his life—his work and family—and done its duty, and now he found in a small shocked moment that he could not just cruise out, jacket over shoulder, whistling and free.

...

I don't know how to explain my situation to them. I walk past the line of jacaranda trees that line government houses. I turn off the main road and follow the path, to avoid Baba's morning drive to work. There is a small faded house here, right at a corner, with a large rocky garden that stretches downhill to border State House. It used to have a swimming pool, which is now gray and green and empty. It is one of several houses that were given to the children of Old Man Bommet, whose sister was married to the president.

A short gnarled old tree has twisted around and back on itself like a dog leaning to nibble an itch on its back; it has a rich brown bark, few leaves, and orange flowers that look like anemones. It must have been common in this area before memories of Surrey and Anglo-Bangalore changed the landscape in the 1930s: jacaranda and eucalyptus and straight stems, in straight lines. You can find this tree all over the wild parts of the crater forest. I don't know its name.

There are stories about the rising jets of steam, that they are the ghosts of old Maasai warriors trying to make their way to heaven and being pulled back by the gravity of hell. For years there were stories about a giant fog-colored umbrella that rises above the floor when it rains, and covers the crater, so the ground below remains dry. There are also stories, lots of them, about people who disappeared down the crater for days, and were found later, disoriented; they could not remember what happened.

The old pattern has reversed: power was in the hands of the cattle keepers two hundred years ago; now it is in the hands of the squatters, the subsistence farmers, the tillers. They adapted to the changing world faster. A hundred years ago, a surplus of grain would buy cattle. The Gikuyu would buy cattle from the Maasai. By 1920, any surplus was converted into cash, and the economy of the Maasai collapsed.

Our new home, a few hundred meters from the house where I was brought up, is on the last line before the blue gum forest that extends all the way to the rim of Menengai Crater.

I heard them come in last night, the *moran* (warriors), and their cattle. The strong smell of urine and dung flooded our house, and old throaty songs, and the cowbells. They sang the whole night, and for a while I could pretend that time had rolled back, and I sat among them, as a biblical nomad, or much as my great-grandparents would have. I decide to spend some days traveling around, to avoid my parents, to follow a road and think about things other than what is wrong with my life.

What a wonderful thing, I think, if it was possible to spend my life inhabiting the shapes and sounds and patterns of other people.

Chapter Twenty

I've got a part-time job. Driving around Central and Eastern provinces and getting farmers to start growing cotton again. I have been provided with a car and a driver. Baba and some friends have invested money buying an old government cotton ginnery, which is being privatized. He asks me if I want to do some agricultural extension work for them. I say yes. They are starting to have confidence in me. I have been helping Mum in her shop and running errands. I promised myself that I would not read any novels while I was sitting behind the counter in her small florist shop. Sometimes I dash across to the club and sit on the toilet for half an hour with a book and a cigarette, but mostly I have been present in the world. Last week, at breakfast, I was going on and on about some theory or other, and Baba burst out, "I don't understand, I don't understand, you are so intelligent, I don't understand why you are so . . ."

Mum sent a sharp warning to him across the table, and he stood up and left. It's good I am no longer an egg. So much better than the silence.

My colleague Kariuki and I are on the way to Mwingi town in a new, zippy Nissan pickup. The road to Masinga Dam is monotonous, and my mind has been taken over by bubblegum music, chewing away, trying to digest a vacuum.

That terrible song: "I donever reallywanna killthedragon . . ."

It zips around my mind like a demented fly, always a bit too fast to catch and smash. I try to start a conversation, but Kariuki is not talkative. He sits hunched over the steering wheel, his body tense, his face twisted into a grimace. He is usually quite relaxed when he isn't driving, but cars seem to bring out a demon in him.

To be honest, Mwingi is not a place I want to visit. It is a new district, semiarid, and there is nothing there that I have heard is worth seeing or doing, except eating goat. Apparently, according to the unofficial national goat meat quality charts, Mwingi goat is second after Siakago

goat in flavor. We Kenyans like our goat. I am told some enterpris-
ing fellow from Texas started a goat ranch to service the ten thousand
Kenyans living there. He is making a killing.

South African goat tastes terrible. Over the years in South Africa,
I have driven past goats that stared at me with arrogance, chewing non-
chalantly, and daring me to wield my knife.

It is payback time.

This is why we set out at six in the morning, hoping that we would
be through with all possible bureaucracies by midday, after which we
could get down to drinking beer and eating lots and lots of goat.

I have invested in a few sachets of Andrews Liver Salts.

I doze, and the sun is shining by the time I wake up. We are thirty
kilometers from Mwingi town. There is a sign on one of the dusty roads
that branches off from the highway, a beautifully drawn picture of a
skinny red bird and a notice with an arrow: Gruyere.

I am curious, and decide to investigate. After all, I think to myself, it
would be good to see what the cotton-growing situation is before going
to the district agricultural office.

It takes us about twenty minutes on the dusty road to get to Gruyere.
This part of Ukambani is really dry, full of hardy-looking bushes and
dust. Unlike in most places in Kenya, here people live far away from the
roads, so one has the illusion that the area is sparsely populated. We are
in a tiny village center. Three shops on each side, and in the middle a
large quadrangle of beaten-down dust on which three giant wood carvings of giraffes sit, waiting for transport to the curio markets of Nairobi.
There doesn't seem to be anybody about. We get out of the car and enter
Gruyere, which turns out to be a pub.

It looks about as Swiss as one can be in Ukambani. A simply built
structure with a concrete floor and simple furnishings, it nevertheless
has finish—nothing sticking out, everything symmetrical. I notice an
ingenious beer cooler: a little cavern worked into the cement floor, where
beer and sodas are cooled in water. This is a relief; getting a cold beer
outside Nairobi is quite a challenge.

Kenyans love warm beer, even if it is boiling outside. Since I arrived in these parts, I have had concerned barmaids worrying that I will get pneumonia, or that the beer will go completely flat if it is left in the fridge for more than twenty minutes.

The owner walks in, burned tomato red, wearing a *kikoi* and nothing else. He welcomes us and I introduce myself and start to chat, but soon discover that he doesn't speak English or Kiswahili. He is Swiss, and speaks only French and Kamba. My French is rusty, but it manages to get me a cold beer, served by his wife. She has skin the color of bitter chocolate. She is beautiful in the way only Kamba women can be, with baby-soft skin, wide-apart eyes, and an arrangement of features that seems permanently on the precipice of mischief.

We chat, and when I ask her what brought her husband to Mwingi, she laughs. "You know Europeans always have strange ideas. He is a mKamba now; he doesn't want anything to do with Europe."

I can see a bicycle coming in the distance, an impossibly large man weaving his way toward us, his short rounded legs pumping furiously.

Enter the jolliest man I have ever seen, plump as a steaming mound of fresh *ugali*, glowing with bonhomie and wiping streams of sweat from his face. There is a familiar expression of mischief on his face— something familiar to me, I don't know why, as a Kamba thing, only with him it is multiplied to a degree that makes it ominous. His face has no irony, also a Kamba thing to me. Gruyere's wife tells me this is the local chief. I stand up and greet him, then ask him to join us. He sits down and orders a round of beer.

"Ah! You can't be drinking tea here! This is a bar!"

He beams again, and I swear that somewhere a whole *shamba* of flowers is blooming. I try to glide into the subject of cotton, but it is brushed aside.

"So," he says, "so you go to South Africa with my daughter? She's just sitting at home, can't get a job—Kambas make good wives, you know, you Gikuyus know nothing about having a good time."

I can't deny that. He leans close, his eyes round as a full moon, and tells me a story about a retired major who lives nearby and has three young wives, who complain about his sexual demands. So, it is said that parents in the neighborhood are worried because their daughters are often seen batting their eyelids whenever he is about.

"You know," he says, "you Gikuyus cannot think further than your next coin. You grow maize on every available inch of land and cover your sofas with plastic. Ha! Then, in bed! Bwana! Even sex is work! But Kambas are not lazy, we work hard, we fuck well, we play hard. So drink your beer!"

I decide to rescue the reputation of my community. I order a Tusker. Cold.

What a gift charisma is. By eleven, there is a whole table of people, all of us glowing under the chief's beams of sunlight. My tongue has rediscovered its French, and I chat with Monsieur Gruyere, who isn't very chatty. He seems to be still under the spell of this place, and as we drink, I can see his eyes running over everyone. He doesn't seem too interested in the substance of the conversation; he is held more by the mood.

It is midday when I finally excuse myself. We have to make our way to Mwingi. Kariuki is looking quite inebriated, and now the chief finally displays an interest in our mission.

"Cotton! Oh! You will need someone to take you around the district agricultural office. He! You are bringing development back to Mwingi!"

We arrive at the district agricultural office. Our meeting there is blessedly brief, and we get all the information we want. The chief leads us through a maze of alleys to the best butchery/bar in Mwingi. He, of course, is well known there, and we get the VIP cubicle. Wielding his potbelly like a sexual magnet, he breaks up a table of young women and encourages them to join us.

Whispered aside: "You bachelors must surely be starving for female company, seeing that you have gone a whole morning without any sex."

We head off to the butcher, who has racks and racks of headless goats. I am salivating already. We order four kilos of ribs and *mūtura*, blood sausage.

The *mūtura* is delicious—hot, spicy, and rich—and the ribs tender and full of the herbal pungency that we enjoy in good goat meat.

After a couple of hours, I am starting to get uncomfortable at the levels of pleasure around me. I want to go back to my cheap motel room and read a book full of realism and stingy prose. Coetzee maybe? That will make me a Protestant again. Naipaul. Something mean-spirited and bracing.

"No, no, no!" says Mr. Chief. "You must come to my place, back to the village. We need to talk to people there about cotton. Surely you are not going to drive back after so many beers? Sleep at my house!"

Back at the chief's house, I lie down under the shade of a tree in the garden, read the newspaper, and sleep.

···

"Wake up! Let's go and party!"

I am determined to refuse. But the beams from his face embrace me. By the time we have showered and attempted to make our grimy clothes respectable, it is dusk.

There is only space for two in the front of the pickup, so I am sitting in the back. I console myself with the view. Now that the glare of the sun is fading, all sorts of tiny hidden flowers of extravagant color reveal themselves. As if, like the chief, they disdain the frugal humorlessness one expects is necessary to thrive in this dust bowl. We cross several dried riverbeds.

We are now so far away from the main road, I have no idea where we are. This lends the terrain around me a sudden immensity. The sun is the deep yellow of a free-range egg, on the verge of bleeding its yolk over the sky.

The fall of day becomes a battle. Birds are working themselves into a frenzy, flying about feverishly, unbearably shrill. The sky makes its last stand, shedding its ubiquity and competing with the landscape for the attention of the eye.

I spend some time watching the chief through the back window. He hasn't stopped talking since we left. Kariuki is actually laughing.

It is dark when we get to the club. I can see a thatched roof and four or five cars. There is nothing else around. We are, it seems, in the middle of nowhere.

We get out of the car.

"It will be full tonight," says the chief. "Month end."

Three hours later, I am somewhere beyond drunk, coasting on a vast plateau of semisobriety that seems to have no end. The place is packed.

More hours later, I am standing in a line of people outside the club, a chorus of liquid glitter arcing high out, then down to the ground, then zipping close. The pliant nothingness of the huge night above us goads us to movement.

A well-known *dombolo* song starts, and a ripple of excitement overtakes the crowd. This communal goose bump wakes a rhythm in us, and we all get up to dance. One guy with a cast on one leg is using his crutch as a dancing aid, bouncing around us like a string puppet. The cars all around have their inside lights on, as couples do what they do. The windows seem like eyes, glowing with excitement as they watch us onstage.

Everybody is doing the *dombolo*, a Congolese dance in which your hips (and only your hips) are supposed to move like a ball bearing made of mercury. To do it right, you wiggle your pelvis from side to side while your upper body remains as casual as if you were lunching with Nelson Mandela. In any restaurant in Kenya, a sunny-side-up fried egg is called *mayai* (eggs) *dombolo*.

I have struggled to get this dance right for years. I just can't get my hips to roll in circles like they should. Until tonight. The booze is helping, I think. I have decided to imagine that I have an itch deep in my bum, and I have to scratch it without using my hands or rubbing against anything.

My body finds a rhythmic map quickly, and I build my movements to fluency before letting my limbs improvise. Everybody is doing this, a solo thing—yet we are bound, like one creature, in one rhythm.

Any *dombolo* song has this section where, having reached a small peak of hip-wiggling frenzy, the music stops, and one is supposed to pull one's hips to the side and pause, in anticipation of an explosion of music faster and more frenzied than before.

When this happens, you are supposed to stretch out your arms and do some complicated kung-fu maneuvers. Or keep the hips rolling and slowly make your way down to your haunches, then work yourself back up. If you watch a well-endowed woman doing this, you will understand why skinny women often are not popular in East Africa.

If you ask me now, I'll tell you this is everything that matters. So this is why we move like this? We affirm a common purpose; any doubts about others' motives must fade if we are all pieces of one movement. We forget, don't we, that there is another time, apart from the hour and the minute? A human measurement, ticking away in our bodies, behind our facades.

Our shells crack, and we spill out and mingle. I care so much for these things that sit under the burping self-satisfaction of the certificated world. Maybe I am not just failing; maybe there is something I have that I can barter, if only for the approval of those I respect. I have lived off the certainty of others, have become a kind of parasite. Maybe I can help people see the patterns they take for granted. Cripples can have triumphant stand-ups.

I join a group of people who are talking politics, sitting around a large fire outside, huddled together to find warmth and life under a sagging hammock of night mass. A couple of them are university students; there is a doctor who lives in Mwingi town.

If every journey has a moment of magic, this is mine. Anything seems possible. In the dark like this, everything we say seems free of consequence, the music is rich, and our bodies are lent brotherhood by the light of the fire.

Politics makes way for life. For these few hours, it is as if we were old friends, comfortable with each other's dents and frictions. We talk, bringing the oddities of our backgrounds to this shared plate.

The places and people we talk about are rendered exotic and distant this night. Warufaga . . . Burnt Forest . . . Mtito Andei . . . Makutano . . . Mile Saba . . . Mua Hills . . . Gilgil . . . Sultan Hamud . . . Siakago . . . Kutus . . . Maili-Kumi . . . the wizard in Kangundo who owns a shop and likes to buy people's toenails; the hill, somewhere in Ukambani, where things slide uphill; thirteen-year-old girls who swarm around bars like this one, selling their bodies to send money home or take care of their babies; the billionaire Kamba politician who was cursed for stealing money and whose balls swell up whenever he visits his constituency; a strange insect in Turkana that climbs up your warm urine as you piss and does thorny unthinkable things to your urethra.

Painful things are shed like sweat. Somebody confesses that he spent time in prison in Mwea. He talks about his relief at getting out before all the springs of his body were worn out. We hear about the prison guard who got AIDS and deliberately infected many inmates with the disease before dying.

Kariuki reveals himself. We hear how he prefers to work away from home because he can't stand seeing his children at home without school fees; how, though he has a diploma in agriculture, he has been taking casual driving jobs for ten years. We hear about how worthless his coffee farm has become. He starts to laugh when he tells us how he lived with a woman for a year in Kibera, afraid to contact his family because he had no money to provide. The woman owned property. She fed him and kept him in liquor while he lived there. We laugh and enjoy our misfortunes, for we are real in the group and cannot succumb to chaos today.

Kariuki's wife found him by putting an announcement on national radio. His son had died. We are silent for a moment, digesting this. Somebody grabs Kariuki's hand and takes him to the dance floor.

Some of us break to dance and return to regroup. We talk and dance and talk and dance, not thinking how strange we will be to each other when the sun is in the sky, and our plumage is unavoidable, and trees suddenly have thorns, and around us a vast horizon of possible problems reseal our defenses.

The edges of the sky start to fray, a glowing mauve invasion. I can see shadows outside the gate, couples headed to the fields.

There is a guy lying on the grass, obviously in agony, his stomach taut as a drum. He is sweating badly. I close my eyes and see the horns of the goat that he had been eating force themselves through his sweat glands. It is clear—so clear. All this time, without writing one word, I have been reading novels, and watching people, and writing what I see

in my head, finding shapes for reality by making them into a book. This
is all I have done, forever, done it so much, so satisfyingly. I have never
used a pen—I have done it for my own sensual comfort. If I am to grow
up, I must do some such thing for others.

Self-pity music comes on. Kenny Rogers, Dolly Parton. I try to get
Kariuki and the chief to leave, but they are stuck in an embrace, howling
to the music and swimming in sentiment.

Then a song comes on that makes me insist that we are leaving.

Some time in the 1980s, a Kenyan university professor recorded a
song that was an enormous hit. It could best be described as a multiplic-
ity of yodels celebrating the wedding vow:

Will you take me *(spoken, not sung)*
To be your law-*(yodel)*-ful wedded wife
To love to cherish and to *(yodel)*
(then a gradually more hysterical yodel): Yieeeeei-yeeeeei . . . MEN!

Then just *amens*, and more yodels.

Of course, all these proud warriors, pillars of the community, are
at this moment singing in unison with the music, hugging themselves
(beer bottles under armpits), and looking sorrowful.

Soon, the beds in this motel will be creaking, as some of these men
forget self-pity and look for lost youth in the bodies of young girls. I am
afraid. If I write, and fail at it, I cannot see what else I can do. Maybe I
will write and people will roll their eyes, because I will talk about thirst,
and thirst is something people know already, and what I see is only bad
shapes that mean nothing.

...

It is late afternoon. Sunlight can be very rude. I seem to have developed
a set of bumpy new lenses in my eyes. Who put sand in my eyes? Ai!
Kariuki snores too much.

Somewhere, in the distance, a war is taking place: guns, howitzers,
bitches, jeeps, and gin and juice.

"Everybody say heeeey!"

The chief bursts into my room, looking like he spent the night eating fresh vegetables and massaging his body in vitamins. This is not fair.

"Hey, bwana chief."

Is that my voice? I have a wobbly vision of water, droplets cool against a chilled bottle, waterfalls, mountain streams, taps, ice cubes falling into a glass. Oh, to drink . . .

"Sorry about the noise—my sons like this funny music too much. Now, tell me about all this cotton business."

I like this job.

Chapter Twenty-One

A few minutes ago, I was sleeping comfortably in the front of a Land Rover Discovery. Now, I am standing outside in the cold, next to my bags, as the agricultural extension officer who gave me a lift here makes a mad dash for the night comforts of Narok town. Driving at night in this area is not a bright idea. We have been growing leased wheat and barley here for years. My father farms here to help pay our school fees. It is hard work, but I have always liked the adventure of Maasailand. There is a lot of time to read, too. My bags are full of library books.

When you are traveling in an unfamiliar landscape, for the first few moments, your eyes cannot concentrate on the particular. I am overwhelmed by the glare of dusk, by the shiver of wind on undulating acres of wheat and barley, by the vision of mile upon mile of space free of power lines. My focus is so derailed that when I return to myself, I find, to my surprise, that my feet are not off the ground. The landscape had grabbed me with such force that for a moment it sucked up my awareness of myself. It occurs to me that there is no clearer proof of the subjectivity (or selectivity) of our senses than moments like this.

Seeing is almost always only noticing.

Rotor blades of cold are chopping away in my nostrils. The silence, after the nonstop drone of the car, is as clingy as cobwebs, as intrusive as the loudest of noises. I have an urge to claw it away from my eardrums.

I am in Maasailand.

Not television Maasailand. We are high up in the Mau Hills. There are no rolling grasslands, lions, or acacia trees here; there are forests, impenetrable woven highland forests, dominated by bamboo. Inside, there are elephants, which come out at night and leave enormous pancakes of shit on the road. When I was a kid, I used to think that elephants, like cats, used dusty roads as toilet paper, sitting their haunches on the ground and levering themselves forward with their forelegs.

The cold air is irritating. I want to breathe in, suck up the moist mountainness of the air, the smell of fever tree and dung—but the process is just too painful. What do people do in really wintry places? Do they have some sort of nasal Sensodyne?

I can see our ancient Massey Ferguson tractor wheezing up a distant hill. They are headed this way to pick me up.

Relief. They got my message.

A week later, I am on a tractor, freezing, as we make our way back to camp from the wheat fields. We have been supervising the spraying of wheat and barley in the scattered fields my father leases.

There isn't much to look forward to at night here, no pubs hidden in the bamboo jungle. You can't even walk about freely at night because outside is full of stinging nettles. We will be in bed by seven to beat the cold. I will hear stories about frogs that sneak under your bed and turn into beautiful women, who entrap you. I will hear stories about legendary tractor drivers—people who could turn the jagged roof of Mount Kilimanjaro into Lauryn Hill's Afro.

I will hear about Maasai outside our camp, so near and so far from us. I will hear about so-and-so, who got two hundred thousand shillings for barley grown on his land, and how he took off to the Majengo slums in Nairobi, leaving his wife and children behind, to live with a prostitute for a year.

When the money ran out, he discarded his suit, pots and pans, and furniture. He wrapped a blanket around himself and walked home, whistling happily all the way.

Most of all, I will hear stories about Ole Kamaro, our landlord, and his wife Milka.

Baba has been growing wheat and barley in this area since I was a child. All this time, we have been leasing a portion of Ole Kamaro's land to keep our tractors and to make camp. I met Milka when she had just married Ole Kamaro. She was his fifth wife, thirteen years old. He was very proud of her. She was the daughter of a big-time chief from near Mau Narok. Most important, she could read and write. Ole Kamaro bought her a pocket radio and made her follow him with a pen and pencil everywhere he went, taking notes.

I remember being horrified by the marriage. She was so young! My sister Ciru was eight, and they played together one day. That night, Ciru had a nightmare that Baba had sold her to Ole Kamaro in exchange for fifty acres of land.

A few years of schooling were enough to give Milka a clear idea of the basic tenets of empowerment. By the time she was eighteen, Ole Kamaro had dumped the rest of his wives.

Milka leased out his land to Kenya Breweries and opened a bank account where all the money went. Occasionally, she gave her husband pocket money. Whenever he was away, she took up with her lover, a wealthy young Gikuyu shopkeeper from the other side of the hill who kept her supplied with essentials like soap, matches, and paraffin.

Milka is the local chairwoman of the KANU Women's League and so remains invulnerable to censure from the conservative element in the area. She also has a thriving business, curing hides and beading them elaborately for the tourist market at the Mara. Unlike most Maasai women, who disdain growing crops, she has a thriving market garden with maize, beans, and other vegetables. She does not lift a finger to take care of this garden. Part of the cooperation we expect from her as landlady depends on our staff taking care of her garden.

...

Something interesting is going on today, and the drivers are nervous. Sang tells me about a tradition among the Maasai: women are released from all domestic duties for a few months after giving birth. They are allowed to take over the land and claim any lovers that they choose. For some reason I don't quite understand, this all happens at a particular season, and this season begins today. I have been warned to keep away from any bands of women wandering about.

We are heading back from work. I am sitting with the rest of the team in the trailer behind the old Massey Ferguson tractor we use to carry supplies and workers. We get to the top, turn to make our way down, and there they are, led by Milka, a troop of about forty women marching toward us dressed in their best traditional clothing.

Milka looks imperious and beautiful in her beaded leather cloak, red *khanga* around her waist. The *khanga* features a giant cockerel, in the president's party colors. Milka is, after all, the leader of the KANU Women's League. This is her cultural dress: the party colors on twin rectangular cloths that were once Swahili traditional dress and have now entered all of Kenya. Around all this are rings, necklaces, and earrings. Because Milka is in charge of the party women's league, she is the leader of all local women. She is, too, a cultural leader. There is an old woman among them; she must be seventy, and she is cackling with glee. She takes off her wrap and displays her breasts, which resemble old socks.

Mwangi, who is driving, stops and tries to turn back, but the road is too narrow: on one side there is the mountain, and on the other, a yawning valley. Kipsang, who is sitting in the trailer with me, shouts, "Aiiii. Mwangi bwana! DO NOT STOP!"

It seems that the 1990s tradition involves men making donations to the KANU Women's League. Innocent enough, you'd think, but the amount of these donations must satisfy them or they will strip you naked and do unspeakable things to your body.

So we take off at full speed. The women stand firm in the middle of the road. We can't swerve. We stop.

Then Kipsang saves our skins by throwing a bunch of coins onto the road. I throw down some notes, and Mwangi (renowned across Maasailand for his stinginess) empties his pockets, throwing down notes and coins. The women start to gather the money, the tractor roars back into action, and we drive right through them.

I am left with the picture of a toothless old lady diving to avoid the tractor. Then she stands up and looks back at us, laughing, her breasts flapping like a flag of victory.

...

I am in bed, still in Maasailand.

I pick up my father's *World Almanac and Book of Facts 1992*. The language section has new words, confirmed from sources as impeccable as the *Columbia Encyclopedia* and the *Oxford English Dictionary*. The list reads like an American infomercial: jazzercise, assertiveness training, bulimia, anorexic, microwavable, fast-tracker.

The words soak into me. America is the cheerleader. They twirl the baton, and we follow. There is a word there, *skanking,* described as "a style of West Indian dancing to reggae music, in which the body bends forward at the waist and the knees are raised and the hands claw the air in time to the beat; dancing in this style."

I have a brief flash of us in forty years' time, in some generic dance studio. We are practicing for the senior championships, in a Kenya that is formatted and large, where work has digested us all, wearing plastic smiles on our faces as we skank across the room, counting each step like good students. The tutor checks the movement: shoulders up, arms down, move this way, move that: Claw, baby. Claw! In time to the beat, dancing in this style.

...

Langat and Kariuki have lost their self-consciousness around me and are chatting away about Milka.

"Eh! She had ten thousand shillings and they went and stayed in a hotel in Narok for a week. Ole Kamaro had to bring in another woman to look after the children!"

"Hai! But she sits on him!"

Their talk meanders slowly, with no direction—just talk, just connecting, and I feel that tight wrap of time loosen, the anxiety of losing time fades, and I am a glorious vacuum for a while, just letting what strikes my mind, strike my mind, then sleep strikes my opening mind.

...

Ole Kamaro is slaughtering a sheep today.

We all settle on the patch of grass between the two compounds. Ole Kamaro makes quick work of the sheep and I am offered the fresh kidney to eat. It tastes surprisingly good: slippery warmth, an organic cleanliness.

Ole Kamaro introduces me to his sister-in-law Suzannah, and

tells me proudly that she is in form four. Milka's sister. I spotted her this morning staring at me from the tiny window in their *manyatta*. It was disconcerting at first, a typically Maasai stare, unembarrassed, not afraid to be vulnerable. Then she noticed that I had seen her, and her eyes narrowed and became sassy—street-sassy, like a girl from Eastlands in Nairobi.

Her breasts are sharp and bounce around under a T-shirt, quite indifferent to their effect.

So I am now confused how to approach her. Should my approach be one of exaggerated politeness, as is traditional, or casual cool, as her second demeanor requested? I would have opted for the latter, but her uncle is standing eagerly next to us.

She responds by lowering her head and looking away. I am painfully embarrassed. I ask her to show me where they tan their hides.

We escape with some relief.

"So where do you go to school?"

"Oh! At St. Teresa's Girls in Nairobi."

"Milka is your sister?"

"Yes."

We are quiet for a while. English was a mistake. Where I am fluent, she is stilted. I switch to Swahili, and she pours herself into another person, talkative, aggressive. A person who must have a Tupac T-shirt stashed away somewhere.

"Arhh! It's so boring here! Nobody to talk to! I hope Milka comes home early."

I am still stunned. How bold and animated she is, speaking Sheng, a very hip street language that mixes Swahili and English and other languages. Here, so far from road and railway Kenya.

"Why didn't you go with the women today?"

She laughs. "I am not married. Ho! I'm sure they had fun! They are drinking *muratina* somewhere, I am sure. I can't wait to get married."

"So, do you use Suzannah pomade?"

She blushes and laughs.

"*Kwani?* You don't want to go to university and all that?"

"Maybe, but if I'm married to the right guy, life is good. Look at Milka. She is free, she does anything she wants. Old men are good. If you feed them, and give them a son, they leave you alone."

"Won't it be difficult to do this if you are not circumcised?"

"*Kwani*, who told you I'm not circumcised? I went last year."

I am shocked, and it shows. She laughs.

"He! I nearly shat myself! But I didn't cry!"

"Why? Si, you could have refused."

"Ai! If I had refused, it would mean that my life here was finished. There is no place here for someone like that."

"But . . ."

I cut myself short. I am sensing that this is her compromise—to live two lives fluently. As it generally is with people's reasons for their faiths and choices, trying to disprove her is silly. As a Maasai, she would see my statement as ridiculous.

In Sheng, there is no way for me to bring it up that would be diplomatic; in Sheng she can only present this with a hard-edged bravado, because it is humiliating. I do not know of any way we can discuss this successfully in English. If there is a courtesy every Kenyan practices, it is that we don't question each other's contradictions; we all have them, and destroying someone's face is sacrilege. If South Africans seek to fill the holes in their reality through building a strong political foundation, we spend a lot of time pretending our contradictions do not exist. To be a new thing in South Africa is normal. We know we sit on top of a rotting edifice; we are terrified of questioning anything deeply. There is nothing wrong with being what you are not in Kenya; just be it successfully. Almost all Kenyan jokes are about people who thought they had mastered a new persona and ended up ridiculous. Suzannah knows her faces well. We chat the whole lazy afternoon.

. . .

I spend whole days watching the combine harvester roll, acres and acres of dry wheat sucked in, *crutch*, and shat out as grain. Weetabix is unbeatabix. I read books out in the sun, now at the top of the familiar escarpment, looking down on Nakuru's flamingos, Amigos Disco, dreams, and distant chatter. I help bag the grain and sew it, following the lead of the workers.

I am starting to scribble my thoughts, to write these moments. It is when this is all done that I do what I do best. I look up, confused and fearful, all accordion with *kimay*; then soak in the safe patterns of other people, and live my life borrowing from them; then retreat—for reasons I don't know—to look down, inside the safety of novels; and then I lift my eyes again to people, and make them my own sort of confused pattern.

I am no sharp arrow cutting through the career ladder. It's time to try to make some sort of sense of things on the written page. At least there, they can be shaped. I doubt myself the moment I think this.

Chapter Twenty-Two

It is time. Christmas 1995 is arriving. In January a new term starts. I have decided to go back to South Africa and try to finish my degree. If I manage to focus enough, for just one year, I can cover all of my missing courses. I can't start again. I have been fine the past few months, so much so that it is hard to explain to myself why I have been so . . . unable. I am nervous. I do not know what I will do if I start to fail again. First, we are on our way, by road, to Uganda, for my grandparents' wedding anniversary. The drive through the Mau Hills, past the Rift Valley and onward to Kisumu, bores me. I haven't been this way for ten years, but my aim is to be in Uganda. We arrive in Kampala at ten in the evening. We have been on the road for more than eight hours.

Mum asked me if I thought I was ready to go back to school. I said yes. "Are you sure?" She was looking straight at me. I did not flinch. "I am ready, Mum," I said. She smiled.

This is my first visit to Uganda, a land of mystery for me. I grew up with her myths and legends and horrors, narrated with the intensity that only exiles can muster. This is the first time that my grandparents will have all their children and most of their grandchildren at home together; more than a hundred people are expected.

My mother—and the many relatives and friends who came to visit—has filled my imagination with incredible tales of Uganda. I heard how you had to wriggle on your stomach to see the *kabaka*; how the Tutsi king in Rwanda (who was seven feet tall) was once given a bicycle as a present, and, because he couldn't touch the ground (being a king and all), he was carried everywhere, on his bicycle, by his bearers.

Apparently, in the old kingdom in Rwanda, Tutsi women were not supposed to exert themselves or mar their beauty in any way. Some women had to be spoon-fed by their Hutu servants and wouldn't leave their huts for fear of sunburn.

I was told about a trip my grandfather took when he was young, with an uncle, when he was mistaken for a Hutu servant and taken away to sleep with the goats. A few days later his uncle asked about him, and his hosts were embarrassed to confess that they didn't know he was "one of us."

It has been a year of mixed blessings for Africa. This is the year that I sat in a bar in Cape Town during the Rugby World Cup in the Cape and watched South Africans reach out to each other before giving New Zealand a hiding. Mandela, wearing the number 6 rugby jersey, managed to melt away, for one night, all the hostility that had gripped the country since he was released from jail. Black people, traditionally supporters of the All Blacks, embraced the Springboks with enthusiasm. For just one night, most South Africans felt a common nationhood.

It is the year that I returned to my home, Kenya, to find people so far beyond cynicism that they looked back on their cynical days with fondness.

Uganda is different. This is a country that has not only reached the bottom of the hole countries sometimes fall into, it has scratched through that bottom and free-fallen again and again, and now it has rebuilt itself and swept away the hate. This country gives me hope that this continent is not, finally, incontinent.

This is the country I used to associate with banana trees, old and elegant kingdoms, Idi Amin, decay and hopelessness. It was an association I had made as a child, when the walls of our house would ooze and leak whispers of horror whenever a relative or friends of the family came home, fleeing from Amin's literal and metaphoric crocodiles.

I am rather annoyed that the famous seven hills of Kampala are not as clearly defined as I had imagined they would be. I have always had a childish vision of a stately city filled with royal paraphernalia. I had expected to see elegant people dressed in flowing robes, carrying baskets on their heads and walking arrogantly down streets filled with the smell of roasting bananas, and intellectuals from a 1960s dream, shaking the streets with their Afrocentric rhetoric.

Images formed in childhood can be more than a little bit stubborn.

Reality is a better aesthetic. Kampala seems disorganized, full of potholes, bad management, and haphazardness. It is the kind of African city that so horrifies the West in all of us. The truth is that it is a city overwhelmed by enterprise. I see smiles, the shine of healthy skin and teeth; no layabouts lounging and plotting at every street corner. People do not walk about with walls around themselves as they do in Nairobbery.

All over, there is a frenzy of building. A blanket of paint is slowly spreading over the city, so it looks like one of those Smirnoff adverts where inanimate things get breathed into Technicolor by the sacred burp of 40 percent or so of clear alcohol.

It is humid, and hot, and the banana trees flirt with you, swaying gently like fans offering coolness that never materializes.

Everything smells musky, as if a thick, soft steam has risen like broth. The plants are enormous. Mum once told me that, traveling in Uganda in the 1940s and 1950s, if you were hungry you could simply enter a banana plantation and eat as much as you wished. You didn't have to ask anybody. But you were not allowed to carry so much as a single deformed banana out of the plantation.

...

We are booked in at the Catholic guesthouse in Kampala. As soon as I have dumped my stuff on the bed, I call an old school friend, who promises to pick me up.

Musoke comes at six and we go to find food. We drive past the famous Mulago Hospital and into town. He picks up a couple of friends and we go to a bar called Yakubu's.

We order beers and lots of roast pork brochettes, and we sit in the car. The brochettes are delicious. I like them so much, I order more. Nile beer is okay, but nowhere near Kenya's Tusker.

The sun is drowned suddenly, and it is dark.

We get onto the highway to Entebbe. On both sides of the road, people have built flimsy houses. Bars, shops, and cafés line the road the whole way. Many people are out, especially teenagers, hormones flouncing about, puffs of fog surrounding their huddled faces. It is still hot outside; paraffin lamps light the fronts of all these premises.

I turn to Musoke and ask, "Can we stop at one of those pubs and have a beer?"

"Ah! Wait till we get to where we are going. It's much nicer than this dump!"

"I'm sure it is, but you know, I might never get a chance to drink in a real Entebbe pub, not those bourgeois places. Come on, I'll buy a round."

Magic words.

The place is charming. Ugandans seem to me to have a knack for making things elegant and comfortable, regardless of income. The ethical universe of the past is strong here in this country that is more Catholic, Anglican, and Muslim than Kenya. At the same time, here the old kingships and their institutions are still alive.

It's strange how things turn around. Uganda was my childhood bogeyman, and now Kenya teeters, and Ugandans everywhere are asking me what is wrong with us.

...

I sleep on the drive from Kampala to Kisoro.

From Kisoro, we begin the drive to St. Paul's Mission, Kigezi. Ciru is sitting next to me. She flew from South Africa and met us in Entebbe. Chiqy has been to Uganda before and is taking full advantage of her vast experience to play the adult tour guide. At her age, cool is god.

I have the odd feeling we are puppets in some Christmas story. It is as if a basket weaver were writing this story in a language of weave, tightening the tension on the papyrus strings every few minutes, and superstitiously refusing to reveal the ending—even to herself—until she has tied the very last knot.

We are now in the mountains. The winding road and the dense papyrus in the valleys seem to entwine me, ever tighter, into my fictional weaver's basket. Every so often, she jerks her weave to tighten it.

I look up to see the last half hour of road winding along the mountain above us. We are in the Bufumbira range now, driving through Kigaland on our way to Kisoro, the nearest town to my mother's home.

There is an alien quality to this place. It does not conform to any African topography that I am familiar with. The mountains are steep and resemble inverted ice cream cones. The hoe has tamed every inch of them.

It is incredibly green.

In Kenya, *green* is the ultimate accolade a person can give land: green is scarce, green is wealth, green is fertility.

Bufumbira green is not a tropical green, no warm musk, like in Buganda; nor is it the harsh green of the Kenyan savanna, that two-month-long green that compresses all the elements of life—millions of wildebeests and zebras, great carnivores feasting during the rains, frenzied plowing and planting, and dry riverbeds overwhelmed by soil and bloodstained water. Nairobi underwater.

It is not the green of grand waste and grand bounty that my country knows. It is not the Protestant nation of taming and saving that Kenya is trying to become. This is a Catholic nation—ritual and form matter more.

This is a mountain green, cool and enduring. Rivers and lakes occupy the cleavage of the many mountains that surround us.

Mum looks almost foreign now. Her Kinyarwanda accent is more pronounced, and her face is not as reserved as usual. Her beauty, so exotic and head-turning in Kenya, seems at home here. She does not stand out anymore; she belongs. The rest of us seem like tourists.

As the drive continues, a sense of where we are starts to seep into me. We are no longer in the history of Buganda, of Idi Amin, of the *kabakas*, or civil war, Museveni.

We are now on the outskirts of the theater where the Hutus and the Tutsis have been performing for the world's media. My mother has always described herself as a Mufumbira, one who speaks Kinyarwanda. She has always said that too much is made of the differences between

Tutsi and Hutu, that they are really more alike than not. She insists that she is Bufumbira, speaks Kinyarwanda.

"Forget the rest," she says.

I have only one memory of my father's father, Guka. We are sitting outside his black wooden house, and he sits on a chair in a black jacket, tall, thin, and dark, with charcoal smudges around his large slanting eyes, like Jimmy. His knuckles stand out from his long fingers and he has the long forehead of all the Wainainas, all the many cousins, all his twelve children. His hairline is shaped like a W, which everybody, except me, has.

I sit on a sharp knee and he tells me he will come to Nakuru to visit us.

The same year, on Jimmy's birthday, we are gathered to open presents in Baba and Mum's room in the morning. Presents are always in the boot of Baba's car. The phone rings. Guka is dead. Baba's mother, my grandmother, died in 1963, and talking about her always makes Baba sad. I never met her.

•••

I ask my mother where the border with Rwanda is. From this high hill, we can see Congo, and Rwanda. Mum points out the border, where Mount Muhavura, a giant inverted ice cream cone, stands above all the other mountains, like something out of a sci-fi novel. The countries are both closer than I thought. Maybe this is what makes this coming together so urgent. Life has urgency when it stands around death. There is no grass as beautiful as the blades that stick out after the first rain.

In the 1960s, when Mum's father, my grandfather, retired, he wrote the family genealogy. He knew his ancestors dating back nine generations: Sserubabaza, son of Mbayiki, son of Bidudu, son of Mutiamwa, son of Ruhetsi, son of Biraro, son of Masunzu, son of Rubunga, son of Nzogoma.

As we move into the forested area, I am softened by the smell and by the canopy of mountain vegetation. I join the conversation in the car. I have become self-conscious about displaying my dreaminess and absent-mindedness these days.

I used to spend hours gazing out of car windows, creating grand battles between battalions of clouds. There is a conspiracy to get me back to earth, to get me to be more practical. My parents are pursuing this cause with little subtlety, aware that my time with them is limited. Baba wanted to know if I have a problem with drugs. It is necessary for me to believe that I am putting myself on a gritty road to personal success when I leave home. Cloud travel is well and good when you have mastered the landings. I never have. I must live, not dream about living.

We sat down a few days ago, Baba and I, in the dining room, with the college manual to talk about my school. We made a deal. I need only three courses to graduate if I change my major from finance to business management. The plan is simple. I will go and finish, and hold my breath until it is done. I will keep things simple. I believe I can do it only because I can't look at them and say I can't. I have been fine for months. It is hard to imagine being lost again. I don't say anything about the stories that I am writing. Baba is retiring this year. I can't fail.

•••

Mum is the great-great-granddaughter of a man called Bidudu and his wife Nyabijana. Nyabijana gave birth only to daughters, and this made Bidudu very frustrated. When he finally got a son, he called him Bisanukuli, which means "this time it seems to be the truth."

Bisanukuli was also called Rukara—which refers to a very dark shade of black skin. People here believe that people born with the darkest skin are those who become truly "infura"—people with large hearts, people who are remembered down generations for acts of grace, courage, and wisdom, so that memories of their lives serve as values for new generations.

Bisanukuli kept both these names and he was addressed by either of them by people. Rukara, however, was the more formal name.

Bidudu was a wealthy man, with many subjects, servants, and a large herd of cattle called "Akatabuze." He had a taste for travel and adventure.

In the late 1800s, during the third dynasty of the Rwanda Kingdom, in the reign of King Rwogerase wa Rwabugiri, Bidudu moved his people from his home in a place called Nduga, in what is now Rwanda, to this place, in the mountains of Bufumbira. Rwanda is an old kingdom. The first king, Mwami Ndahiro, started to rule in the twelfth century.

For Bidudu, there was no end to Rwanda—he believed that Rwanda ended only where "the sky was held up by pillars." Wherever one went, one kept one's citizenship.

When Bidudu landed here, in Bufumbira, Nyabijana gave birth to a second son, Mbayiki.

Mbayiki and his wife Nyiramivumbi had twins: Sserubabaza, my great-grandfather, and Bujunjuri.

Mbayiki was poisoned and died a young man.

Their fifth child was Rwirahira.

As a child, Rwirahira was fond of mixing up his food on the plate. His family nicknamed him Binyavanga, which has something to do with mixing things up. The name stuck. He was the first in the family to be baptized and join the Catholic Church, the first to go to school. He became one of the first schoolteachers in this part of the country.

Binyavanga was thirty when he was baptized a Catholic. He took the name Cosma and was one of the first teachers in Kigezi District. In 1935 he married a woman of the Abagyesera clan named Modesta Kamondo from Bunagana in what is now Congo. Binyavanga and Modesta had twelve children.

Their daughter Rosemary, the beautiful one, was a traveler too. She married in Kenya. Her second son, according to her husband's custom, is called Binyavanga, after his maternal grandfather. My grandfather is surprised that I am called Binyavanga. His people do not name that way. It is a strange idea to him—that the son of his daughter carries his name. He does not know how mixed up that young man is.

Among us Gikuyu, your name is a kind of fate. You hear women call their sons Daddy, or call their daughters Mummy—said enough times, you grow up seeing yourself in the image of the one you were named after. But I do not know my grandfather. I do not speak his language.

Being Binyavanga is to me also exotic—an imaginary Ugandan of some kind resides in me, one who lets me withhold myself from claiming, or being admitted into, without hesitation, an unquestioning Gikuyu belonging.

...

We are in Kisoro, the main town of the district, weaving down roads between people's houses. We are heading toward Uncle Kagame's house. I have a dizzy vision of a supernatural movie producer slowing down the action before the climax by examining tiny details instead of grand scenes. I see a narrator in the fifth dimension saying, "And now our Christmas movie: a touching story about the reunion of a family torn apart by civil war and the genocide in Rwanda. This movie is sponsored by Sobbex, hankies for every occasion" (repeated in Zulu).

My grandmother embraces me. She is very slender, and I feel she will break. Her elegance surrounds me and I feel a strong urge to burrow into her secrets, see with her eyes. She is a quiet woman, and unbending, even taciturn, and this gives her a powerful charisma. Things not said. Her resemblance to my mother is strong.

My grandfather is crying and laughing, exclaiming when he hears that Chiqy and I are named after him and his wife (Kamanzi and Binyavanga). We drink *rgwagwa*, banana wine laced with honey. It is delicious, smoky and dry.

Ciru and Chiqy are sitting next to my grandmother. Jim could not make it; he has a new job. I see why my grandfather was such a legendary schoolteacher.

At night, we split into our various age groups and start to bond with each other. Of the cousins, Manwelli, the eldest, is our unofficial leader. He works for the World Bank.

Aunt Rosaria and her family are the coup of the ceremony. They were feared dead during the war in Rwanda and hid for months in their basement, helped by a friend who provided food. They all survived; they walk around carrying an expression that is more common in children— delight, sheer delight at life.

Auntie Rosaria's three sons spend every minute bouncing about with the high of being alive. They dance at all hours, sometimes even when there is no music. In the evenings we squash onto the veranda, looking out as far as Congo, and they entertain us with their stand-up routines in French and Kinyarwanda, the force of their humor carrying us all to laughter.

Manwelli translates one skit for me. They are imitating a vain Tutsi woman who is pregnant and is kneeling to make a plea to God. "Oh please, God, let my child have long fingers and a gap between the teeth; let her have a straight nose and be ta-a-all. Oh Lord, let her not have a nose like a Hutu. Oh please, I shall be your grateful servant."

The biggest disappointment so far is that my aunt Christine has not yet arrived. She has lived with her family in New York since the early 1970s. We all feel her absence keenly, as it was she who urged us all years ago to gather for this occasion at any cost.

She, my aunt Rosaria, and Mum are the senior aunts, and they were very close when they were younger. They speak frequently on the phone and did so especially during the many months that Aunt Rosaria and her family were living in fear in their basement. The family has been through a lot over the years. Although they are very close, they haven't been together since 1961. Visas, wars, closed borders, and a thousand triumphs of chaos have kept them apart. We are all looking forward to their reunion.

...

I have hardly spoken to my mother the past few days. I find her in my grandmother's room, trying, without much success, to get my grandmother to relax and let her many daughters and granddaughters do the work.

I have been watching Mum from a distance. At first, she seemed a bit aloof from it all, but now she's found fluency with everything and she seems far away from the Kenyan mother we know. I can't get over the sight of her blushing as my grandmother machine-guns instructions at her. How alike they are.

I want to talk with her more but decide not to be selfish, not to make it seem that I am trying to establish possession of her. We'll have enough time on the way back. She seems vague lately, less emphatic than I have known her. She has lost weight and tires easily. I tell myself that she is aging.

I've been trying to pin down my grandfather, to ask him about our family's history. He keeps giving me a bewildered look when I corner him, as if he were asking: Can't you just relax and party? He must be wondering why this Kenyan grandson of his should be bothered. Last night, he toasted us all before dancing to a gospel rap song my cousin Laura brought from Kampala. He tried to get my grandmother to join him, but she ducked into her room and locked the door.

Gerald is getting quite concerned that when we are all gone, they will find it too quiet. We hurtle on toward Christmas. Booze flows, we pray, chat, and bond under the night rustle of banana leaves. I am filled with magic and I succumb to the masses. In two days, we feel like a family. In French, Swahili, English, Gikuyu, Kinyarwanda, Kiganda, and Ndebele, we sing one song, a multitude of passports in our luggage.

At dawn on December 24, I stand smoking in the banana plantation at the edge of my grandfather's hill and watch the mists disappear. Uncle Chris saunters up to join me.

I ask, "Any news about Aunt Christine?"

"It looks like she might not make it. Manwelli has tried to get in contact with her and failed. Maybe she couldn't get a flight out of New York. Apparently the weather is terrible there."

The day is filled with hard work. My uncles have convinced my grandfather that we need to slaughter another bull as meat is running out. There is to be a church service in the sitting room of my grandfather's house later in the day.

The service begins and I bolt from the living room, volunteering to peel potatoes outside. About halfway through the service, I see somebody staggering up the hill, suitcase in hand and muddy up to her ankles. It takes me an instant to guess. I run to her and mumble something. We hug. Aunt Christine is here.

The plot has taken me over now. Resolution is upon me. The poor woman is given no time to freshen up or get her bearings. In a minute, we have ushered her into the living room. She sits by the door, facing everybody's back. Only my grandparents are facing her. My grandmother starts to cry.

Nothing is said; the service motors on. Everybody stands up to sing. Somebody whispers to my aunt Rosaria. She turns and gasps soundlessly. Others turn. We all sit down. Aunt Rosaria and Aunt Christine start to cry. Granddad is crying; he looks like he will break. He is ninety-five. Mum is crying. Uncle Henry is trying not to. Aunt Rosaria's mouth opens and closes in disbelief. Soon we are all crying. The priest motors on, fluently, unaware.

One day, I will write about this place.

Chapter Twenty-Three

I am back at the University of Transkei. It is January 1996.

My new confidence lasts exactly one week. When I attend my first Accounting 2 class, we are learning something called disclosures.

Accounting, they say in the textbook, is a perceptual framework. Debit line, credit line, debit line. That is the last class of any kind that I attend. I go out that night to Miles to drink and dance like a jackrabbit. I get violently drunk. They kick me out of the club. I walk and walk. Then I am sitting by a stream. I do not know how I got here; it is more than two kilometers from my room. I am crying, my lungs are chafed, and I am dizzy with self-pity and vomit. There is a cow blowing mist into the air, and I can smell dung.

After a month, my landlord kicks me out. He is not ready for another series of my locked-door adventures. I spend hours online in the campus computer labs. There are already hundreds of writers' groups online. I meet a guy in a supernatural fiction writers' group. His name is Charlie Sweet, and he lives in suburban California. Charlie survived the sixties, but believes the world is coming to an end at the millennium. He has bought land in Duckshoot, California. Meanwhile, he does something called multimedia. His wife is from Japan, and she is on his case a lot. She has just become an Amway distributor. Charlie is building a bunker in Duckshoot.

I am living in the house of a friend, Sylvia. I make a very delicate living typing biographical information into little boxes that are laminated for high school student cards. I get paid ten rand a page. I also babysit for Sylvia, who teaches at the university. I use her computer every night.

I don't phone my parents or write to them. Ciru has gone back home, and is looking for a job there. I am on my own a lot. I am writing every day now. Sometimes I write through the night. No, no, says my self-pity, I am not a spineless flibbertigibbet—there must be some secret mission, something mystical. Maybe, maybe I am some sort of Ben Okri-ish *abiku*, that spirit child in *The Famished Road*.

Months fly past. Things are stable at Sylvia's. I start to write a novel. In it, a tortured young man called Jango, who has an imagination like a helium balloon, finds out that the great brain stem of the world is growing, on the Internet, and he is part of its secret ancient code. At the end of the novel, the young man will meet his genetic mother, Lucy, on a Web site, and the circle will be complete. Digital drums are beating all over the throbbing Net, and Jango shows them, shows them all . . .

Fucking perceptual frameworks! Debits and credits.

I still can't face my parents. I send e-mails to Ciru. Birthday messages and happy cheerful e-mails to everybody. I avoid details. Chiqy had a baby boy, Ciru tells me. Paul. She has left the house. Baba is still upset. I call them, and lie and tell them all is well. I do not ask for money, or fees. Charlie Sweet reads my . . . speculations, and I read his stories, which are semiautobiographical and involve much sex and many chemical substances.

There is a new phrase around: black empowerment. All of a sudden, people I was in school with, who have now graduated, are landing in astonishing places. Like paragliding, black empowerment has the ability to lift you very high, on a front of warm air. One friend started a small design company, and before the paint was dry, the company was listed on the Johannesburg Stock Exchange, and she was featured in a lifestyle magazine looking very aerodynamic in a business suit, going places.

One broke Saturday, I walk all over town, stopping by friends' homes sorta kinda saying hello, and kind of sort of hoping for a good meal and some cold beer. Mrs. Baguma, whose fridge and hospitality are boundless, is not home. Damn. She is the best—never asks you probing questions, just dishes out love and warm food.

I avoid my uncle Henry's. He gave me a job once, easy stuff, helping him with some research, and I let him down badly. There are thousands of African immigrants in Umtata, which was the capital of Transkei, once an independent homeland and now part of the Eastern

Cape Province. There are always baptisms and gatherings. We all know each other.

I cross the railway line, into town, and knock on Alice Bosa's door. Alice is Ugandan, the granddaughter of a famous poet, Henry Barlow, whose poem "Building the Nation" we studied in school:

> Today I did my share
> In building the nation.
> I drove a Permanent Secretary
> To an important urgent function
> In fact to a luncheon at the Vic.
>
> The menu reflected its importance
> Cold Bell beer with small talk,
> Then fried chicken with niceties
> Wine to fill the hollowness of the laughs.

I find a friendly gathering: Alice, George Majola, an old friend who was a few years ahead of me studying commerce, and Alice's nephew Kiwanuka, who it turns out now works for George. I assume it is something to do with George's family, which is wealthy and well connected here in Umtata. There is beer and brandy, and meat is grilling on the stove. Outside, cars with many, many valves are grinning smugly at Umtata's peeling paint and piss-stained walls.

George now lives in Durban and owns an architectural firm. "Oh," I say. "I didn't know you did architecture?"

He shrugs.

"So what are you building?" I ask, reaching my finger out for a plump dripping rib.

"A convention center," he says.

Oh. I am trying to think what a convention center is. In my head, it is a kind of community hall that contains badminton courts, anger-management courses, table tennis, township youths carrying happyface satchels that open to release role models and awareness workshop folders and income-generating schemes and empowerment agendas, all of this air-conditioned by sophisticated convention currents.

George snaps his briefcase open and takes out a flyer. It is very glossy, in full fashion-magazine color. He looks at me from the flyer, in a sharp suit, eyes facing the sky in a Visionary™ pose, Go-Gerrit, his body says, looking at his target with a squint, like the Six Million Dollar Man. Gentlemen, we can rebuild him. We have the technology. Next to his left shoulder is a picture of a mud hut. Next to his right shoulder, a bionic building swooshes to the sky like Nike—glass and steel and sky. The Durban Convention Center! Breathtaking architecture! Epic settings! Panoramic foyer! African flair! UB40 concert! Where Africa and the world meet. Sit there agog, you failing fucker, eating our ribs greedily! Wipe your mouth!

I wipe my mouth. On the top of the flyer, right above his glowing head: "George Majola was born in a mud hut. When he grew up, he built the largest conference center in the Southern Hemisphere."

A mud hut? Hmm. Here I was thinking their four-bedroom home with a double automatic garage door in Fort Gale was built by a very good credit rating. Goodness. I don't think George is more than twenty-eight years old.

I open a new beer and chew my bone.

George has decided to come home to the Eastern Cape and give something back. He is giving a series of PowerTalks, motivational workshops for GoingSomewhere people. That's what the flyer is for. He has a bootful of them in his car, just above the valves, which are sitting right next to my green gills and my bobbing Adam's marble. I can drink! The Windhoek beer chugs down my throat effortlessly.

So George had hired some slick Durban marketing and PR consultants to promote his talks in Umtata and East London. They are doing nothing! No bookings!

Now. Me, what do I have to lose, and my patterns are in good order, look, no dribbling! So I let the golden liquid speak; it trickles out of my throat like piss, warm and good and full of bullshit and beautiful . . . AySssymmetrical Guerrilla Marketing, Finding Your Center, Speaking the Right Brand-gauge.

He is startled. Do you want to market my talk?

Lift one eyebrow, tilt your head like Steve Austin, and look straight at somebody through your left squinty eye, and sound impatient, like he has lost his marbles, like you are a *hughagh* guy who leads from the front and that is the guy you want giving you cover when you run out of ammo, and the going is tough, so the tough get going, *hughagh*.

This is a technique for making people fall inside your patterns, or burst out laughing.

Alice is looking at me strangely.

"It's a busy time," I say. "Let me call up some people and see whether we can make this work. I don't want to promise anything until I have a strategy and a team. How much can you offer?"

He speaks. My face remains still. Agog is a marble bumping up and down my throat, a swollen epiglottis. I sip some more beer. That is more money than I need to live for six months.

"Hmmm," I say, still squinting bionically, hands televisioning like itain'tworthmytime, that won't even cover my costs. He nods in agreement and his offer starts to climb up like black empowerment; soon it is paragliding in the sky, wheeee, and my stomach is billaboinging in fear.

I nod and step outside, worried I will throw up in excitement. I light a cigarette and think to myself that, truth be told, George Majola has always been a sweet guy, not a malicious bone in him at all, and he must have some idea of my situation, if only from my wild scribbled hair and greedy fingers, and he is offering me this with grace.

Like how Sylvia Nkanyuza offered to let me stay rent free in her house; like Sylvia's father, a physics professor who left South Africa in the fifties unable to get a job in Verwoerd South Africa and who was adopted in Nigeria where they lived for many years, and he taught a generation of Nigerian physicists at Ibadan. He often turns up at Sylvia's house when she is traveling, to chat, see that I am okay. He always brings beer, refuses to let me buy any. Like Victory's endless free beers and small loans; like how DoomDoom let me sleep in his small room for two months and showed me how to use a computer; like how Chuma Koyana took me home to their lovely place in East London one long holiday; like how Chuma's mother took care of me as if I were her own son; like Kaya's uncle asking me, a Kenyan he did not know, but an African they trusted, to tell Kaya his mother had died; like how Mrs. Baguma asks no questions; like how my uncles brought us here and watched over us. This is how to become an African. This town—full of doctors and teachers and professors and nurses and civil servants from all over the continent, and from all over this country—has taken good care of me, and given me more than I have given back.

George and Alice come and stand with me, and we chat about this and that, and watch the meat grilling. The door to her house is open, and music is playing.

...

I call up Chuma. He has a new Golf GTI, which he always needs money to service. Chuma is like family to me. He too is presently jobless. But he is better subsidized than I am, by an inheritance from his late father, a lawyer who died in the 1970s.

We draw up a thing of beauty. It has charts, projections, colors, and trenchant analyses cut and pasted from the Internet. George loves it. He gives us a fat deposit for expenses. And several giant boxes of his posters.

We spend the next few weeks driving all over the Eastern Cape, talking to "contacts," the media and other important people. Chuma knows everybody, so the work is easy. Mostly we attend parties. We call up George to report, and he tells us he has something to tell us. Can we drive to Durban?

Sure.

We drive to Durban—six hours from East London. He hosts us in his firm's corporate flat. He says he has decided to cancel the tour. Work. Priorities and . . . he looks uncomfortable. We are nervous. I look at him and keep my lifted eyebrow bi-ronic.

But—but . . . of course he will pay us in full. Do we mind staying in that flat, and partaking of its black Johnnie Walker whiskeys and minty black powerments, and being driven around Durban for a few days as his corporate guests while he organizes the money? There is a big Empowering launch tonight at the beach. You are invited. Many celebs and free drinks floating on the swimming pool and bikinis and DJs.

Hmm, my eyebrow sighs, like timeismoney.

I look down and notice a hole in my shoe. "Oh," he says, "and here is a small something for now." The envelope has crisp notes.

After three days George brings the money. Himself. Lovely man. We get the money. I walk into a secondhand-book shop: three floors of heaven. I buy more than a hundred books that day.

I decide to pack immediately when I get back to Umtata, and move to Cape Town.

Chapter Twenty-Four

Hayibo. What is up with Brenda Fassie? Why can't she stay dead?

We have pounded her right into toothless history. We laugh and gossip-column her. Three years ago her lesbian lover, Poppie Sihlahla, died, an overdose of crack cocaine. In Hillbrow! Once Struggle Central, now Hillbrow is the drug-dealing capital of Africa, where the broken are robbed by the new and hungry. We can see now, how broken she is. Her son, Bongani, says he tries to hide drugs from his mother.

How could we ever have followed her?

She storms out of rehab, after only one day there, and speaks to journalists, saying, "I went there, and they made me wear a uniform and said I should say, 'Hi, my name is Brenda and I am a junkie.' Me! Me! Brenda Fassie! No way."

She is finished.

Finished. We are listening to bling music, which thumps and talks about hip and hop, gold and going places. There is no past, everything is sampled. Kwaito.

She is finished. Bubblegum.

But . . . she isn't.

It is 1998. I have been in Cape Town for a year, and things are moving. I started a small catering business with a friend, making African food—all those years of free meals taught me a thing or two about peanut butter chicken and Nigerian *ogbono* soup. We are failing mostly, but things are moving, a few deals here and there.

It is a chilly day, lunchtime, and the wind is blowing like mad. I haven't slept, but I need to find a cheap phone to call Mum. I have news.

I board a black taxi in Sea Point, in Cape Town, and two white women keep asking the taxi driver to play some song. He puts it on, and the taxi falls silent.

It is Brenda's new song. In Xhosa.

It is strange. There hasn't been any real crossover music in South Africa, except Mango Groove. Artificial Tropicana juice has been drunk by generations of Day-Glo bright, banana-leaf-wearing natives of a rainbow nation, who dance and sing daylight come and me wan' go home. That is the general idea behind Mango Groove—a white woman with a group of anonymous blacks in faux tropical clothes cheerleading her.

Cape Town whites listen to rock music and the ethnic music of all places not in South Africa. The word *edgy* appears a lot in music magazines, music that takes people outside themselves to some cliff, so one can bungee jump off and get the "energy," drum and bass and techno and a thing called ambient. Urban black South Africans love R&B, and Kwaito, reggae, and gospel.

One day, a couple of months ago, I was living in a backpack hostel, and the common phone booth was ringing early in the morning. Somebody picked up and called me to the phone. "It's your father," he said.

I pick up the phone. "Hello."

Baba was in Johannesburg. He had been in Australia on some work thing and had changed his ticket to try to come to South Africa for a day or two to see if he could find me. Somebody had told him I was in Johannesburg. Then Ciru called a friend, and they gave him this number.

"I . . ."

"Don't say anything. Just listen. You have to stop worrying about us, and what we think, or what we want. Do what you need to do . . ."

I am quiet.

"But—call your mother. She . . . you know she worries."

I panic. There is something in his voice. They are hiding something. "Is she okay? I can . . . come home?"

"Oh no, no. We are fine. Kenya is bad but we are fine. Don't risk losing your papers . . ."

He doesn't ask what I am doing. Then he drops the bombshell. Ciru also had a baby two weeks ago. His name is William. "Oh," I say. I am surprised. He is quiet on the phone. "She is old enough," I say. "She can support herself." He sounds tired. I wonder if I will ever manage to survive having children.

Mum and I speak a few times. I tell her about the writing. She sounds happy, wary, and encouraging. She doesn't ask what I am writing about. Baba told me that the diabetes is back. I ask her about it, and she says she is fine. She sounds frail. She talks about the grandkids a lot. Paul is talkative and William is the quiet one. Everybody calls Paul Bobo. "He looks like you when you were a baby," she says. Jimmy got married, to his girlfriend Carol, and I missed the wedding. I am not going home until I make something of myself.

Baba has retired now, and they have moved to a new place they are renting while they build the new house. Sometimes she has to go to Baba's new office to receive a call while they wait for a landline. She can't drive herself. Politics is terrible, more clashes, and the 1997 election was rigged. Moi is back and the opposition is broken.

I am working around the clock, writing, cooking, looking for catering contracts, not getting them. Charlie Sweet and I still share work. I am still trying to make my dreadful novel work. Last night, Charlie and I were e-mailing back and forth. I started to write to him about my trip to Uganda. A long, long e-mail. He is quiet for a few hours, and it is nearly dawn.

He doesn't e-mail. Then the phone rings. It is Charlie.

"This is beautiful," he says.

I can hear my jaw creaking open, its rusty hinges groaning.

"Your mother . . . she . . . wow . . . man, you really should publish this somewhere big."

I work through the morning. Cut and shape it. I spend some time looking around the Internet for newspapers and magazines. I want to send it somewhere before I sleep and get all accordion and *kimay*.

The *Sunday Times* is South Africa's biggest and richest newspaper. I read the weekend magazine travel section. Yes, I could try for that. There is an e-mail address at the bottom of the page. I attach the story. It is just after 9:00 a.m., and I am about to shut down the computer when a reply arrives. "How much money do you want for your story?" asks a gentleman called Andrew Unsworth, who is the subeditor. "It's quite long," he says, "but I think we can make room for it. Love it. Love it. It runs on Sunday."

So, I am sitting in this taxi, floating. The two white women are saying, "Oh, oh. It's so so beautiful, this new Brenda Fassie song." Not a word in English in this first real crossover song in a new South Africa.

It's the way the song begins—a church organ, playing on a scratchy old record, a childhood memory of a sound, for the briefest moment, then come her first few words, slurred like she is drunk and far away, lost inside an old shortwave radio. The first word is *vul'indlela*—clear the path—delivered in a soft, childlike candor, and for the next few sounds, we are left alone with her voice, pleading to us softly, *vul'indlela*, let me in.

The country has all its defenses up. Everybody is screaming and jostling for space. Young hip-hoppers with trousers showing the crack in their buttocks have announced the end of innocence, the death of the village, the end of the struggle; young white kids shrilling, "Emigrate, we are emigrating to Australia because of affirmative action, which is racism in reverse." At the supermarket last week, the cashier, a colored woman, shut her till when she saw me and told me to join a new queue.

"But . . . but . . . ," I said.

She laughed. "What will you do?" she asked. "Go report me to Mandela?"

All that disappears for a moment, as the first ten seconds of the song turn us all into mush.

The song starts to thump, and Brenda continues to twist the gut, sounding like she is sixteen again, and our shoulders are popping in this taxi. Everybody in this car is in exactly the same place. I hide my tears.

South Africa is starting to make something new. In Brenda's new video, she is pouting, a crown on her head, her fake teeth flashing, her lips lopsided, a mischievous child, a brassy woman, a tomboy, a cartoon, refusing to fall, carried forward by song only. I am sure Wambui—powerful and unbeatable Wambui—is still in Kenya, still somebody's maid. Wambuis do not become Brenda Fassies in Kenya.

I am a writer. I am now a published writer. I am going to call Mum, call Baba, and tell them that my story, about us in Uganda, will be online for them to read.

Later, Brenda will say, of this new album, *Memeza* (Shout), "I'd been shouting and shouting and no one wanted to hear me. When I sing this song, *vul'indlela*, I want to cry."

Chapter Twenty-Five

It is 1960, Mum is sixteen, and she is at home. Standing on Grandpa's balcony, looking down the big hill at the train of cars and trucks and vans crawling in circles up the steep old road, driving toward them, coming from Congo, where my grandmother, Modesta, was born. The cars are piled high with luggage and mattresses and furniture, and boxes and trunks and bags.

It is all over the radio. Congo is shaking. Rebellion is spreading like fire.

Independence is a fever, and it is all over the continent.

Last night a family came to their house, dressed in torn clothes, some in sleeping clothes, pajamas and nighties. They were tired and weak, and Mum found it heartbreaking. She helped feed them and fetched water for them to drink and wash. They parked their cars outside, to rest. In every direction, eighty thousand of them flee as Congo erupts. Some refugees are staying in the cathedral a few hundred meters away. In the 1930s, when my grandfather was baptized, he gave land to the church for the cathedral.

Mum is about to sit her O-levels. She will do well. She is waiting to go and study at Makerere University, in Kampala. Ever the mouse nibbling in people's cupboards for books, I once found, stole, and read her school autograph book. One of her friends said, "Rosa, I hope you meet your handsome sailor."

From where Mum sits, this road leads deep into Congo, to Kigali, Rwanda, and the same road will take the refugees who are able to go to Kampala, then Nairobi, then Mombasa—and to South Africa, Rhodesia, and Belgium. Cars run out of fuel along the way and are abandoned. The famous Ugandan poet Okot p'Bitek buys a Rolls-Royce for next to nothing in Kisumu. In the 1960s, V. S. Naipaul wanders down this road and says it will all go back to bush.

In Nairobi, a young man, all of twenty, with a wide smile and big eyes, has a job as a tea broker for Brooke Bond. In a few days, he will buy his first car from one of the refugees. He likes fast cars. He broke his leg on a motorcycle. He loves the English language.

His name is Job Wainaina. His big sister, Rebecca, is already a famous playwright. Rosemary, standing on the hill, does not know that soon she will head down the same road as these refugees, to Nairobi and Kianda College, to do a secretarial course.

She will not go to university.

Sometime in the early 1950s, many years ago, Modesta, my grandmother, and her sister are at home cleaning and cooking and a neighbor comes to the door all fearful and excited and says that a strange white man is on their property.

My grandmother is a shy woman, a stern woman. She is around thirty years old. They find the man walking around, digging at the ground, as if he is looking for something. He is Belgian. Grandmum takes a stick and starts to beat him. She hits him as hard as she can. He is on the ground begging, and she hits him. Those who know her have never seen her so fierce.

Grandad finds out that there is a black stone on their land, that this black stone is very valuable. This stone sends their eldest son, Damian, to university; it sends Rosalie to Switzerland to study, and Christine to France. Christine sends Mum her first pair of shoes from France. Mum is thirteen and has never worn her own shoes. Mum works hard in school and excels in her exams. She is called to Uganda's top high school, in Buganda, Mt. St. Mary's Namagunga, where she wears her new shoes. One day she sees the king of Buganda, King Freddie, who shakes her hand. He is handsome in his military royal clothes, hand in pocket like an Englishman. She never stops talking about it.

All the Binyavanga children do very well in school. Many of them go to the top schools, in Buganda. Kamanzi and Henry are always at the top of their class at St. Mary's Kisubi. Eventually they move to South Africa. They teach at universities there.

Modesta is very close to her daughter Rosemary, who, at sixteen, is already dangerously beautiful. Rosemary is quiet and dreamy and can be stern, like Modesta. Among the children, it is Rosemary who helps enforce Modesta's rules. She does all her work, on time. She helps take care of the babies—Bernadine and Gerald and Innocent. She is almost another mother to them.

Like her mother, she can be strict and gets into no mischief. She is not confused like her son will be. She is very stubborn; when she believes something, nobody can sway her. When she was young, she used to have fits; when she cried she would faint sometimes.

If you ask her now, she will say that she will marry somebody in Kampala, after university. They will build a home near her parents. She is the good daughter who stays behind and helps her parents. Standing here on the hill and watching Belgian Congo fall, and Lumumba's Congo rise, she does not know that Uganda too will fall and break, long after she has left.

The black stone's value on the world market has fallen. There is not enough money to send Mum to university. She agrees to wait for a couple of years. She goes to Nairobi, to do a secretarial course at Kianda College, which is famous all over East Africa. She lives with her cousin Barnabas, who is a friend of the deposed king of Rwanda. The king, who is very tall, is always flirting with Rosemary. Rosemary is not interested. There is another friend of Barnabas. His name is Job. He has a wide smile. A car. She is not her father's favorite child. It is her sister Rosalie who is close to her father. But she loves her father terribly. She will speak of him all the time to her childen. Job, like her father, is warm around people, makes them laugh. Takes her quietness out of her. Sometimes Job drives past Kianda College in his car and finds her at the bus stop. He looks surprised to see her. Oh! It's you? Do you want a lift?

They marry, in the district commissioner's office. She wears a simple suit. His family is very Protestant. Her family is very Catholic. She is the first of the sisters to marry. Her sister Christine will say, "I was so worried. Rosemary was so in love with Job, we were worried about her. I had never seen her like that."

Standing here, on the hill, she does not know that she and her husband will take in her own younger sister and three brothers, support some through school, college, and university when Uganda is bleeding. She will start a hair salon to help to raise money for family. She will be known for her willingness to put her own dreams behind and serve her family. She will drive a tractor one day, pregnant with baby Chiqy, to deliver diesel to the farm. She will grow wheat and barley with her husband for extra money when Kenya starts to stumble.

Her son Kenneth, named after her father, Binyavanga, is a strange one. She defends him, more than she should. He lives inside his dreams, and is always stumbling. He never accepted God, and sometimes it looks as if he can disappear inside chaos. He has a sweetness that disarms her; in a way they are friends. He never made it difficult; even when he was lost in his world, he would never say so. He shrugs and smiles and tries to please, following people.

He cannot say no. He has her dreaminess, her absentmindedness. Her stubbornness. He does not have her will, her spine, or her refusal to accept uncertainties, to transcend them. He stands and falls into the tangle of his doubts. Always stands and falls and dreams. She too wanted to make beautiful things and maybe that is why she let him go, when sometimes she could have been sterner with him.

She is not there, when her son's Cape Town phone rings. It is Uncle Henry, who has not spoken to her son in years. Uncle Henry, now a professor of business management at the University of the Witwatersrand, says, "Hello, Kenneth."

"Yes," says Kenneth.

"Are you . . . how are you? Kenneth . . . are you sitting down? I am sorry to tell you, your mother, Rosemary . . . she passed away today, in Kenyatta Hospital."

Rosemary Kankindi is the third daughter of Cosma Binyavanga. She married Job Muigai Wainaina, of Kenya, and they have four children:

James Muigai Wainaina
Binyavanga Wainaina
June Wanjiru Wainaina
Melissa Kamanzi Wainaina
She has two grandchildren.
From both her daughters. Paul Muigai, and William Wainaina.

Chapter Twenty-Six

Nairobi in 2001 is one big bar.

It's been a year since Mum died. I came for the funeral and found I could not leave. To leave means changing my name, getting a new passport. It means not being sure I will get a visa. It means witnessing change in a place that will never let me be part of it. South Africans are infatuated with their own new trajectory. Like Americans, they see the whole world in their country, and seem perpetually surprised that other people are in their country. I will always be a foreigner. Even after ten years. I am tired of moving around. I want to be home. Just to be home. I don't want people being born, people dying with me away. My baby sister is all grown up and I do not know her.

I live in a small room in a private student hostel called Beverly Hills, in Eastlands, next to one of Nairobi's largest slums.

Hostels like these are popular with college students and the newly employed. They are cheap and secure. Water is rationed. That first night I left the dry taps open, and I woke up to see my laptop floating in four inches of water. The screen died. I bought a cheap secondhand PC screen in the city, and now it is working.

I spend my day indoors, writing, and leave my room when I smell the first onions and Royco Mchuzi Mix frying for people's supper. I walk into Mlango Kubwa to buy something cheap to eat. To meet and chat with people.

Congo rumba music squeals out of a rusty corrugated-iron shack; it seesaws up and down my stomach, wrapped around beer-fueled laughter, the squeals of barmaids. Early-evening light makes beasts of faces. Eyes and teeth gleam; gums and tongues rejoice, as paraffin light laps at the cooling air, and the tentative scuttle out of their holes to feed. A group of three Somali women walk, like mice, huddled together, heading for the mosque in Eastleigh. I follow.

Two Congolese men are standing outside the bar, their pants hiked up to their chests, short and stocky in designer fur coats, skin bleached a flat and dead yellow, lips black and smoky. There is a Kenyan joke about the Congo man whose trousers are so high that he can access his wallet only by reaching over his shoulder. The men are laughing and talking to each other in Lingala, in a closed world of two, a sound that jangles like the music in my head.

I am writing a lot, and getting commissions here and there. I have started writing fiction, which I love the most. My only regular source of income is the one hundred dollars a week that Rod Amis, the editor of an online magazine, g21.net, pays me for contributions. I have abandoned my bad speculative fiction novel. I am trying to build skill by writing short stories.

The elections are in a year, and we are all wondering whether we will survive that long. Many people have filled the streets many times to campaign for political change. Finally the constitution is amended, so an elected official can only serve two terms. This is Moi's second term. He has promised to retire. We don't really believe it.

I make my way through the zigzag paths of Mlango Kubwa's main avenue, Biashara Street. The soapy, gagging smell of an open drain rises up and catches me by surprise. I walk, in a hurry, breathing with my mouth, a childhood habit designed to bewilder ambitious microbes. The gaudy hand-painted colors of small-scale marketing wriggle; they splash to woozy life in the muddy puddles that line the path.

Tens of thousands of people—on foot and bicycles, unloading from thumping *matatus*—are swarming past us down Mlango Kubwa, through Eastleigh, the frontier of formal Nairobi, on paths made spongy from years of fresh produce and litter, to Mathare, in a thick downhill flow.

Dark is thick now, and I walk more lightly. I take this route most days, to catch the flickering streams of people. There is something beautiful about the moments when people are removed from themselves by the imminent: the rush to do small forgotten things; the unpacking of mobile shops; children shrieking, cut loose from routine; the flood of black China-made bicycles, hurling warning bells and threats at children; the sharp clicks of roofs contracting in the cooling air. I come out every evening at this time to buy some supper; to buy some dope, sometimes to buy a beer.

I spent the past few weeks polishing a short story for the Caine Prize for African Writing. It is about a young girl (Girl Child, Gender!) who is questioning the world, and her mother's values (Empowerment).

I mine every sexy African theme I can think of. The Caine Prize, based in England, is worth fifteen thousand dollars, and you get an agent and fame and lots of commissioned work.

Whenever I walk here, I always look out for Joga's murals.

I stumbled on his work a few weeks after moving here; after my eyes adjusted to the flow of things, I could set aside the hundreds of small dramas unfolding before me, and I was able to focus on the particular. Joga's older works were smoky, sometimes difficult to see clearly. In one bar, I found a large mural painted on chipboard, mounted on the wall. The bar was full of old Gikuyu men and women: waistcoats and plastic eyeglasses and headscarves, the odd walking stick. Sluggish traditional accordion music from the Kenyatta-era 1970s scratched its way out of old speakers. There were murals everywhere. Friesian fields; overlarge udders; lush countrywomen trampolining on soft kikuyu grass; gnarled old trees gathered in a semicircle of wisdom.

Escape here, says the hand-painted ad; sample a little bit of rural home. Two drunk men try to carry a cow into a *matatu*, their legs waggling like earthworms. In the distance, coffee plantations gleam, like gold.

After a few months, this mural disappeared. The bar owner was bored with it and threw it away. He bought a pool table and a VCD player.

Every few weeks I go to Nakuru and spend some time with Baba. We have a beer at Njoro Golf Club, eat there even, and talk. He is the chairman of the club, and spends a lot of time there restoring things and making them work again. It's strange to us—we are all used to seeing each other through my mother's gentle public relations. It is hard to believe this Baba who makes mistakes, who can be unsure of himself, who is not up and out of the house at 8:00 a.m. every day. The new people at Pyrethrum Board have been mismanaging things, and it is hard for him to stand aside and watch what he has worked for be destroyed by incompetence. The new managing director is from Moi's tribe. A diplomat, with no experience working with farmers. I get angry and flap my hand about when Baba tells me this, and he remains measured and sensible, writes reports, and goes to Nairobi often and discreetly to meet ministry people and suggest ways to keep Pyrethrum Board alive.

I stop at a tin and clapboard and recycled tin barbershop, which is asymmetrical and coiled around a get-together of wiggling paths, made slick by large advertorial murals—painted, again, by Joga.

Mash and Ndizi stand outside, as they do every day, eyebrows offering suggestions whenever eye contact is made with a potential customer. Kalamashaka, the original rappers in Sheng, growl out of a music system that sits outside: "I'm so thirsty Sprite cannot quench my thirst / I'm so tired trying to maintain an image . . ."

Kalamashaka live up the road, in Dandora. Only here, in the slums of Nairobi, has some sort of three-in-one language developed, Sheng, and slowly hip-hop musicians are bringing Sheng to life all over the country: angry burning songs about the struggle of life in a falling city, on new FM radio stations that have opened the previously restricted airwaves.

Joga's work on this barbershop has a metallic aspect. Master P's golden face leers, filling a whole wall, gold glinting on his teeth, on his fingers, around his neck.

There is a small portrait of Osama bin Laden on the door, and the rest of the walls and the stand-alone sign on the ground are taken up by paintings of soft slick African American haircuts. On quiet nights I have turned a corner and a giant Joga face—ruby-colored lips parted to whisper green-card lottery dreams in an air hostess voice—slaps me to attention.

Mash has a face like a Cadbury drinking chocolate advert, shiny yellow cheeks and dimples. A James Hadley Chase novel, *No Orchids for Miss Blandish*, peeks out of the side pocket of his denim jacket. We met a few weeks ago, at an open-air book exchange near the KBS depot. Ndizi, his business partner, has remained elusive, sliding away smoothly whenever I try to pin him down, always friendly, always aloof.

K-Shaka rap: "Are you thinking of bringing a ridiculous cast to my funeral / Please hide the machete before thoughts start roaming."

We chat, and my eyes wander. Paths zigzag, crash into shops, and swerve off, so at ground level you can't see any farther than a few meters, an instinctive maze fulfilled by a naked citizenry, a protection from surprises: Police. Authorities.

When Mungiki militias took over in this area, they started to build straight roads and demolish shacks. They said that straight roads make it hard for thieves to hide. Most of us think Mungiki are the lowest of the low. Fanatics. Mafiosos. Mash is a Mungiki supporter; he says crime has stopped and young men have something to believe in, something to do.

All the systems that function here are built on small relationships. You—your branded individuality and its costumes, and your manner, and the trade or activity this costume represents—are the institution that matters. You negotiate your power in every conversation.

Joga comes out of the barbershop to say hi. He often hangs out here. He has changed. The awkward nineteen-year-old I met a year ago, wearing the shyness of the village, is gone. He is now a celebrity. Eastleigh, only a few hundred meters away, has "discovered" his work, and he has new commissions nearly every day. He has his first contracts with the formal city, and the respect that this brings.

He no longer wears paint-splattered jeans; he has on a trendy fleece jacket, baggy pants, and Nikes. He has acquired that loose-walking way that is referred to as cool. He will stop and lean against a wall, slouching slightly. He will not stare at anybody, like he used to, with eyes that declared his shyness; he will let his glance sit lightly on whoever addresses him. The glance will acknowledge that person's contribution, and the shutters will close.

He nods his head to one side, one eyebrow lifting in greeting. I nod back.

"Nimemaliza," he says to the group, and we follow him inside, to see a huge two-meter by two-meter portrait of Jay-Z.

"Ni kaa photo." It's like a photo, says Ndizi. I look at it, and there are little cartoon emphases: gleams exaggerated on his teeth, cartoon bursts of diamond bling! Jay-Z's features are exaggerated, for effect. Joga does not see a difference between his pungent cartoon images and photographs.

I grew up with people whose lives dived down from television satellites, and shot past us. Going Somewhere People. We followed: all of us scrumming to enter the bottleneck beyond which international-level incomes are offered. We are threatened, every minute, by failure, if we question the stepping-stones of certainty presented to us, if we fail to be fluent in the fashions of MTV and London and New York.

Joga does not know what an art gallery is; he does not seem to believe me when I tell him about the Nairobi art scene at Kuona and the French cultural center. Even here, he has never apprenticed under anybody. He taught himself; his whole evolution as an artist has been mediated only by his translation of what he sees and hears.

Which face do you pick to meet chaos? The one built from the ground up, baring all your past, all your scars? Or the adopted one, wired to a certain manner that you have discovered will open doors to the scholarshipped, resuméd, backed-up, buffered world out there and the piece of stamped paper that promises that you will inherit the earth?

Me, I am like a squirrel, looking for opportunity all over the Internet. My story "Hell Is in Bed with Mrs. Peprah" is accepted by a small American magazine, and I celebrate.

But I find out that it won't be published in time for the Caine Prize deadline. The magazine, in Nebraska, can only pay in contributor copies.

In a panic, the day before the submission deadline, I ask Rod Amis to publish my girlchild story for me on g21.net.

He says he can't publish fiction. I send him a quickly reedited version of the Uganda story I published in South Africa.

We decide to call it "Discovering Home."

Rod submits it, and gets a snooty e-mail from the Caine Prize people in England, saying they only accept stories published in print.

I am furious. I write back, telling them only one anthology has been published in Africa in the past year. Where do they find published stories? I ask.

They don't respond. Fuck them, says Rod. Bloody colonizers. Yes. Yes, I say.

Joga is stuck in the same place I am. Can only see his pictures as photographs because, like me, he receives ideas from some far-off capital. Nobody here will pass up a chance at gold and bling and puppy dog jeans. Does he have any idea how fresh his work looks, after the elaborate mimicries of the other Nairobi? I hand over some money to Mash, and Ndizi passes me the rolls of *bhangi*. His dreadlocks splash spaghetti shadows on my shirt.

"Why do they call you Ndizi?"

His laugh sounds like paper rustling on a radio microphone.

"Ndizi kaa Sundaymorning."

An answer and no answer. A Jamaican accent smudges the seams of his Sheng. His voice has the rich musical undertones of a Luo. I turn and head back slowly for home. I laugh to myself. Joga is better off than I am. Rod can't afford to pay me a hundred dollars a week anymore, so I can't even afford to live in this slum.

I last three months.

I go home and ask Baba if I can stay with them in the new house. Ciru has a job, with an Internet start-up. Chiqy works for a mobile phone company in Nairobi. Her son, Bobo, lives with us while she sets herself up. I babysit my nephews and write and cook. I do small features for local magazines in Kenya. I meet online and make friends with a young Nigerian woman, Chimamanda Adichie, who is also trying to get published. We critique each other's work. Soon, we are e-mailing every day. I meet Muthoni Garland online and other Kenyan writers—a community starts to connect and talk. Soon we are talking about publishing, about starting a magazine.

I am online all day and all night. Baba complains about the bills. An uncle is sent to speak to me. He has this new machine. It can take cheap alcohol and seal it in small sachets. "You talk well," he tells me. "You can do sales and marketing and make some money."

I am about to say yes when the e-mail from the bloody colonizers comes.

Dear Caine Prize Shortlisted Guy, called Binya . . . vanga. Do you want to come to England, and have dinner in the House of Lords, and do readings, and go to the Bodleian Library for a dinner of many courses, with wine, and all of London's literati? At this dinner, you will find out if Baroness Somebody Important will give you fifteen thousand dollars in cash, and even if she doesn't, you should come because being shortlisted and having dinner at the House of Lords and such is like a big deal, a really big deal. Will you come?

Oh yes. I go.

I win the Caine Prize, and cry, bad snotty tears, and come back with some money. A group of writers and I start a magazine, called *Kwani?*—which means so what?

Chapter Twenty-Seven

I am traveling a lot now, sometimes on magazine assignments. I always look for reasons to travel in Africa.

One day a very nice Dutch man calls me up. "Are you Binya-wanga? The writer?"

"Yes."

"Oh, I heard about your work. I work for the European Union Humanitarian Something. I want to produce a book about Sudan, about sleeping sickness in Sudan."

"I don't really do development writing," I say.

"Oh, no no. We want a proper . . . African writer to write a book about what he sees. You know, literature. We will publish it and pay for everything. You will go with a photographer. It will be something different. Powerful. Literature and photographs."

"You mean you will pay, and I can write whatever I see?"

"Yes."

"And you can say that in the contract?"

"Yes."

So I go to Sudan, and come back shell-shocked. I start to write. I fictionalize parts of it. I met a South Sudanese doctor who worked for the SPLA. He would work the whole morning and get violently drunk in the afternoon. Sometimes his superiors would send him to Nairobi to get in shape, then return him to the front to patch broken bodies together and throw them back to the war. He refused to leave his work and get a decent job somewhere. I decide to make him a poet. It is the first poetry I have written.

I send the finished text to the nice Dutch man.

He is quiet, for a long time. Then I am called to a meeting. His supervisor is in town, from Brussels. The EU is very jittery about the book. They say that EU policy says there is only one Sudan, but my story says South Sudan!

They are also concerned about language ... some ... improper ... unseemly . . . language. Many things are not in line with EU policy. They have a proposition. Scrap the book. Keep the money. What they can do is fund an awareness-raising photo exhibition. And for the exhibition, I can write a few paragraphs—within the parameters of EU policy on Sudan, of course. You keep your full fat fee, of course. I tell them to fuck off in seemly language. I raise the money elsewhere, and *Kwani?* publishes the book.

I start to understand why so little good literature is produced in Kenya. The talent is wasted writing donor-funded edutainment and awareness-raising brochures for seven thousand dollars a job. Do not complicate things, and you will be paid very well.

...

Moi has been voted out. We have our first proper democratic government since the 1960s. I came down from Nairobi, where I am now living, two days ago, to my hometown, Nakuru, to vote. I decide to take a trip up Moi's heartland, through Baringo, and all the way to Pokot, beyond the tarmac, where I have never been, and where I am told people ask you, did you come from Kenya?

The road extends out into the distance, knobbly gray tarmac, straight and true, and making equal: Nakuru town; the agricultural showground; the dead straight line of jacaranda and their morning carpet of mushy purple on rich, brown damp earth; ex-president Moi's palace and its attached school in Kabarak; plains of grain and cattle; stony, sky land, hot and dry; a pile of lonely casks of fresh milk, slowly souring by the side of the road; another pile of recycled bottles filled with dark, beer-colored Baringo honey, waiting for a market that is not coming; an arm reaching out to show off a wriggling catfish to the odd city car; a huddle of schoolgirls in purple school skirts swollen by the wind into swaying polyester lamp shades, giggling; goats seated in the center of the road just past Marigat town; dried riverbeds; groups of shining Vaselined people walking or cycling by the side of the road, to church, sometimes ten or more kilometers away; ten or twelve tribes, three lakes. The whole unbroken line of human evolution here, in the base of the Rift Valley, as I head out to visit Pokot.

This road was the promise of a president, for his people. The honey projects, the milk, the irrigation scheme not far from here that once produced eggplants the size of small pumpkins—all these things failed to find markets.

· · ·

Until a few weeks ago, Moi was every policeman, the photo on every wall; he was all the cash in the bank, the constitution. We wanted him gone; we were afraid of life without him.

Voting day was probably the quietest day in Kenya's history. From Nairobi, I took a *matatu* to my hometown. There was virtually no traffic; all the streets were empty. The tin-shack cities were ghost towns, as were the pyrethrum plots at the fog-dark, freezing height of the escarpment. I looked down and saw little patches of green and brown, tea and coffee and pyrethrum and cattle: fields of dreams.

A few days later, the largest crowd in Kenya's history gathers, in Uhuru Park, to inaugurate a new president. Moi's car is pelted with mud. When he stands up to speak, he is booed, and mud is thrown at him.

If, before this, we had wondered whether we could easily become a noncountry if we challenged the status quo, this fear died that day.

We began to become something resolute and possible. We started to want again. But wanting, too, brings its own risks.

There is a stake now, and people are passionate.

· · ·

I have never been to Pokot before, so I can't really say I am looking for familiar things. I know this road, have seen these sights change so many times. When you are locked in your room, sluggish and lost inside yourself, the person you were who lived in the world is vague and distant to you. Standing in the world now, I can feel the echo of my long sleep— small familiar movements are startling; memories excite, everything is just a little too bright, my Umtata room is already far away. I tingle at the most mundane things, and I am still wary of hanging around people I know: friends, and family.

The *matatu* drives past the turnoff to Kabartonjo, and the road rises a few thousand meters in minutes. To our left are the Tugen Hills, which run all the way to Kabartonjo; from there you can look down from a great height on the Lukeino triangle, on the lakes of this area, the massive Kerio Valley.

...

When I got into the *matatu* this morning, the conductor, a young, shabbily dressed man, had been slapping the vehicle, eyes narrowed and shrewd, sometimes urging people on with a hand on the back, sometimes grabbing people from the side of the road, all the time in Gikuyu— bawdy and rustic, laughing hoarsely when somebody shrugged away in annoyance. We left, and he marinated chatter in Gikuyu, and in Gikuyu-accented English.

We had just passed the police post at an industrial area when the driver turned to the young man sitting next to the door in the backseat of the fifteen-seat Nissan and addressed him in Kalenjin, and he replied in the same language. I was so startled I turned back, and his eyes caught mine and he laughed, then broke into Kalenjin for the benefit of the passengers, swinging his chin to point at me, laughing softly, his smile now open and friendly, teasing, rather than mocking. It is an excellent way to defuse our present political tensions—he is telling us all is fine. He has good reasons to do this; there have been clashes between Kalenjins and their neighbors every election since 1992.

It is marvelous to watch. The man's body language, his expressions, his character even, change from language to language—he is a brash town guy, a Gikuyu *matatu* guy, in Gikuyu, and even in Kiswahili. When he speaks Kalenjin, his face is gentler, more humorous, ironic rather than sarcastic, conservative, shy eyes. By the time we pass Kabarak, the newer passengers are helped in with more courtliness and less rush, things piled on the roof; one older woman is helped in, his eyes respectful.

Some frail old threads gather as the woman sitting next to me sighs, long, in the middle of saying something to the driver. Her shoulder slumps, and she says, "Mpslp, ai, aliniuthii"—the *mpslp*, a sort of pulling in of saliva, a completely familiar movement, and one I haven't noticed since I left, years ago. The thing about it is how complete it is, how Kenyan it is, not just the sound, but the way her neck swings, her shoulders move up the droop quickly, as she says, "Oh, that man!" He really offended me, her slack shoulders say. Even now she can only soften and succumb to this offense, for like me, or you, she suggests, we are vulnerable to being offended and being defeated by the offense: and this moves us all, for she has told us all too that she trusts our common reaction enough to know that we too would not put up a wall of pride at offense, or begin an escalation of conflicts. We sigh with her. For a moment we become a common personality, and she is chatting back and forth with people all over the *matatu*.

Her name, she says, is Prisca Cherono. It is possible to be alone, says her shrug. I am always afraid of falling into and getting tangled by my messy shapes. When I wake up to an awareness of place and time, I find I have gone far away from others, and I do not have the confidence to make my way back. In a way, writing keeps me close to people. I feel comfortable taking huge leaps of perception, and knowing that I can come back to what I have written, and build it into a defendable shape.

These simple shrugs bring me back.

If, in the soft quiet after Prisca's shrug, she turns back to me in the fifteen-seater, and asks me some small intimacy, which my individual person would not appreciate—like, why are you so fat? your body remembers—she has made a community by sharing her vulnerability, and my community person will find himself being gracious and open.

I say, "Oh, I lived in South Africa. They have a lot of fast food."

"Oh," she will say. "I heard it is like America there," and the whole car will pause and picture this.

We live by these acts, in any part of this country, where neither our anthem nor our tax base nor our language nor our view of the world is in any way universal.

It often feels like an unbearable privilege—to write. I make a living from simply taking all those wonderful and horrible patterns in my past and making them new and strong. I know people better. Sometimes I want to stop writing because I can't bear the idea that it may one day go away. Sometimes I feel I would rather stop, before it owns me completely. But I can't stop.

I look out, and there is a horizontal placenta of cloud, dirty pink and brown, and somewhere in this distance, shafts of cloud-colored rain are falling. On both sides of me, there is a wall of blue mountains, the escarpments of the Rift Valley. There is a trail of goat shit on the road.

Grace is a funny thing, and I don't mean just the grace that refers to swans. Let us imagine that as Prisca begins to speak to the whole now-open vehicle, a Bavarian tourist in the car says something poisonous, like, "Please shut up, madam. Can't you see I am reading?" The moment this happens, this man senses the small shifts and stiffness inside the vehicle, the sudden silence of fifteen chattering people. His confidence in his body evaporates. His fingers do not know what to do as they fidget, and his throat clears, gurgling defenses. He knows exactly what he has destroyed, but not at all what she said or did, or what that meant.

He could go quiet and look fiercely into his book, face red, and soon he will be lost inside it, and the open chatter will rise again and seal him off. Or he may choose to be brave and stretch out an arm, which we are all so suddenly acutely aware of—it stands outside our common experience. If this wiggling thing cannot read the common body, its actions are unpredictable. It is so easy for people to turn on you. Here in Kenya, where only our interactions keep us together. Now that the state is failing, we are held together by small grace, by interpersonal relationships, by trusting body language.

I lean back and let my fantasy loose. We are tense, as this foreign object reaches forward. Perfectly physically familiar, this hand becomes an immediate animal threat, an inhuman object. It is no longer a warm symbol of a preferred greeting. It is a thing that can hurt flesh. We may choose to hurt it first. It knows this and is tentative, and those long pale wrinkled things that spread like a fan from a palm flutter for a moment, and then pat the shoulder of the woman, too hard or too softly, self-consciously, and the woman jerks sharply with an inhaling of breath to catch his eyes, and we inhale sharply too, and his eyes are jump-ing now, clueless, and he looks down and his shoulders have slumped, and this immediately releases our tension. He mumbles, "Sorry, sorry mama," and there is silence for a moment as we let him marvel with us, at his own bravery, for he has found his way to us blindfolded. We avert conflict every day with the smallest of things. If there is no law, no order, what keeps us together? Faith in the future? Not really. But we have built a common body language of a sort. We have to be alert and extra considerate to each other. That thread is what we hang on to.

So now, somebody, the conductor maybe, and this becomes a truly appropriate word—*conductor*—his job is to speak all our languages, move his body to arrange us, persuade us, collect from us. He takes charge and sends us all into a new series of patterns by saying, "Hallo mzungu," and jerking about in a deliberately simple-patterned way, a parody, close to our idea of a television Bavarian clumsiness, and we all burst out laughing at this joke with no punch line, constructed only out of movements that are incongruous, a word I am already associating with my brief religious ideology, based entirely on patterns and conduc-tors. So many innocent people have died in this Rift Valley, killed by neighbors. We can't just trust the moods of moments, the memories of love and life.

During these minutes, we climbed up a whole wall of an escarp-ment, which every year yielded to scientists more and more ancient hominids and early human permutations, and ten or twenty languages hidden in the hills out there. In this distance many languages are spoken whose history is unwritten, things are known that have yet to be shared. We drive past lakes and parks and towns, and these remain invisible, as we register with no conscious attention little sighs and slumping shoul-ders and a pat on a shoulder.

And so, I register the irony of a swaying conductor, moving to be irreverently German; achieving this is only doing it ever so slightly wrong. He is confident enough to use the smallest of signals to suggest that he is not proposing violence or offense by this parody, but is defusing dangerous awkward patterns, killing their threat. And we all get it; even the imaginary cliché Bavarian leans back and laughs. I want to wander, and see people and places. I want to move and watch and not stop.

...

I spend the night in Baringo town. The next morning, I hire a private taxi and wander past the tarmac to Pokot. All around us are mountains and dust and rocks—stones, rocks piled as far as the eye can see. The Pokot, 150,000 in number, are farmers or herders (often not the two together), and live mostly in this hostile land. The altitude changes rapidly, from three thousand meters above sea level to eight thousand feet. Everything around me is a memory of water. The dry riverbeds, the millions of dried petrified trees, the camels. Hot dry wind. Water-carved gullies and channels. The stone dams look silly and useless. Every few years, when the rain comes, this is a green place, lush and impassable. Bridges, cars, people, cattle, and camels get washed away.

We stop at a small village center to buy cigarettes and consult with the chief. The Pokot elders congregate around the car, and all burst out laughing when they see me. They are convinced I am a woman, even though I have a beard. Only Pokot women dreadlock their hair. I am astounded at how healthy they look. Not a sign of sickness or malnutrition. They are all lean and beautiful. The women are well oiled and gleaming, with twisted locks, and the married women have enormous disks of beadwork around their necks. Some wear old leather smocks, beaded and earth colored. One older man has a round disk of beads woven into the top of his head. The rest of his scalp is bare. I see another man with a plug below his lower lip—this I know was traditionally meant for lockjaw.

Here, outside the tarmac, they ask us if we come from "Kenya."

The second-longest bone in our bodies is called the tibia, a Latin word that also refers to the musical instrument by the same name, as flutes were once made from the tibiae of animals. There are two bones in our lower legs, the fibula and the tibia. *Fibula* means "clasp" or "brooch" in Latin. The idea, among the Latin-speaking ancients, was that the fibula was the clasp, and together they made a brooch.

In Pokot, an essential word, *korok*, allows me to glimpse, in a small way, how this landscape is seen through Pokot eyes. The word *korok* is three things: the tibia, a unit of physical space, and a unit of social space. It is not clear to me, or to the anthropologist who first wrote about this, Francis P. Conant, whether the tibia as a concept in Pokot has anything to do with the other versions of the same word.

There are two clear features of land here: rocky mountain, in the not-far-off distance, long walls of mountain height, running vertical in folds, and intensely flat, parched land, covered in small rocks.

Each fold is a shoulder of sorts, and in between the shoulders, rainy-season streams and channels of rainwater will run to the plains, fanning out as they descend, making them wider at the base than at the top of the mountains. This is a *korok*, and a fundamental unit of measuring society and physical space. A *korok* can also be a slight elevation between two streams of water. So, a *korok* can equally be a shoulder rising a thousand feet and bordered by water and a slight slope of twenty or so feet marked out by flowing water. I am reaching here—at the possibility that the way these physical spaces lock into each other is similar to the idea of *korok* as the tibia, the brooch. Maybe the lesson here is opposite to this: a simple reminder that words carry such pungent worldviews.

The car swoops down into a riverbed, surrounded by trees, and my skin is assaulted by thousands of shadows of leaf petals.

George, the taxi driver, says the people here get a lot of food aid from various international donors. He also says that the Pokot have been much less affected by modern life than their cousins the Maasai— and that the Pokot have remained away from the usual tourist beat.

We drive past a change in vegetation. There are succulents straight out of an undersea documentary—cacti and short stumpy baobab trees with pink and white flowers. The subchief tells me that they eat the leaves of the cacti as greens when there is a drought. In the distance, there is an enormous range of mountains, the Mau Escarpment of the Rift Valley.

There are opposite questions also, for those who live outside such nations within this nation, and who are poor. Life is measured as a poverty that wholly defines you; you are measured only by your worth, and you know it, like the worker bees of South Africa.

Asking the Maasai, who still own vast herds and vast lands, to give this up to the other Kenya is asking them to become peasants. The smallholder cash-crop farmer, the coffee grower, the tea grower will say, "Argh, you people, you do not work hard and look for opportunity." The trust land guy will say, "How many of you made it out of poverty?"

Most of you have not. And will not. Most of you come here to hide, or beg the Maasai to take you as wives, or lease small patches of ground for potatoes.

Maybe we are better off here than you are. It isn't working for any of us. We are all worse off than we were twenty years ago. Fifty years ago.

George tells me he has worked all over Kenya. But ended up back here running a small transport business in Marigat.

"We are cursed by a culture that is too strong," George says. "We do not want to go forward and change. Many people go to school and are clever in school. Pokots are always breaking records in Marigat high school. But most Pokot leave all that to come back and live in their culture. When I finished at university, they sent me to Maasailand, but I couldn't live there. Then they sent me to Kericho, but eventually I came back home. I can only live here."

We stop under a dry riverbed, in the shade of enormous acacias, to eat watermelon and icebox mango. The wind outside is so fierce and dry that my lips are on fire when the watermelon touches them. There is a group of children playing nearby, and they congregate to get a share of the fruit. We chat with them in Kiswahili. I ask them whether they are afraid of snakes. They laugh. Do they play outside like this at night? "Oh yes," they say. "We go out at all hours. Nighttime is better because it is not so hot. If we find a snake, we kill it."

We climb out of this dried oasis, and we are back on a plain of dust and rock. George shows me an enormous circle of stones, around a hundred feet in diameter. He tells me that this was the last gathering place of the Maasai in this area. They had faced years of drought, and after they had been defeated by the Pokot, they had a great meeting in this circle. Then they gathered up their cattle and moved on to Laikipia. This was the beginning of the end of their influence over the interior of Kenya.

In Pokot, the machine that produces warriors is as efficient as it was a hundred years ago. Thank God it has not been called to action against us on the other side. I am not sure how we could stop it.

In this dry place, where land has not been reshaped by development, it is still easy to imagine what that day was like. Vast herds of wealth, cattle stamping and sniffing in the dark. I can see the stones piled like a wall, woven with branches of thorn. Another surround of thorns where the young cattle were kept. The large tree to the left, the only tree around a lookout point. The recently circumcised warriors, bellies swollen from stuffing themselves with meat, eyes ready for war. Sullen that the elders have said they must give in and move. Eager to spill an enemy's blood, to prove themselves. Young boys and girls restless and excited, sensing that something without precedent for them was about to take place. That this is the beginning of a new history; that they will tell the last stories of this place. Night was cold, and they sang the whole night.

Chapter Twenty-Eight

> When we reached there, she picked a stick and began to scratch the
> ashes with it, and there I saw that the middle of the ashes rose up
> suddenly and at the same time there appeared a half-bodied baby, he
> was talking with a lower voice like a telephone.
>
> —from *The Palm-Wine Drinkard*, by Amos Tutuola

I am going to Lagos. The Lagos airport is famous. I had a good picture
of it in my head: sun-bleached and moisture-drenched plastic and concrete; a "modern" 1970s building thrusting up like an oil-gushing new
nation; now a kind of mental hospital, with mazes littered with crumpled
paper dreams and sleeping refugees; long empty corridors; screams in
the head; numberless identical doors, broken lights; musty bureaucrats
with red eyes flashing at me hungrily; multilingual lightnings and thun-
derings: DO YOU KNOW WHO I AM . . .

I was promised beasts full of eyes, be-fore and be-hind, with horns
charging and goring passport-wielding lambs that gamboled down its
rusting tongue. I knew that some would glide through, in lace gar-
ments and diamond-studded head wraps, bodyguards, some Shell Oil
types maybe.

I was promised thousands of flailing desperate arms lifted for the
attention of the sleepy-eyed three-biro-in-pocket man chewing a roast
plantain as large groups of people in sackcloth wait for the small silent
room with bottomless plastic seats that smell of fear, where you sit for
hours and look at a scowling hole in the wall, muzzled with gauze, behind which aliens in dirty khaki uniforms glide and chew with dead
sleepy eyes, stamping and stamping, as you finally stand behind the
snarl and say, "A beg. A beg. A beg. Oga. Master? Sir? Madam?"

This is what I was promised, and I was prepared.

I am going to be a postmodern African here; able to sweet-talk, able to see coherence: all that chaos is surely an artichoke? Inside there is the small tender and functional heart of Nigeria? Gentle. Fractals and mazes. Yes. Old civilizations. I will find coherence here.

The Virgin Nigeria flight from Dakar is okay. Not good. Not bad. Business class is full. The woman sitting next to me has the largest piece of hand luggage I have seen since Air Malawi used to do a cheap four hundred fifty–dollar flight from Johannesburg to Nairobi. She is in her sixties and reads a book by T. D. Jakes all the way. She prays before we take off, and prays softly again, in tongues, as we land.

I find I cannot be a jaded and flexible traveler. I break a rule by carrying her bag into the airport for her.

Not a sign of Armageddon. I go up the escalator smoothly, happy MTN adverts everywhere, green Naija colors, rolling CNN on television screens. I am stamped, smiled at, welcome bordered. I can see the odd sign of bendy machineries and machinations—but that morning Lagos airport is friendly and working.

I am picked up by my host. It is early morning, and we cut through the traffic without any problems. I try to fit into his groove and harrumph in a *Time* magazine way about the economy, stock markets and democracy and mortgages. We stick to this airbag talk, the air-conditioned car moving smoothly into the freeways. We smell of good dry cleaners and car polish, and we fly on wide soaring asphalt from land to island, land to island, looking at skyscraper skylines.

"How was Senegal?" he asks.

I cannot find anything *Time* magaziney to say about Senegal, so I talk about the Mourides, and his eyes open wide and he tells me his favorite book in the world is by Chiekh Anta Diop. Soon we are Pan-Africaning and literati-ing all over the place. He works in a strange bank, this man; it turns out the boss likes literature. That is why they are funding these writers' workshops I am here to help run: in job interviews at Fidelity Bank, one of the new financial powerhouses in this country; interviewees are asked what they last read. And they don't mean *Time*.

"I used to be a journalist," he says. "I am a Pan-Africanist. Afrocentric."

Traffic lights stop us, and a swarm descends on the window bearing all manner of machinery, trays and coils and wires and spikes holding produce. Grins plaster the windows. James Eze continues chatting about the African revolution. People are knocking on the window, and magazine covers are plastered next to me: pink and red lips pout at the window.

The headgear on the celebrity magazine covers! One woman is wrapped in gold and purple lamé cloth; her head looks like a Dubai hotel. There is the Leaning Tower of Pisa wrapped around another head. There is more bling on that head than in a Las Vegas casino.

I have to buy one . . . how many *naira?* James thrusts the car forward, and the guy chases us at full speed. He is laughing and sweating, his body wound and ready, a striding cable. He catches up with us, banging a poor overdressed celebrity woman's head on the window. James loans me some cash, frowning disapprovingly.

It is called *Ovation* magazine: Didn't she look graceful and debonair? . . . The world exclusive on business tycoon Alhaji Asoma Banda. . . . He is suave, he is articulate, he is a businessman par excellence, he is an exemplary family man and above all, he is a billionaire. . . . Welcome to the world of . . . president/CEO of Zenon Petroleum & Gas.

We drive into Lagos Island. And the city changes: thirty-story warrens, and caves, and leaning, cramped buildings clawing for space, and everywhere people: crisp and ironed in tailored clothes in all colors all speeding toward the stationary bicycle future . . . you can see them, like weaver birds, goods laid up below the bridge, climbing up. I am waiting to see somebody claw up the side of the expressway, shouting a sales pitch jubilantly, arm raised high and laughing as blood drips down his nails.

. . .

A few weeks ago, I was in Frankfurt. I happened to be staying at the same hotel as the bodyguards of the Nigerian president, who was in Germany for a visit.

One evening we stood together smoking outside the main entrance, and they chatted.

"The cigarettes here are bad."

"Very bad," the rest agreed.

"Not like Nigerian cigarettes."

"No, no . . ."

"But the gym here is very good!"

The rest nod.

"Why?" I ask.

"It is very hard to go to the gym in Abuja, you know . . ."

"Very hard. Very hard."

"Why?" I ask.

"You don't have that problem in Kenya?"

"What problem?"

"Women."

"Hmm . . . what about women?"

They all laugh. But the main guy does not. He looks quite upset.

"They bring many problems. Many problems."

"Like what?"

"We are in a special situation, you know . . ."

"Oh?"

"All those big men's wives . . . they come to the gym . . . and if you say no . . . they finish you, and if you say yes, the big men will finish you. Abuja gyms are very difficult."

...

We are driving in Lagos. We are lost on some highway. The traffic defies belief, all hooting. We are late. I am in a taxi, going to meet an old friend. There are a million motorbike taxis buzzing around us. The driver hails one, who sweeps toward us and runs alongside as the driver asks for directions. The motorbike swoops to the front and we follow. For twenty minutes we follow, and then he points out our destination and swoops away, waving. No money changes hands.

No way in hell this can happen in my country.

...

Twenty thousand motorbikes hooting, a million collapsing yellow metal taxis—all held up by talk, talk, move, move . . . beeeep, push car puush, arms flap up and down, neck tendons are guitar strings tightened, my jaws thrust forward yapping.

Signs, notices, and billboards all rapturous: Victory Ncobo, Xtra-Ordinary Value, Heaven, Crusade, Powering Forward, Transform Your World, Life's Pleasures in Full Measure, Move You Ahead in Life!

A billion tons of concrete and metal and glass and wood and paper teeter—structural adjustments—and eight million people are running at full speed, pushing at full strength, talking in surround sound: all the energy required to keep the machine moving. If they all stop, metal will twist, concrete will fall into the sea.

We are Atlas, says Lagos. We will carry this thing.

...

The Kenyan *mssslp* is short and soft and is all about resignation. *Mpslp*, oh I am sad, my shoulders sag, what can you do? The West African *mssssssslp* starts with the forehead leaning forward; eyes lift, tighten, and shoot, like blowtorches; eyebrows gather together for the thunder-clap. It starts at the back of the tongue, mouth pouted, saliva pulled loudly in, long and slow, an inhaling hiss. It is disdain, contempt, head swings back, you turn and leave, hips swinging if you are a woman, shoulders squared and jaw forward if you are a man: you are not worth my attention.

...

Francis, one of our drivers, is in a good mood today. Like everybody in Lagos, it seems, he is always immaculately presented. Ironed and crisp in a navy suit and fresh haircut. He opens the boot of the car and shows me a massive box. "A hundred thousand million *naira*," he says. "A television. Brand-new. I have been saving for months."

"So, where are you from?"

"Enugu."

"Are you married?" He turns to me, eyes a little wild.

"Nooo. I am the firstborn.

We cruise onto the freeway. He puts on a cassette. An American born-again gospel song. He taps the steering wheel and sings along . . .

Jesus . . . Jesus . . . his head swinging from side to side. Then his phone rings. He turns down the stereo.

He listens for a while, mmming and ahhhing, then explodes, banging the steering wheel.

"I have no moni."

Long loud conversation in Igbo.

Then: "Nooo. No. I have no moni-o."

He cuts the phone. Curses. "Argh. Moni. Moni. Always moni. My sister she has her own husband. But always moni. Moni this, moni that. Moni moni always moni. Sisters, children, school fees, food, wedding, funerals. Moni. Moni. Moni." Curses.

Mssssssslp.

After a while, he puts the cassette back on, adds the volume . . . Jesus . . . Jesus . . . the gospel choir is crescendoing now, there is much clapping. Soon Francis is tapping the stereo again and singing along.

Mssssssslp. He goes again. *Mssssssslp.* He sighs, and turns down the volume, and picks up his phone.

"How much?" he says.

...

We are in a suburb of Lagos near the airport, going to see Lagbaja, the Masked One, a high-life musician popular with university students and intellectuals for his political lyrics. He wears a mask and has his own nightclub called Motherlan'.

We keep passing nightclubs. People dressed to the nines, music thump-thumping from large buildings. But sometimes there are families with children. I ask my friend, "You mean you guys go to nightclubs with children?"

He laughs. "That is not a nightclub. Those are all night churches."

Chapter Twenty-Nine

In 2005 we are three years into Kibaki's government, and there is tension. Many things have happened. Many good things—but tribalism is increasing. Kibaki is Gikuyu, and non-Gikuyus feel his government betrayed a gentleman's agreement made when a coalition of political groups came together to remove Moi's party from power in 2002. Raila, who was promised the post of prime minister and who had proposed Kibaki for president, is given the ministry of roads. There is a feeling that a powerful group of people around Kibaki, some of them from Kenyatta's time, are determined to secure the grip of Gikuyus in power. We all thought that these sorts of games were over. They brought us to the brink. But our politicians are still playing them. Now that Kibaki has lost the trust of non-Gikuyus, Gikuyus are terrified that if he loses power we will be victimized. The beneficiaries of all these games are the political classes and their children. Most Gikuyus remain poor; most Kenyans remain poor.

Five years ago, in 2000, I landed at home, for my mother's funeral, and found myself in a small steamy office of a security official at the Mombasa airport. I did not have a yellow fever certificate. A group of red-eyed officials had cornered me as I picked up my luggage. I tried to plead, using my mother's death, patriotism, Kiswahili, hand-wringing, ah bana, please, I said, head tilting sideways, Boss, Chief, Mkubwa, Mzee, Mamsap, Sir. There was no yield. A long shabby man just stared at me, smiling. So I reached into my pocket and gave him one hundred dollars. As I walked away, I could hear them smirk behind me.

In 2002, less than a month after the election, I walked through the airport and found to my surprise that all officials smiled, said hi, welcomed me home. "Where are you coming from?" a woman asked me, smiling. "Many people are coming home now," she said. If I asked anybody, of any tribe, so, how are things? I could expect a familiar answer, sometimes gossip: they stole the mayor's chain. We were the most optimistic country in the world. Much bar talk was even sympathetic about Moi—people were angry that during the inauguration, the crowds, the largest in Kenya's history, had thrown mud at Moi. How unseemly. There were stickers with the flag everywhere. All the cool twenty-something designers for the Sheng-speaking new and detribalized generation of Kenyans were making baggy clothes with the flag placed proudly somewhere funky, a toned buttock, a hood, a bandanna.

If you carry a Kenyan passport and are leaving Kenya to go to London, with a valid visa, on our national carrier, there is a particular little humiliation you need to go through: you are pulled aside, by somebody from our national carrier, and asked to explain why you need to go to London. You are asked questions; your passport is photocopied and examined closely.

Tourists with better geopolitics sail past you.

So, one day, two years ago or so, well into Kibaki's season as president, a young woman, with a good middle-class accent and that breathy singsong air hostess voice, looked at my passport, then looked at me, then looked at my passport, then looked at me, then asked me, "What tribe are you?"

I was startled. Something was wrong with this pattern. She manifested no tribe at all in her body language, in her English even. She was a young Nairobi girl in an air hostess uniform. In many years of flying, nobody had ever asked me what tribe I belonged to. Of course, this is not to say that tribe did not matter.

If I belonged to the same tribe as the red-eyed crew who waylaid me those years ago for a yellow fever certificate, I would have escaped, but they would not have asked overtly. And I would not have asked them.

I would have been clued in to them; it is easy enough to tell who shares your mother tongue. What we would do is start to chat casually in our mutual tongue, in low voices—all of us conscious, for no clear reason, that this was a way of dealing between ourselves, and it is okay, but it can be shameful if it is too public.

So I thought maybe this young woman was not serious. So I asked her, jokingly, whether the authorities in England had blacklisted Gikuyus. No. She laughed. "But . . . but," she asked, "this name of yours, Binya-minya-faga, where is it from?" She was smiling her air hostess smile, head tilted to the side happily.

"Nakuru," I said, naming my hometown. The name Binyavanga originated in Uganda. I was not about to make this easy for her. She jabbed me happily with her elbow. "Haha," she said. "Haha, you are sooo funny, but, really, where is that name from? I just want to know."

I switched to Kiswahili. This is easy enough to deal with in stern Kiswahili. "My sister," I said, looking very brotherly and concerned about her manners. "Yaani, what is your business with this?" Kiswahili, the language of an old civilization, used to handling diverse people, full of rhetoric and manners, is perfect for revealing unreason. It is our national language, and it is more painful to be accused of ethnic bigotry in Kiswahili. In Kiswahili we feel a brotherhood and we are in the habit of this. If you fail with this approach, then real shit is coming.

"Are you doubting that I am a Kenyan?" I looked her straight in the eye. In Kiswahili this is devastating.

She was taken aback. The queue behind me was impatient.

Backtracking, she said, "Oh. No. Ai! You mean it is wrong to ask? Kwani I can't just ask you? I am just asking? Your last name is Gikuyu . . . where is the other name from?"

She still did not let me move. Finally I lost it and said, "Are you saying I can't check in until I answer your question?" She pouted and let me pass, and for a second I saw her small sneer.

After the incident with the air hostess, three years into Kibaki's reign in Kenya, my name has begun mysteriously to twist tongues. Binyawho? Manyabanga? Sometimes people laugh at it. All the people who find their tongues unable to pronounce my name are Gikuyus. My own tribe. Some members of my family. Friends even. One person stops me on a street to tell me how happy he was to see me in the newspaper— but that name of yours, my friends are asking, you are half what?

Now that we have a Gikuyu president, for the first time in my life, to be Gikuyu is a public event. You are tagged and measured, and then people let you in; there is a national conversation taking place, and this conversation is happening in Gikuyu, for Gikuyu, and of Gikuyu.

The rest of Kenya has become the Tribes. There is a text message being sent to Gikuyus calling Luos and people from western Kenya "beasts from the west." This sort of thing is being peddled even among the middle classes. The direct targets of this are the Luo, personified by Raila Odinga, who is becoming the devil in hundreds of text messages and Web sites. For decades the public face of Kenya's struggle for identity has been symbolized by the battles of towering Gikuyu politicians fighting towering Luo politicians. In our vague unthinking way, we Gikuyus have come to see Luo meaning the coming of communism and emotionalism, and the collapse of order.

To be Gikuyu, it is said, now every day, in nearly every forum in which Gikuyus gather, is to be reasonable. We are the invisible middle-class objectivity of Kenya. For others to belong among us, they have to behave like us. We do not need to examine ourselves.

We need to tame the tribes.

Years ago, I sat with an old man I respect, and he told me that Kenya would work wonderfully if we had an overt policy to develop people according to their tribal abilities. Positive tribalism, he called it. The Luhya are strong, and they make good laborers. They also speak English very well, he conceded. The Luo are very artistic and creative. They are good tailors. The Kamba make good soldiers because they are loyal. The man went around the pizza called Kenya, naming every slice and according it grace. It completely escaped him that every skill coincided nearly perfectly with the first acts of labor division introduced by the British, that he was, in fact, affirming exactly how we were defined and given roles to play in colonial Kenya. These identities were, in his mind, our permanent tribal personality. I asked him, so what will the Gikuyu do in this utopian Kenya? He was surprised, and frowned. It had not occurred to him. The Gikuyu just were, and everybody else was ethnic.

Something slipped into his generation's view of a possible Kenya. Those early Gikuyu technocrats under Kenyatta inherited, nearly exactly, the British idea about who does what. Who runs things. Who can. Who can't, and why not. The tribes were primeval and could not escape their fate. This impartial and objective view is always presented as the conclusion of a long and thorough analysis, which, by complete coincidence, comes up with the finding that if you look at it all, all of Kenya, analytically, especially now that our president, Kibaki, is Gikuyu, any reasonable person will come to the conclusion that we Gikuyus are the best people to allow the tribes to develop.

I am home from teaching in America. Paul and William, my nephews, are eight and seven. Jimmy is doing well. He has two daughters. His house is full of kids running around. I laugh at him and say how he used to tell us he would live alone like a hermit. He tells me the economy is doing well. He is a legend now, in Nairobi retail banking circles.

He finished a triathlon and was on the company billboard.

Mary Rose, his eldest, is named after Mum. She looks just like Jim. She has the same high energy. Emma, the baby, is a flirt.

In the past two years, during political campaigns, text messages called on the members of the House of Mumbi (the mother of the Gikuyu Nation) to let things "stay at home." *Ka mucii* was whispered from cab driver to passenger, from politician to market trader. Text messages flew everywhere. John Githongo, Kenya's anticorruption czar, who broke ranks with a corrupt Gikuyu elite, was branded a traitor.

Wink wink. Nod nod. It is our season. Kibaki season.

Over the past two years, people complain that nice middle-class Gikuyus are now speaking in their language in office corridors. It is a strangely schizophrenic place to be. Many Kenyans assume I am not Gikuyu and share their concerns with me. Meanwhile, an equal and opposite paranoia about the Gikuyu is starting to spread around Kenya. Many Gikuyus freely share with me their newly discovered contempt for everybody else. The mood is triumphant. We are back. Kenyatta's face is on our currency.

For it has come to be, now, in this fever, that part of what it means to be a Gikuyu is to be not a Luo. To be Gikuyu is to be not a tribe. And to be a Kenyan is to be not Gikuyu. We are saying we are the template of Kenya, and you other people had better fit yourselves in. If you behave, we will be nice to you.

I say my hellos. I say my good-byes. I can't wait to leave.

Chapter Thirty

She took her own certainty along by stooping under everything: stooping under her own history of the heart, stooping under the stares in Mamprobi, and stooping under her own lowering world.

—from *Search Sweet Country*, by Kojo Laing

I arrived in Accra, Ghana, yesterday. This is my first time in West Africa, on writing assignment for a World Cup anthology. Years are flying by now, as my writing career starts to take shape. It is 2006.

I spend much of the first night in a cybercafé in Osu, trying to find out as much as I can about Togo. The café is full for most of the night, full of young men, mostly, all well dressed, and, from my sideways glances, all looking for scholarships or at dating Web sites.

I am going to Togo tomorrow, to sniff around for a World Cup–related book project. Togo is suddenly in the headlines because its team, against all predictions, has qualified for the World Cup.

What a happy, happy city. People are laughing and greeting and laughing and greeting. Working, selling, building.

Many Google trails yield much information.

The French, since the days of de Gaulle especially, love fatherly African dictators who love French luxury goods, and French military bases. It makes them money, makes them feel they have their own commonwealth that gives them a feeling of international drama; it makes for good dinner-party talk and much student agitation. Omar Bongo, of Gabon, imported a French chateau; Emperor Bokassa had a Louis XIV–style inauguration and died in Bangui; Léopold Sédar Senghor died in France; and Félix Houphouët-Boigny of Ivory Coast built the biggest Catholic basilica in the world in his home village.

Gnassingbé Eyadéma, who died recently, was cut from the same market fabric. He managed to remain in power for thirty-eight years with no small help from the French, who ignored most of the abuses of his government and gave him much military aid for decades. Chirac called him a friend of France.

Nations that have cut themselves off from any way of measuring themselves against the normal transactions of their population become comical, in a crocodile-grinning, Idi Amining way. The constituency of these leaders was France, their cold war partners, their clan insiders, and the executives of the main extractors of their main overseas export. A Togo Web site reports that a former Mitterrand aide was arrested in Lomé for selling arms.

...

I meet Alex at breakfast in Accra. He is a carver of wooden curios who has a small shop at the hotel. His uncle owns the hotel. He spends his days at the gym, playing soccer, and making wooden sculptures of voluptuous Ghanaian women. For tourists. He shines with beauty and health and fresh-ironedness. He seems ready, fit and ready. I am not sure what for. We chat. He doesn't speak very much. I ask him if he can help get me somebody. He plays finger football on his mobile phone and finds me somebody to take me to Lomé.

Later, in the evening, we get in his uncle's Peugeot, and he drives me to meet my guide. I am struck, again, by the fluidity of his body language, and even more by his solemn maturity. There does not seem to be anything he cannot handle.

But his attitude toward me is overly respectful. He plays boy to my man. Does not contradict anything I say. It is disturbing. Before we get to the suburb where his friends are hanging out, he turns to me and asks, his face awed, and suddenly boyish, "Have you been to America?"

...

We find them, Alex and I, at dusk, a group of young men sitting by the road, in tracksuits and shorts and muscle tops. They are all fat-free and pectoraled and look boneless, postcoital, and gray after a vigorous exercise session at the beach, and a swim and a shower. One of them has a bandage on his knee and is limping. They are all fashionably dressed.

I ask around. They all come from middle-class families. They are all jobless, in their twenties, not hungry, cushioned in very small ways by their families, and small deals here and there.

Hubert is a talented soccer player. Twenty-one years old, he is the star of a first-division team in Accra. In two weeks he will go to South Africa to try out for a major soccer team. His coach has high hopes for him.

"I am a striker."

He looks surprisingly small for a West African football player. Ghanaians are often built like American football players. I conclude that he must be exceptionally good if he can play here.

"Aren't you afraid of those giant Ghanaian players?" I ask, nodding my head at his hulking friends.

He just smiles. He is the one with the international offers.

Hubert agrees to take me to Togo for a couple of days. He is mortified by my suggestion that I stay in a hotel. We will sleep in his mother's house in Lomé. His father died recently. Hubert is in Accra because there are more opportunities in Ghana than in Togo.

"Ghana has no politics."

...

I offer Alex a drink. To say thanks. We end up at a bar by the side of a road. A hundred or so people have spilled onto the road, dancing and talking rowdily and staggering. Alex looks a little more animated. They are playing hiplife—Ghana's version of hip-hop, merged with highlife. It is a weekday, and the bar is packed with large, good-looking men, all in their twenties, it seems. There are very few women. We sit by the road and chat, watching people dance in the street. This could never happen in Nairobi—this level of boisterousness would be assumed to lead to chaos and anarchy, and it would be clipped quickly. Three young men stagger and chase each other on the road, beers in hand, laughing loudly. Alex knows a lot of the guys here, and he joins in a little, in his solemn way.

I notice there are no broken bottles, no visible bouncer. No clues that this level of happiness ever leads to meaningful violence.

After a while, we find a table on the pavement. I head off to the bar to get a round of drinks. Some of Alex's friends have joined us. "You don't drink Guinness?" they ask, shocked. Guinness is MANPOWER.

When I get back, I find that a couple has joined the table: a tall man with large lips and a round, smooth baby's face, and a heavily made-up young woman with sharp breasts and a shiny short dress.

The rest of the table is muted. They do not meet the woman's eye, although she is their age. The man is in his thirties. He shouts for a waiter, who materializes. His eyes sweep around, a string of cursive question marks. People nod assent shyly. He has a French African accent.

Alex introduces us. He is Yves, from Ivory Coast. He is staying at the same hotel that I am.

Yves laughs, his eyes teasing. "Your uncle's hotel. Eh."

Alex looks down. Nobody talks to me now. It is assumed Yves is my peer, and they must submit. They start to talk among themselves, and I turn to Yves.

"So. You are here on business? Do you live in Côte d'Ivoire?" I ask.

"Ah. My brother, who can survive there? There is war. I live in South London. And in Chad. I also live in Accra sometimes."

"Oh, where do you work?"

"I am in oil—we supply services to the oil companies in N'Djamena."

We talk. No. He talks. For a full hour. Yves is thirty-three. He has three wives. One is the daughter of the president of Chad. The other is mixed race—a black Brit. The third lives here in Accra. I wait for him to turn to his girlfriend by his side. He does not. And she does not react. It is as if she is worried the makeup will crack if she says anything. It is impossible to know what she is thinking. He has money. She will wear the mask he needs. Every so often, he breaks from his monologue to whisper babyhoney things in her ear.

Yves knows Kofi Annan's son. He claims to be on a retainer for a major oil company, seeking high-level contacts in Africa. He looks at me, eyes dead straight and serious, and asks me about my contacts in State House. I have none to present. He laughs, generously. No problem. No problem. Kenya was stupid, he says, to go with the Chinese so easily.

This is the future. But most people do not see this . . .

He turns to Alex. "See this pretty boy here? I am always telling him to get himself ready. I will make it work for him . . . but he is lazy."

Yves turns to the group. "You Ghana boys are lazy—you don't want to be aggressive."

The group is eating this up eagerly, smiling shyly and looking somewhat hangdog. The drinks flow. Cuteface now has a bottle of champagne.

Later, we stand to head back. Yves grabs Alex's neck in a strong chokehold. "You won't mess me in the deal, eh, my brother?"

Alex smiles sheepishly, "Ah no, Yves, I will do it, man."

"I like you. Eh . . . Alex? I like you. I don't know why. You are always promising, and nothing happens. You are lucky I like you."

Alex looks very happy.

We separate at the hotel lift, and Yves slaps me on the back.

"Call me, eh?"

Early the next morning, we take a car from the Accra bus rank at dawn. It is a two-hour drive to the border. You cross the border at Aflao, and you are in Lomé, the capital of Togo.

...

Gnassingbé Eyadéma was a Kabye, the second-largest ethnic group in Togo. The Kabye homeland around the northern city of Kara is arid and mountainous. In the first half of the twentieth century, many young Kabye moved south to work as sharecroppers on Ewe farms. The wealthier Ewe looked down on the Kabye but depended on them as laborers. Eyadéma made sure to fill the military with Kabye loyalists. It was called "the army of cousins" and was armed by the French. Alex is Kabye.

Eyadéma threw political opponents to the crocodiles.

Lomé is hot, dry, and dusty. People look dispirited, and the city is rusty and peeling and bleached from too much brine and sun and rough times. Hubert points out a tourist hotel to me. It looks like it has been closed for years, but the weather here can deteriorate things rapidly. The tourist industry collapsed after the pro-democracy riots in early 2005.

Hubert is not Ewe. And he supports Faure Gnassingbé: "He understands young people."

It turns out that his family is originally from the north.

We take a taxi into town and drive around looking for a bureau that will change my dollars to CFA francs. One is closed. We walk into the next one. It has the characterless look of a government office. It smells of old damp cardboard. They tell us we have to wait an hour to change any money.

In the center of the city, buildings are imposing, unfriendly, and impractical. Paint has faded; plastic fittings look bleached and brittle. I have seen buildings like this before—in South African homeland capitals, in Chad and Budapest. These are buildings that international contractors build for countries eager to show how "modern" they are. They are usually described as "ultramodern"—and when they are new, they shine like the mirrored sunglasses of a presidential bodyguard. Within months, they rust and peel and crumble. I see one called Centre des Cheques Postaux, another Centre National de Perfectionnement Professionnel.

There are International Bureaus of Many Incredibly Important Things, and International Centers of Even More Important Things. I count fourteen buildings that have the word *développement* on their walls.

In Accra, signs are warm, quirky, and humorous: Happy Day Shop, Do Life Yourself, Diplomatic Haircut.

Everywhere, people are wearing yellow Togo team shirts.

We decide to have lunch. Hubert leads me to a small plot of land surrounded on three sides by concrete walls. On one side of this plot, a group of women are stirring large pots. On the other, there is a makeshift thatch shade, with couches and a huge television. A fat gentleman, who looks like the owner of the place, is watching *Octopussy* on satellite television. There are fading murals on the walls. On one wall, there are a couple of stiff-looking white people waltzing, noses facing the sky. Stiff and awkward, cliché white people. An arrow points to a violin, and another arrow points to a champagne bottle. It is an ad for a hotel: L'Hotel Climon. 12 chambres. Entièrement climatisé. Non loin du Lycée Française.

One another wall, there is an ad for this restaurant.

A topless black woman with spectacular breasts—large, pointy, and firm—serves brochettes and a large fish on a huge platter. A black chef with sparkling cheeks grins at us. A group of people are eating, drinking, laughing. Fluent, affluent, flexible. I order the fish.

When we are done, we make our way out and look for a taxi. There are more taxis than private cars on the road. Hubert and the taxi driver have a heated discussion about prices; we leave the taxi in a huff. Hubert is furious. I remain silent—the price he quotes seem reasonable—but Nairobi taxis are very expensive.

"He is trying to cheat us because you are a foreigner."

I assume the taxi driver was angry because Hubert did not want to be a good citizen and conspire with him to overcharge me. We get another taxi, and drive past more grim-looking buildings. There are lots of warning signs: Interdit de . . . Interdit de . . .

One.

Interdit de Chier Ici. No shitting here.

A policeman stands in front of the sign, with a gun.

In several hand-painted advertisements women are serving one thing or another, topless, with the same spectacular breasts. I wonder if they are all by the same artists. Most Ghanaian hand-painted murals are either barbershop signs or hair salon signs. Here breasts rule. Is this a Francophone thing? An Eyadéma thing?

It could be that what makes Lomé look so drab is that since the troubles that sent donors away, and sent tourists away, there have not been any new buildings to make the fading old ones less visible. They have gone: the licks of fresh paint, the presidential murals; the pink and blue tourist hotels with pink and blue bikinis on the beach sipping pink and blue cocktails. The illusions of progress no longer need to be maintained. The dictator who needed them is dead.

We drive past the suburb where all the villas are, and all the embassies. Nearby there is a dual carriageway, sober charcoal gray, better than any road I have seen so far. It cuts through bushes and gardens and vanishes into the distance. This is the road to the presidential palace that Eyadéma built. It is miles away. It is surrounded by lush parkland, and Hubert tells me the presidential family has a zoo in the compound. Eyadéma was a hunter and loved animals.

We drop off my luggage at Hubert's home. His mother lives in a large compound in a tree-lined suburb. The bungalow is shaped like a U. The rooms open to a corridor and face a courtyard where stools are set. His mother and sisters rush out to hug him—he is clearly a favorite. We stay for a few minutes, have some refreshments, and take a taxi back to the city center.

Driving past the city's main hospital, I see the first signs of sensible commerce: somebody providing a useful product or service to individuals who need it. Lined along the hospital wall are secondhand imported goods in this order: giant stereo speakers, some very expensive looking; a drum set; bananas; a small kiosk with a sign on its forehead: Telephon Inter-Nation; dog chains; a cluster of secondhand lawn mowers; dog chains; five or six big-screen televisions; dog chains; crutches; steam irons; a large faded Oriental carpet.

An hour later, we reach the market in Lomé, and finally find ourselves in a functional and vibrant city. Currency dealers present themselves at the window of the car—negotiations are quick. Money changes hands, and we walk into the maze of stalls. It is hard to tell how big it is—people are milling about everywhere; there are people sitting on the ground and small rickety stalls in every available space.

There are stalls selling stoves and electronic goods, and currency changers and traders from all over West Africa, and tailors and cobblers and brokers and fixers and food and drink. Everything is fluent, everybody in perpetual negotiation, flexible and competitive. Togo's main official export is phosphates, but it has always made its money as a free-trade area, supplying traders from all over West Africa.

Markets like these have been in existence all over West Africa for at least a millennium. There are traders from seven or eight countries here. Markets in Lomé are run by the famous "Mama Benzes"—rich trading women who have chauffeur-driven Mercedes-Benzes. These days, after years of economic stagnation, the Mama Benzes are called Mama Opels.

Most of the stalls are bursting with fabrics. I have never seen so many—there are shapeless splotches of color on cloth, bold geometrics on wax batik, pinks on earth brown, ululating pinstripes. There are fabrics with thousands of embroidered coin-size holes shaped like flowers. There are fabrics that promise wealth: one stall owner points out a strange design on a Togolese coin and shows me the same design on the fabric of an already busy shirt. There are fabrics for clinging, for flicking over a shoulder, for square shouldering, for floppy collaring, for marrying, and some must surely assure instant breakups.

We brush past clothes that lap against my ear, whispering; others lick my brow from hangers above my face.

Anywhere else in the world the fabric is secondary: it is the final architecture of the garment that makes a difference. But this is Lomé, the duty-free port, the capital of Togo, and here it is the fabric that matters. The fabric you will buy can be sewed into a dress, a shirt, an evening outfit of headband, skirt, and top in one afternoon, at no extra cost. It is all about the fabric. There are fabrics of silk, of cotton, from the Netherlands, from China, mudcloth from Mali, kente from northern Togo.

It is the stall selling bras that stops my forward motion. It is a tiny open-air stall. There are bras piled on a small table, bras hanging above. Years ago, I had a part-time job as a translator for some Senegalese visitors to Kenya. Two of the older women, both quite large, asked me to take them shopping for bras. We walked into shop after shop in Nairobi's biggest mall. They probed and pulled and sighed and exclaimed—and I translated all this to the chichi young girls who looked offended that a woman of that age could ask questions about a bra that had nothing to do with its practical uses. We roamed for what seemed like hours, but these Francophone women failed to find a single bra in all the shops in Sarit Centre that combined uplifting engineering with the right aesthetic.

They could not understand this Anglophone insistence on ugly bras for any woman over twenty-five with children.

Open-air bra stalls in my country sell useful, practical white bras. All secondhand. Not here. There are red strapless bras with snarling edges of black lace. I see a daffodil-yellow bra with curly green leaves running along its seam. Hanging down the middle of the line is the largest nursing bra I have ever seen, white and wired and ominous. I am sure the white covers pulleys and pistons and a flying buttress or two. One red bra has bared black teeth around a nipple-size pair of holes. Next to it is a corset in a delicate ivory color. I did not know people still wore corsets.

A group of women start laughing. I am gaping. Anglophone. Prude.

It takes an hour for Hubert and me to move only a hundred meters or so. Wherever I look, I am presented with goods to touch and feel. Hubert looks grim. I imitate him. Heads down, we move forward. Soon we see a stall specializing in Togo football team jerseys. There are long-sleeved yellow ones, short-sleeved ones, sleeveless ones. Shirts for kids. All of them have one name on the back: Togo's superstriker, Sheyi Emmanuel Adebayor.

I pick out a couple of jerseys and while Hubert negotiates for them, I amble over to a nearby stall. An elegant, motherly woman, an image of genuine Mama Benzhood dressed in pink lace, smiles at me graciously. Her stall sells shirts, and looks cool and fresh. She invites me in. I go in and stand under the flapping clothes to cool down. She dispatches a young man to get some cold mineral water. I admire one of the shirts. "Too small for you," she says sorrowfully. Suddenly I want it desperately, but she is reluctant. "Okay. Okay," she says. "I will try to help you. When are you leaving?"

"Tomorrow," I say.

"Ahh. I have a tailor—we will get the fabrics and sew the shirts up for you, a proper size."

It is here that my resolve cracks, that my dislike of shopping vanishes. I realize that I can settle in this cool place—cast my eyes about, express an interest, and get a tailor-made solution. I point at possible fabrics. She frowns and says, "Nooooo, this one without fancy collars. We will make it simple—let the fabric speak for itself." In French this opinion sounds very authoritative. Soon I find I have ordered six shirts. A group of leather workers present an array of handmade sandals: snakeskin, crocodile, every color imaginable. Madam thinks the soft brown leather ones are good. She bends one shoe thing into a circle. Nods. Good sole.

Her eyes narrow at the salesman and she asks, "How much?"

His reply elicits a shrug and a turn—she has lost interest. No value for money. Price drops. Drops again. I buy. She summons a Ghanaian cobbler, who reinforces the seams for me as I sit, glues the edges. In seconds all is ready. She looks at me with some compassion. "What about something for the woman you love?" I start to protest—no. No—I am not into this love thing. Ahh. Compassion deepens. But the women's clothes! I see a purple top with a purple fur collar. A hand-embroidered skirt and top of white cotton. It is clear to me that my two sisters will never be the same again if they have clothes like this.

I get two outfits for each of them.

I can't believe how cheap the clothes are. Now my nieces—what about Christmas presents for them? And my brother Jim? And my nephews. And what about Jim's wife? These women in my life—they will be as gracious and powerful as this madam in pink lace, cool in the heat. Queens, princesses. Matriarchs. Mama Benzes. Sexy. I spend four hours in her stall, and spend nearly two hundred dollars.

On the way from the center of Lomé, I see an old sign by the side of the road. Whatever it was previously advertising has rusted away.

Somebody has painted on it, in huge letters: TOGO 3 – CONGO 0.

We head for Hubert's home. The beach runs alongside a highway, and hundreds of scooter taxis chug past us with 5:00 p.m. clients, mostly women, who seem very comfortable.

Hubert's eldest brother has spent the day lying under a tree. He had a nasty motorcycle accident months ago, and his leg is in a cast. He is a mechanic and has his own workshop. His wife lives here too, and his two sisters. We shake hands and he backs away. There are metal rods thrust into the cast. He must be in pain. The evening is cool, and the earthen compound is large and freshly swept. It is a large old house. This is an upper-middle-class family. Hubert tells me he is uncertain. His father is from the north, and after Eyadéma died, he is not sure how safe his mother is in the capital, which is in the south.

Hubert's mother and sisters are happy to see him home, and have cooked a special sauce with meat and baobab leaves and chili. Hubert's mother, a retired nurse, is a widow. Hubert is the last born, and it is clear he is the favorite of his sisters. The rooms at the front of the house open to the garden, where some of the cooking takes place to take advantage of the cool.

We all stand around the kitchen. Clearly Hubert and his brother do not get along, but what is most curious is the family setup. His mother is the head of the household. His father is dead. His brother—a good ten years older than Hubert—behaves like a boy in his presence.

Talking about money with Hubert has been tricky. He agreed to come with me, but said we would come to an agreement about money later. He has made it clear he will be happy with anything reasonable I can afford. He is not doing this because he is desperate for the money. He seems comfortable with the arrangement I offered—and is happy to do things, trusting my good faith, and giving his. He does not eat much.

As an athlete, he is very finicky about what he eats. His mother does not complain. I dig into the sauce. It's hot. Awkwardly, I make him an offer.

I find out I am to sleep in his room.

It is very neat. There is a fan, which does not work. There is a computer, which does not work. There are faded posters of soccer players. There are two gimmicky-looking pens arranged in crisp symmetry on the table, both dead. There is a cassette player plugged in and ready to be switched on, but I can see no tapes. There is no electricity—I am using a paraffin lamp. The bedroom is all aspiration. I wonder, before I go to sleep, what his brother's bedroom looks like.

In the morning, I try to make the bed. I lift the mattress and see, on the corner, a heavy gray pistol, as calm and satisfied as a slug.

Chapter Thirty-One

It is 2006. Winter. I have finally become acceptable to a respectable institution. For the past few months, I have been teaching creative writing and literature at Union College in Schenectady, in upstate New York.

All my life, my body has been a soft and comfortable beanbag, nicely worn into the right shape for my mind to wiggle around, to lean back, sigh and dream. No longer. Something happenened. This winter my body has been causing havoc. It has become one of those American chairs—fat and cushy, with numerous moving parts and levers that can chew your fingers; chairs that have gears and buttons and heart monitors, chairs that, at a push of a button, start vibrating maniacally.

I have lost a lot of weight and I wake up several times a night to the sight of a million dripping icicles of confectionary outside my window. I am so hungry I am faint. Only crunchy crystals of sugar will do. Or oozy sugar. Or any sugar. My throat went and got all imperialist on me. It wants to drink the whole Hudson River. It is sure it can drink it all. It must be something wrong with the heating, and winter energy cravings. What do I know about this new American weather, these old upstate houses? Every night, I eat, drink, piss madly, then turn into a late-night cheerleader on amphetamines. I race out of the house with doughnut fuzz on my lips and I jump on my bicycle. The cold means nothing; the dark means nothing. I pedal furiously, all the way down to the Stockade, and ride along the river, and between the old Dutch houses, and climb back up the hill to my house, soaked with sweat and full of energy, my body burning from inside, cold on the outside.

It is Friday. I wake up at 2:00 a.m. and eat three frozen chocolate croissants and drink a liter of water. I clean the house, which is filthy. The previous owner left behind more cleaning chemicals than I have ever seen. I spray and wipe, spray and wipe, and I am dizzy with chemical haze. One of the kitchen cleaning sprays says it kills the HIV virus, which must surely lurk inside loose coffee grounds in the sink. I am still restless and find random things to drop into that wonderful whirring metal chewing machine inside this American sink that has twin power jets. No dribbles here.

After taking a shower, pissing, drinking more water, I get on my laptop and start browsing randomly, to kill time.

We are a year and a bit away from the presidential and parliamentary elections in Kenya, and Kenyans are already arguing on the blogosphere—this time it is not about water, power, or the constitution. All of a sudden, Kenyans, usually skeptical, are becoming unusually fierce in defending leaders who share their ethnicity. For Gikuyus, Kibaki is the most wonderful person ever. For Luos, Raila was manufactured in heaven. For Kalenjins Ruto is the next king, Koitalel arap Samoei reincarnated. Our usual irony about all politicians seems to have vanished. Any attempt to be nuanced means being accused of being a traitor, a communist, mixed up.

Next year promises drama. We do not know if our democracy is strong enough for the incumbent, President Kibaki—Gikuyu— to be peacefully removed from power by a strong candidate, Raila Odinga—Luo.

Things are getting hot in Togo too as we get closer to the World Cup. The Togolese soccer federation is run by Rock Gnassingbé, brother of the president and son of the late Eyadéma.

Now, soccer itself is not a negotiable object. Democracy is, treasuries are, French government loans and grants, the lives of all citizens, the wombs of all women—all these things can bend comfortably to the will of the first family, but the fates of the national soccer team belong to the people. Nobody has ever successfully banned the playing of soccer in Africa.

It is easy to see why: soccer is a skill one can cultivate to the highest levels with nothing but plastic and string and will.

Arjukumar K Patel is online early in the morning, somewhere in an anxious Gujarati-speaking Kenya. On a Canadian Immigration Web site, he has this to say:

I am originally INDIAN born but settled in kenya & holding KENYAN CITIZEN i dont have any digree, but i have work experiance for more then nine years in tyre business, is there any chance to get job in canada? i have my first cousin who is a CANDIAN CITIZEN can he apply permenant resident for my family? please advice me thank you.

I grab an apple and carry my laptop to the living room, and put on the television. Somebody is selling a TOTAL solution to WEIGHT LOSS. I change the channel. Goodness. The teeth of Americans are truly wondrous. Look at Lionel Richie's teeth, as he zigzags across the stage in sequins and shoulder pads singing in broken Kiswahili presented in a bad Jamaican accent. "Jambo nipe centi moja, oooh Jambo Jambo."

Hallo, hallo, give me one cent, hallo, hallo.

Tension is high, and next year's election is going to be close. We hoped to have a new constitution in place before the election. This will not happen. Now that the main players are so divided, and Kenyans too, we agree on nothing. We had one referendum for Kibaki's constitution, and he lost. Kibaki lost the trust of non-Gikuyus. Our doddering colonial constitution gives the presidency the powers of a medieval king. It is very difficult, under the present constitution, to remove an incumbent president from power. Kenyatta and Moi made sure of that. We have to trust that Kibaki will behave with grace and allow a relatively level playing ground.

A soccer player seeks to find chinks in the structural arrangements of an opposing team—needs to make his body and mind flexible; needs to have an eye that does not just understand the structure of the opposition but also can seduce, fake, deceive, con, charm. Can score and secure victory by finding a hole, a gap, seeing avenues where zigzag paths exist; sweet-talking your way through the barbed wire of the Port Area that serves the whole of West Africa; bullshitting your way into the fat cat's office; seducing, with a nimble tongue, the stiff and proud daughter of the fat cat; and then you have access to the duty-free goods of a subcontinent. Strolling through gates manned by violent giants into the inner sanctum, the president's zoo, his home, and the treasury of your country. At any time, a giant monster, or a team of them, will be ready to bring you down with all the violence they know how to produce. Your tongue, the flexibility of your limbs, your sexiness, the timbre of your voice; your understanding of the structure of power you face—these are your only tools.

This intelligence is not harbored in the mind. Repeated practice transfers the ideas of the mind into the instinct of the body. No gun to the head can make this body perform.

Now Lionel Richie is Swahili Jamaicanly saying we are going to part-ay, *karamu*, fiesta, forever. When his mouth is closed, it puffs out with interesting possibilities—to my dentally naturalist eye. It promises dramatic teeth, tall and craggy-faced Mau Maus on horses galloping along the raw pink highway of Kenya. They stand in a semicircle at the jawline of the Ngong Hills, looking down at the capital, grimy and determined. They pause for a moment—for the heroic bronze sculpture they hope they will commission to celebrate this hilly revolutionary moment. Teeth facing forward, they gallop down the hill, then storm the city with sharp pointy things heading straight for the biggest-dick building: Kenyatta Cornflakes Center. "Everyone you meet," calypsos Lionel, "they are partying on the street, all night long." Yeah. Mouth closed, Lionel Richie promises on-your-mark, get set, go teeth.

To be a successful sovereign citizen of urban Togo (or Brazil, or Nigeria, or Kenya)—one who is not allied to French scholarships and French departments, to administrative authority and the "private sector"; one not allied by clan or tribe or family relationship to the Gnassingbés or the Kibaki family—one needs to cultivate a certain fitness, a certain rhythm. Your body, your tongue must respond quickly to an environment that sometimes shifts every few minutes. You must constantly invent new strategies to thrive the next day. These strategies need to be drilled into the body, so they are used subtly and suddenly when they are required.

What is so sublime about the truly great soccer players is the ability of a single individual to completely bewilder a nation: Maradona over

Germany and England. Zinedene Zidane against everybody, restrained only by his own pride, his other sovereignty, his realization at the very climax of his art and career that soccer is only a game, and he, a paid performer.

The *Nation* newspaper online today announces that the Gabonese Pygmies may soon be learning Chinese because of iron ore. Famous Brands, the South African Company that brought Debonairs Pizza to Kenya, has just bought 49 percent of Wimpy UK. Kenya's economy has grown by 6 percent, but the poor are worse off than they were last year. Fifty percent of Kenyans are living under the poverty line. Nyanza Province, Raila Odinga's Luo-speaking political heartland, has a life expectancy of forty-four years; Central Province—Gikuyus who support Kibaki—has a life expectancy of sixty years.

Now Lionel is smiling. The mouth stretches sideways—looking to lock onto the gold happyhooks that hang down his earlobes. I look closely. There are no battle-weary warrior teeth. Sitting on top of the soft pink crown of his empire is a troop of thirty-two little drum majorettes, pearly and white, light bouncing off their medals as they squeal with teenage self-satisfaction. Ohh Jambo Jambo.

A cobbler should be able to attack you before you see him, see a chink in your fine leather before you can slap him away. A Kenyan market trader needs to be able to pack up all wares in a minute once a city council *askari* in civilian clothes has been spotted. Must do this, and turn over enough money for tomorrow's stocks and today's bribe, and yesterday's children's medication, and this month's tax to a city council that collects taxes efficiently and will never allow you to trade freely, will never invest your taxes in any infrastructure.

Teenagers, the *Nation* online lifestyle magazine informs us, are at a critical stage of their life. Lesbianism is rampant in our schools and must be eradicated by role models. The Kenyan stock market is booming. Kenya's second-oldest brokerage firm is issuing bouncing checks. It has six hundred thousand account holders. Every listed company is oversubscribed. Kenyans are buying stocks like crazy: diaspora Kenyans, up-and-coming Kenyans, and newly rich Kibaki Kenyans. It is hard to say that things are not better. Government departments work. There are tax collection records. You can get your national exam results by text message. The largest bank in Kenya is a microlending bank. New sky-scrapers are all over Nairobi. There is an epidemic of pyramid schemes that the police cannot stop.

Many Kenyans have lost their life savings.

Aiii! I can't take another winter day indoors.

The moment the sun is up, I take a taxi to the Amtrak train station in Albany. I will spend the weekend in New York City.

...

I have a window seat, near the toilet, and four ripe apples. There are slabs of ice floating on the Hudson River. The train follows the Hudson all the way to the city. Outside, the rest of the water is a flapping duvet of gold and white light. The train smells bad. A woman sits on her own. She has an ear-length red perm, polished into a flowing thing, with threads of silver. She has the shoulders of a dancer. A bottle of water rests by her side, and some fruit. She is fresh and wholesome in the very dirty Amtrak carriage.

I take out my laptop and continue browsing. Luos in America and Gikuyus in America have crowded the chat rooms—all screaming at each other with very bad spelling. I can't stop looking at the woman, she moves so well, looks so . . . television. She is in her forties and has a Roman column of a neck, long and leaning forward a bit. It is held up by tight cords and wires that thrust down from a chin held high. Eyes smoulder, nearly shut, low rumbling charcoal clouds of mascara starting to promise rainfall. It must be a breakup. By text message maybe.

I am sure I have diabetes. I have all the symptoms. Pentecostals are announcing and denouncing a new Kenyan prophet. His name is Pastor Owuor. He says he has a PhD in molecular biology, from Israel. But now God speaks to him. The woman's fingers tap and fiddle with the bottled water, tendons running up and down her black fingers, like piano keys. The train clip-clops and whinnies as it turns. I turned thirty-six last month. Diabetes hit Mum's side of the family, all twelve of them, when they were in their thirties. Mum got it when she was thirty-four. Mum's mum got it in her nineties, but she ate boiled food and lots and lots of fresh vegetables.

A thousand morning suns have split the trees and turned the Hudson River into a highway of light. Maybe the woman is a musician, at Bard College, or Vassar. Jazz. Yes, jazz.

Next December, the pastor says in giant rallies all over Kenya, an earthquake will destroy Nairobi. Bridges, towers will crumble like dust; blood will flow and the river will burst its banks.

In Togo, Rock has been caught with his hand in the cookie jar. The whole of Togo is furious. Rock decides to call a press conference, to announce a major sponsorship deal. There are balloons in the press conference room, and a few bespectacled Dutch businessmen, I imagine, one who has known and bribed and loved the Gnassingbés for forty years, and his Dutch ancestors have known and bribed fat, rich, and violent warlords for a couple of hundred years—so waxy Dutch cloth, of quite astonishing expense, is bought by millions of West Africans. In the room there are long, lithe hostesses serving Gnassingbé bottled water and Gnassingbé biscuits, and they are dressed in tight print fabrics and head knots that would silence Erykah Badu. They are Mama Opels in training.

In the room there are a few sullen Eyadéma grandsons in mummy's soft yellow skin and pouty pink lips and giant gold chains and OutKast's wardrobe; in the room there are tight-faced fat women, still Benzing, powdered, with round surgically blanked faces; fat football officials in shoulder-padded shirts, and patrols of multicolored pens in their front left pockets; and at the back of the room, standing, right in front of the red-eyed soldiers bearing guns, are lean, underpaid local journalists with ruled notebooks and Bic pens.

International correspondents with their long Dictaphones, and dirty jeans, and five hundred words before whiskey, are slouched over the red velvet chairs, in the VIP section in the front, looking for the Story: the Most Macheteing Deathest, Most Treasury Corruptest, Most Entrail-Eating Civil Warest, Most Crocodile-Grinning Dictatorest, Most

Heart-Wrenching and Genociding Pulitzerest, Most Black Big-Eyed Oxfam Child Starvingest, Most Wild African Savages Having AIDS-Ridden Sexest with Genetically Mutilatedest Girls . . .

The Most Authentic Real Black Africanest story they can find for Reuters or AP or Agence France.

But: this time, because this is the World Cup, a billion or two viewers, and endorsements, and there is a pretense that everybody comes in there somewhat equal, they will actually look for a normal story about normal human beings doing normal things. This is the only time CNN will show you a former favela resident playing and thriving and normal and actually speaking for himself, and not shooting, or shooting up, or in the throes of unbearable CARE International–seeking suffering.

Sitting next to the foreign correspondents are their dark, slinky girlfriends, the better-educated daughters of some Ma Benzes, one of whom nearly became Miss Togo, another who nearly won her region's Face of Africa competition.

A twenty-five-piece army band starts to play. Trumpets (the elephant is about to speak).

Rock announces that a Dutch textile company has bought the rights to print cloth with the Hawks' logo on it. In Togo, the words *cloth* and *Dutch* are nearly as electric as the words *World Cup*.

Market women are salivating. Mercedes-Benz dealers start sending text messages to East London and Düsseldorf.

Snap snap. An android mobile phone takes a picture of the sample fabric on display. Somebody sneaks out of the room—an Ivorian, perhaps—and calls his guy in Abidjan, tells him to catch a flight to the fabric factories of Guangzhou, China, tonight to have five containers in Lomé by the weekend.

Tomorrow, the Chinese traders in Lomé market will do the same. Cheaper.

But soccer wins over the drools of fabric.

A journalist asks Rock about the players who are holding him hostage. He loses his temper in a George Bushish way and accuses the journalist of being unpatriotic.

Rock loses the war against error. Togo is humiliated in the Cup of Nations.

The Hudson has split into two. One branch glides away from us, and the train follows the larger branch; there are chunks of ice piled up against the aging railway line. Kenyan rivers have not yet been tamed by engineering. They gush and spill and dry up, no sedate movements. The train clatters into a tunnel. The woman is talking on the phone, and there is traffic running up and down the cables on her throat as the clock ticks just above a collarbone and tears are pouring down her cheeks.

In front of a huge crowd in Thika town, Pastor Owour says there will be rivers of blood in the city in December.

···

The woman is smiling all pearly-teeth, and crying. A full black-skinned Goldie Fawn smile, her phone on her ear. Her voice is too whispery for me to overhear—and her mouth is smiling: thirty-two tap dancers on stage. A cab driver told me, a few weeks ago, that the industrial infrastructure of New York State is being unpacked, crumpled into scrap metal, and shipped off to China down the Hudson on barges. I am going to vote for Raila. I don't love him. Kibaki is sort of okay. A bit sleepy, but there is no way I am voting for a second term for any president while this constitution is still alive. Too much power. I do not want to vote for a better Gikuyuland. I want to vote for a better Kenya. If I can't trust my vote to a leader of another tribe, I may as well take a green card and not go back.

···

Winnie Amayo, who is chatting online today, has nothing to say about the election. She is concerned about the coming earthquake:

> God . . . showed me dead bodies full of blood and other people
> had been shot but they had not died. They were criying but there
> was no body to help them because people were running to other

countries to be refugees. it was at noon time and the blood begun to smell because of the hot sun shine. That smell came into my nose and then I closed my nose then I woke up. I began to cry in prayer telling God to have mercy on us because we have never been refugees but instead we have been hosting refugees in our country. That night I watered my bed with tears.

I can see this Amtrak woman curtsying at seven, after a dance re-cital, this mouth stretched to its tendon-tauting end, in pursuit of hap-piness, a beautifully shaped head held up by cables and columns, and teeth: this mouth is an auditorium, a performance space—and it can hold many pounding crowds of screaming citizens, and lions and gladi-ators. The columns on her throat will hold up her imploding day.

...

I am home in Kenya in the American summer, when Togo meets South Korea in their opening World Cup match.

The entire continent watches, almost every man and woman—a billion of us: in small towns in Germany where day is euros and in-continent old Germans, and night is neo-Nazis; in foreign correspon-dents' sea-facing living rooms in Accra, where long sexy limbs are flying and weave is disheveled and a girl with a long tubular face and pouting lips is screaming, as the foreign correspondent sips whiskey and types, "Africans in the heart of Togo's dark jungle, in the middle of the dead animals of fetish-markets today cheered . . ."

"Africa forgot war and misery today, to celebrate the rare good news . . ."

The entire African continent: some living in musty dormitories in Moscow; dusty and tired and drunk, living among abandoned ware-houses and dead industries of New Jersey; in well-oiled boardrooms in Nairobi and Lagos and Johannesburg; in cramped tenements in the suburbs of Paris; inside the residences of the alumni of the Presidential School of Lomé; in the markets of Accra and the corrugated iron bars of Lusaka; in school halls; and social halls in the giant markets of Addis Ababa; in ecstatic churches dancing in Uganda; on wailing coral balconies in Zanzibar; in a dark rumba-belting, militia-ridden bar in Lubumbashi; in rickety video shops in Dakar; in prisons in the Central African Republic; in miniskirts on red-lit street corners in Cape Town, peering into SuperSport bars; in school halls in Cherengani; in Parliament cafeterias in Harare.

We all jump up and down, and shout and sing when, in the thirty-fourth minute, Kader gives Togo the lead over South Korea with a blistering shot from a very difficult angle.

Chapter Thirty-Two

December 2007. The election is three days away.

I have had enough. Raila's party is now nakedly saying in rallies all over Kenya that their campaign is about forty-two tribes versus one tribe—the Gikuyu. The Gikuyu have become "blemishes" in some parts of the Rift Valley. Blemishes that need to be wiped away. They have gone mad, our politicians. Kibaki has selected his own commissioners for the electoral commission. He has broken his promise to consult the opposition. One woman tells me she has volunteered her own money—and she is not rich—to help rig the election in Raila's constituency. She is Gikuyu.

Almost all the people I know, for the first time in our history, are nakedly and openly beating their tribal chest.

I tear up my voter's card. I board a plane to Lamu, as far away from the poisonous election as I can get and still be in Kenya. The man sitting next to me on the plane is dressed in an African-print shirt with short sleeves. It is a good batik. He does not try to be flashy with it—it is a safe navy color and does not drown his white skin. No fake blond dreadlocks; his hair is brown and cut short. The man has been chatting to me for ten minutes now, and he is irritating. Maybe that's it. Noo. He is speaking in Kiswahili—but his Kiswahili is perfect. First he speaks in Sheng, then he shifts to clean and elaborate coast Kiswahili. My Kiswahili is not very good. My Sheng is not so good. Maybe I am jealous. Noo. That's not it.

It is that he has got it all wrong. His accent is perfect; his tone, rhythm, everything. His timing is wrong. In this country, with its many languages, classes, and registers, much is said by what is not said. There are many understood ways to address someone: sometimes you shift quickly into English; often you speak in a mock Kiswahili, in an ironical tone, simply to indicate that you are not dogmatic about language, that you are quite happy to shift around and find the bandwidth of the person to whom you are speaking.

The man is dogmatic. And his exquisite politeness is rude. He wants me to thank him for his cultural scrupulousness, and is unwilling to let me speak English, or not speak at all. I am not an individual. I am a cultural ambassador. His proper Kiswahili demands that I be more attentive than I want to be—inattention is impossible when somebody speaks in formal Kiswahili. It demands brotherhood and respect. I must nod, and say, "Ndio, ahaa, eh? Yes. Ohh!" Eyebrows up and eyes wide in mock interest.

It is going to be a long flight.

Lamu town is the oldest living Swahili town in Kenya.

Lamu was founded around the twelfth century, and there is evidence that international trade had been taking place there for at least a millennium before then. There were larger and more powerful city-states than Lamu in East Africa's past: Siyu and Pate, for example. These cities are now mostly ruins. What makes Lamu interesting is that the basic architecture remains mostly intact. There are no cars on the island. The narrow streets and the thick-walled stone and mangrove homes remain close to what they were three hundred years ago. The same and yet very different. For in those days, Lamu was much more than a museum. These days it is a world heritage site, acting out its past for its own fond memories, and for the curiosity of others. The town of poetry and trade with India and Persia and China is diminished and poor.

We walk out of the plane and collect our luggage. Patrick, a young beach boy I befriended the last time I was in Lamu, is standing a few feet away, holding a posy of frangipani flowers and looking sheepish in his stubby dreadlocks and baggy jeans. He winks at me. An elderly white woman—she must be at least sixty—rushes past me; they hug, kiss, she oohs and aahs at the flowers.

They walk away looking all aloha.

Young men have come across from the island with carts to take the luggage to the boats. Every hotel has its own cart; most have their own boats. I ask one of the porters about the election. He shrugs. "We will vote for whoever gives us a banquet," he says.

We walk toward the mainland jetty on a dusty red path that is lined with stubbly bush. It is hot, and I am stuffy and irritable. There are sporadic groans and mumbles of sleepy blue water between the bushes, and people are yelling in lyrical Kiswahili, pushing carts, luggage bouncing in discomfort. The sea yawns and stretches, a lazy, prostrate, undulating blue, like a morning. And a few hundred meters across the water, I can see daytime standing up: to the right a longish strip of gleaming white buildings, the shining white tower of a mosque. Lamu Island.

"Boss!"

The man is old enough to be my father. My face immediately becomes solemn and I greet him in as good and respectful Kiswahili as I can manage. It sounds all wrong and stilted. He hoists my bags onto his shoulders from the cart, smiling and bowing. I am not sure what to do. I continue to speak respectfully. My respect is instinctive; his very accent demands it. This is not even a class thing, or guilt. Kiswahili is just a tool for me, as it is for most Kenyans. An inherited language that a hundred million Africans mutilate. Lamu, this small island, is the home of the original dialect of Kiswahili, and of the Swahili civilization.

We walk down the jetty toward the boat. He has all my bags on his back, and I am stupid. Anywhere else in Kenya, we can pretend we are equals if we speak in Kiswahili; it is the national language and invites a feeling of brotherhood that does not really exist. But Kiswahili is Muhammed's mother tongue; he does not know how to play national games with it. Lamu is too far away from Kenya proper—and Kiswahili is old and deep here. He is not reading my signals, and I am resentful. I dig out crumpled notes and place them awkwardly into his hands as I board the boat, turning away from his gratitude.

The main jetty area is covered in orange: flags, posters, T-shirts, campaign banners. People are huddled in groups listening to the radio.

Mr. America in Kiswahili is salamu alaikuming all over the place— and it occurs to me that I am now, to the people of this island, what he was to me when we boarded the plane.

It is evening, and people are dressed up, men in long white *kanzus*, women in black *buibuis*, henna designs on their hands and fingers and feet. A lean blond couple strolls by, both dressed in linen—probably from Shela, the village next to Lamu where jet set celebrities have holiday homes. A group of shirtless teenagers are surrounded by a cheering crowd as they dance a stick fight; there is a donkey race for young boys. Young Bajuni women in green and gold *buibuis* move in giggling huddles, eyes ringed in kohl, gold everywhere. I catch one eye, which bats, moves down shyly, and then covers itself with a flick of fingers and whoosh of fine green cloth. She turns into the fragrant huddle, which swells with speculation.

The town slopes upward gently, and all the narrow twisted paths lead to the seafront. The town is cleaned by rain and water heading downhill. There is a lot of donkey shit. I walk past the long, sea-facing avenue and turn into a thin alley, into the bowels of the town. Buildings lean into each other, scrape each other; walls loom over narrow twisted paths.

Lamu has always had a reputation as a libertarian town. People spend most of their time indoors, and even individual houses are built with the idea of public and private, with increasing layers of intimate space the farther away from the door you are. The doors are thick, tall, and elaborately carved from wood; just outside are benches built into the wings of the main door. It is here that guests are received. There is a heavy metal knocker near the bottom of the door. You knock and sit and wait. Most people don't get to enter the home.

In the old days, traders would come in from India and from the Middle and Far East. As soon as you enter most traders' homes, you will see a small staircase that leads you to the room where foreign traders were hosted sumptuously, but still distant from family. Guests were treated well. They were sprinkled with rose water. Orchards in courtyards had lemon, lime, and banana trees and rose apples. When Ibn Batutta spent time among the Swahili in Mogadishu and Kilwa, he was fed with stews of chicken, meat, fish, and vegetables served on beds of rice and cooked with ghee. He ate green bananas in fresh milk, pickled lemon, ginger, and mangoes.

Lamu became a place of pilgrimage for hippies and gay men in the 1970s. Outside the thick walls, and mostly in the evening, people put on their dutiful appearances: mother, elder, imam, tourist.

...

Patrick makes his way to my hotel at night. We have a beer; he is happy to see me, he says. "Why didn't you call me? I called and you never called back."

"I was busy," I say.

He does not look impressed by my answer. "Are you following the election?"

He laughs. "Me? No. Am just a beach boy."

...

The election rages on the radio. There are pocket radios on everywhere, and people gathered in small groups around them. Yesterday I told off Patrick. He had disappeared with my money for a whole day while I stewed without mobile phone credit. I was furious. There are rumors going around that militias are gathering in the Rift Valley. He was partying somewhere. He shrugged, as if to say, why do you upcountry people and white people, who to us are really the same people, move so aggressively against the tide of things?

While we were talking, a young Kenyan woman, a doctor, joined us for a beer, and we started talking politics. When she left, he asked me if the woman was a Gikuyu. I said no. He said, "Yeye ni mjanja sana."

I told him she was probably Luo. He was confused for a second. Then he nodded, and said, "Ni mjanja kama mzungu."

What he was saying was, she is very cunning, or clever, like a white person. He did not say, or mean, wise, or educated, or even intelligent.

I drink with a banker. He is excited. Kenya has changed already, he says. The old middle-class banks are over. Banking for the masses has arrived; anybody can get credit, open an account. There are hundreds of new good schools, colleges, many new private universities. The biggest new depositors do not live in middle-class Nairobi. They provide services to the masses—food, construction, mobile phone credit, small loans, hardware. The most organized union in Kenya is the primary school teachers' union. They have their own banks—with billions, they are building their own homes. Growth is arriving from below, not from the money of political patronage. Those new moneymakers can force policy. The banker is a big Kibaki supporter. "Raila is dangerous," he says, his face grim. "He can't win, whatever it takes."

"What about the constitution, a new constitution?"

He sniffs. "Ha. We need to stabilize things first." He means let the Kibaki clique consolidate power.

I spend the night walking up and down the jetty and chatting with people. There are radios everywhere, and we follow the results. I hear people say they cannot pay their bills; the cost of food is now impossible. In the morning, I try to draw money from the only ATM in town. It has run out of cash. The count has begun, and it is clear there is rigging. Gangs of angry young men are making roadblocks in Kibera.

The flight out of Lamu is delayed. Nairobi is dangerous.

Why this time? Five years ago we had a near-perfect election. Who knows? Could be the price of oil; the beef in China; paranoia about Gikuyu entitlement; paranoia about Kalenjin entitlement; Luo betrayed again; if they win won't there be reprisals?

Moi; Kibaki; Raila; Ruto; December circumcision ceremonies; trickle-down economics not trickling down enough; instant text messages; xenophobic Texas-, New Jersey–, and London-based Kenyans insulting each other like mad people on the Internet, having discovered xenophobia in chat rooms; high panga sales in our supermarkets; colonialism; Kenyatta's land grab; Moi's land grab; trickle-up corruption; the Federalists; the Centralists; spontaneous combustion; neoliberalism; preplanned combustion; slush money for violence from politicians; slush money for violence from wealthy athletes; Kibaki messing with our electoral commission. Raila will rig! Angry young men; hungry young men; too much democracy too quickly; old men who refuse to cede power; young men who want power too much; too little democracy way too slowly; misplaced grievances; our president, a terrible politician.

Too much hope, too little reform.

While our baggage is being checked, I overhear a conversation between the baggage handlers. Even here, everybody is split. Orange Democratic Movement people stand around their radio. Party of National Unity people stand around their radio. After a dispirited argument about the elections, one of the baggage handlers sighs and says, "These days Kenya is like England."

I laugh, and ask her why.

"I don't know. So many things like England. Now even here in Lamu you see more Kenyan tourists than British . . ."

Her colleagues are nodding.

"Even food in the shops is like England. They way they package it like it is imported. Things are expensive."

One of her colleagues turns to her and says, "Now since which time were you in England?"

"*Mpslp*," she says, blushing, and all politics is silenced for a common moment. "You know what I mean."

The plane lands and we head to board. We are all nervous. It says on the radio that Kibera is burning. There are riot police all over Nairobi.

The final results come out tomorrow. Rigging is rife in both main parties. All the supermarkets have run out of knives and pangas. We are worried. We are not worried. Tourists still frolic on the beach. It is hard to imagine the chaos all those pangas promise. After all, things have been worse before. We don't do all that Uganda stuff, we tell ourselves. It is going to the wire, unfolding live, cameras all over the country bringing the hottest reactions, the angriest protests; they are neck and neck. Kibera is always causing trouble anyway. No sport ever has been so thrilling. Under this constitution it is winner take all. Half the country will feel cut off whoever wins. All monies and plans come from

Nairobi, from the central government. It is possible we will not know who has won until the very last votes are in. The airline steward passes me today's newspaper, and winks.

...

We are sitting in an apartment, a group of friends, artists, watching the election collapse live on television, together with the rest of Kenya. There is pizza, beer, and drama. Politicians and their agents, from both sides, are crowding the electoral commissioner. Kenyatta Cornflakes Center, where the main count is taking place, is surrounded by riot police. We still believe it will be all right. We hear rumors that some close to the president came in at night and fiddled with things. Last night Raila was a million votes ahead. This morning, we woke up and Kibaki had caught up. But we knew it would be close. People do not understand numbers, we say to ourselves. Kivuitu, the head of the electoral commission, is still cracking jokes, so things will be fine. Many key constituencies have not yet delivered their numbers. The commission can't raise them on the phone. It turns out that they are waiting to see the numbers before fiddling with their own numbers and sending them in. Everybody is rigging, and now we are telling ourselves that the media had agents in all constituencies, so they will keep things honest. It is still only just riveting television. Five years ago we had a good and clean election; this one can't be much worse.

It is evening when a sudden energy gathers. Kivuitu clears the room and disappears. A few minutes later, in a small room, without having announced the remaining results, without anybody from the independent press, he announces that President Kibaki is the winner. The whole room is quiet; the whole of Kenya is quiet. Then, suddenly, all screens shift to State House, where a few grim people are seated, as Kivuitu inaugurates Kibaki. No millions of people this time.

Then, there is no news. There is music. Cartoons, and the sun sets and Kenya goes dark. Al Jazeera survives for a while and all we see is numbers, fifty dead, eighty dead, one hundred dead. We hear later that, the moment the president was sworn in, you could hear the screams of people as they rushed down hills and valleys to kill, and all the mobile phones of Kenya were jammed up with text messages full of rumors and threats.

These next few weeks, it does not matter that you have known her all your life and she was the first girl you loved in primary school. Your wife of another tribe. Your blade will cut through her stomach, tear through the Tupac T-shirt, and you will clean that blade and move to another room to look for her baby.

Several Kalenjin militias are marching on foot to Nakuru, and Baba won't leave. I am on the phone with him every hour, begging him. Paraffin and matches cost less than a dollar a day. The ants have crawled out of the logs of Kenya; some will set their own city, Kisumu, on fire, watch it burn and cheer.

You will all sit stunned and watch as your nation—which has broadband and a well-ironed army and a brand-new private school that looks exactly like Hogwarts castle in *Harry Potter*—is taken over by young men with sharpened machetes and poisoned bows and arrows. As you sit in your living rooms, they will take over your main highway, pull people out of cars and cut their heads off. In Nairobi, they will lift up your railway, the original spine, and start to dismantle it. For days there is no news. We are told the generals are about to take it all over. That Raila has the army and Kibaki has the police and the air force. Television news has been silenced. Our president is silent. He is afraid, we hear. There is a joke that he is under his blankets, in Marks & Spencer pajamas, reading P. G. Wodehouse with a torch, and every few minutes his head pokes out and he asks, "Is it over? Have they gone away?"

Last night a whole small army with bows and arrows were killing people a few hundred meters from Pyrethrum Board. There were battles in the lakeside suburbs of Nakuru. "I am not leaving," Baba said.

Chapter Thirty-Three

It is 1983. I am twelve. In two months I write CPE, the national primary school examinations. I spend a lot of time in my room pretending to study. I read a lot of novels. I am in trouble all the time with Mum.

When I masturbate in my bedroom, I do not like to think about people I know. I know I am in love with Khadija Adams, who was Miss Kenya and who is an international beauty star and uses Lux soap. But I can't imagine her breaking glamour and writhing about. I am also in love with Pam Ewing of *Dallas*—but she is too good for sex ideas, and she is sweet and cuddly. I hate Bobby Ewing and really hate Jenna Wade. Alexis Carrington of *Dynasty* makes me giggle when she talks all pouty.

This afternoon, while kids ran around outside the lines of classrooms during games, I used a paperclip to break into Andrew Ivaska's desk. Andrew's parents are Baptist missionaries from America, and he has a whole library of novels. Mum won't let me go to the library. I have been itching the whole day to do something malicious, to jab somebody with a pen. Inside the desk is a brand-new, unread copy of *The Black Stallion* by Walter Farley. I put it in my bag, between the textbooks. As soon as I get home after school, I rush to my room and lock the door.

I am under my orange bedcover. I need forty-five minutes before Mum comes knocking. The kid in the book is called Alex—he is quiet, stubborn, and lonely. One of those people who quietly go about their business, grittily working, scrubbing stables, loving horses and not showing off, and depending on themselves. So then Alex is stuck on this island with a giant black stallion—a wild beast that wants to kill him. In his mumbling cowboy way, Alex decides to ride Black Stallion. Alex has decided to want something impossible. And he wants this impossible thing so much he is prepared to lose everything. He will not admit this, so he pretends to make his lust a mechanical problem: he will find fix-it solutions. How to jump on the back of the animal, how to rig devices to keep him on the back of the beast, how to bribe the horse with various tidbits. As he goes about his business in his fatherless and lonely way, rigging devices, we drip with his want. He will not say how much he wants to conquer the horse. We want to conquer the horse. We want that horse more than anything. I want to be thrown, fall on my back, and limp for days.

The evening chill has landed. I stand and look outside the window. The lake and hills are foggy, like a movie—there are no tin roofs or sudden fields of illegally grown maize to disturb the English countryside look. I can almost imagine horses. Not a cow in sight, no random goats; even our goat is not yet out to pasture. I put on the radio, rush to find General Service. We have two main radio stations, General Service and National Service. General Service is in English. Every morning after the news, they play soft music like ABBA and Boney M. and Kenny Rogers and Lionel Richie. Sometimes an orchestra called James Last, which plays soft misty versions of famous songs. The news is all about President Moi. James Last is good music to masturbate to: I can lie down and see misty television bodies doing naked misty things in the screen of my head.

Ten years ago, this suburb had been, for sixty years, the carefully built illusion of settler bureaucrats. All white, no black Africans allowed to live here. Only servants who would be beaten if they were seen wearing shoes—it made them uppity. The settlers moved out fast after Independence. So fast, their houses were cheap. Baba bought a cottage in Nairobi that is our most valuable family asset. By 1972 Mum could drive us to town and all we would see were kids like us, living in a landscape like this, which was made for people who wanted to imagine an English spring in a stolen land. Kenya from my misty dawn bedroom with General Service seems ageless and ours. The only problem is National Service radio, all those songs in so many languages that suggest some other pungent reality, songs complicated enough to suggest mess and history. This music does not want to conveniently fit the shape of thrusting forward and shaping yourself like the next opportunity; it throbs with undefined past sounds, and shapes and ideas, and it is inconvenient, if only because the Anglo-Kenyan garden does not look like that music sounds.

The one Kenyan musician who is allowed regularly on General Service is Kelly Brown. He has an Afro, glittering clothes, and an R&B dance hit in Germany. He comes from Mombasa but has changed his name. Abdul Kadir Mohammed does not work in 1980s Europop circles. As people disappear into Kenya's newly engineered dungeons, as people die of hunger and disease and roads crumble, we are feverishly passing exams and dancing to Kelly Brown, his Afro bobbing, sequins glittering: *Me and my baby tonite-ah, we hold each other tite-ah, she gives me evuh-rythang, coz she's ma best thing. Oooh ah. Ooo ah. Ah cant gerrinuf of your luuuurve.*

I am supposed to be studying. This is why I masturbate. If I don't masturbate, I will have to spend the day trying to hide my hard-on and never know if people can see it or not, and then my nose gets all sweaty, and then I have to LOOK AWAY from all breasts, and it seems that all the girls have breasts. What can I do to avoid them?

General Service radio is easy to find on medium-wave radio. Exactly at 800 using the dial. National Service is somewhere around 200. I know this because I try as much as possible to avoid it and its *kimay* sounds. I don't know why that Congo music and that bad Kenyan guitar music so distress me; they just do.

The truth is I am not good at pictures; I am much better at words. Any kissing or touching in any book is very powerful. I don't feel the same with television or movies. Films are for everybody, they make you feel what the whole watching world feels. To a film, I am an outsider, a witness marveling at the spectacle unfolding in front of me. The novel's erotic world is not alive on a screen—on glass and plastic and metal. It is not alive on the page either, those are only squiggles cheaply stamped onto dead trees. The whole world of a novel unfolds inside the head, fully entangled with the stinging eyes, the tight chest, the galloping belly. It is fully mine, 100 percent private. When they touch and kiss, the kiss belongs to me, it does not belong to other readers, to the author, to the couple. If it is a well-written kiss, it will be carried in a small, coiled place under the hard bone below my nipples.

I wonder sometimes if there is a third kind of human being. There are real flesh and blood people. There are television and radio people. There are people in books. People in books do not have an actual voice for your ears. You cannot see them. You, the reader, work with a good author to make them move around your head, toss their hair, hate and love, and need things urgently. Russet is an emotion inside me that comes from reading things about horses, and manes, and many hairs tossing, and autumn, a set of impressions, movements, lights. These are my concerns.

It will be years before the dungeons are opened, and we find out the truth. In 1983 every day, several times a day, I play Michael Jackson's "Human Nature" and feel myself brimming in compassion for his sensitivity. We know enough to know things are going on out there, beyond the mist. There are whispers. But there is also *Dallas, Dynasty*, and *Falcon Crest.*

Michael Jackson is beautiful. The nose has not yet fallen. He has managed to make himself into a perpetual present tense: no lineage, no history; he is the maximum of sound and movement and nowness. In 1983, while I read novels, Moi is building his Big Dick Building in secret. Every dictator has to have one. His is called Nyayo House. He knows already that to rule Kenya, he is going to have to shed blood. All those years, we thought he was just hapless, that he tortured because he was floundering. Later, we found out that there was an underground chamber, designed by his people, designed for torture with Nikolae Ceauşescu's help, in that tall tall building. Nobody in the West complains. Moi is a good friend of the West. While we dream shoulder pad dreams, inside those chambers, intellectuals, activists, writers are beaten, waterboarded, testicles are crushed, people are deprived of sleep.

...

It is autumn 2009, as I write this in my bed and breakfast room in Red Hook, New York, near Bard College, where I work. I took a long walk this evening. I walk and step on crushed leaves, watch the first golds and reds in this glorious light. It is such a charismatic season because it looks and feels like the ripening of things—but the leaves are not ripening, they are dying.

It has been a year and a half since Kenya went crazy. During the violence, I refused to fly back to work in the United States in January. It felt like I was abandoning home. But as soon as the peace agreement was signed, I left. I told myself I was done. Done with too much Kenya. I was going to apply for a green card. Visit for holidays. Save up to help get my family out if necessary. Love from a committed distance.

I drank a lot, got angry a lot that summer. I can see myself now, flapping my arms drunkenly in many jagged locations and railing against this and that, and feeling that if I keep talking the ground won't open up and make me lonely.

At a reading and a talk at Williams College, I embarrassed myself and burst into bad snotty tears when I started to talk about Kenya. There is no tissue. Please, please, all podiums, have tissue!

I am tired of being alone.

...

It is the summer of the World Cup 2010, and I am in Ghana enjoying things. I have planned to be home in time for the referendum on the new constitution. I am tentative. Each time I have been home, things have been tense, tribe in everybody's eyes, doubt. Last time, an immigration official at the airport started to speak to me in Gikuyu the moment she saw my surname. Wink wink. No hiding now. We are in conspiracy with one another. Let's help each other, her eyes said. My uncle Henry, who took care of me in South Africa, is dead. Auntie Rosaria, the sweetest of Mum's sisters, died of diabetes complications. Auntie Grace, wonderful, warm, and true Auntie Grace—Baba's big sister—is dead. Baba is fine, but now I worry. Jim has a son, Eddy—a tsunami of energy and laughter. None of my nieces and nephews strongly recall Mum. I wish just one of them had Mum's voice—so she does not just remain in our generation.

I am diabetic and have discovered doctors. My knees were fine, and then I did that American thing that insists on testing for problems you have not felt. I have an MRI and find out that my knees are on the verge of death, and the moment I find this out, they creak and threaten to pop out of their sockets every time I bend them. Then I spend the night in a sleep clinic and they tell me I have probably never slept well, that I breathe badly, that an operation is imminent. I am excited. Maybe this is the cause of my vagueness. Maybe my vagueness is not caused by too many years of soft-focus trash. I have a syndrome. I am a victim of an -osis.

This is growing up, concerns and worries can no longer be suspended, they are just part of the day. Kenya is suddenly all soft and gooey. People smiling, looking you in the eye and saying mushy things like "as a Kenyan . . ." or "in this New Kenya . . ." Shyly, shyly, millions go home to their villages from the city, pay money for buses and gifts, money they do not have, to vote for the new constitution. Even those who vote no do so peacefully. Kibaki is looking dangerously energetic. The fool. But today I like him, beaming like a teddy bear, today I like him. I had planned to be here and leave after the referendum, just for a selfish jolt of good feeling. To leave before I looked too hard and saw ugliness. Now with all of this, I cannot *not* leave.

In a moment of watery patriotism, the day after the referendum, I buy a *benga* compilation, done by Ketebul Studios. It comes with a booklet on the history of *benga*, and a documentary and CD. I am afraid to watch it and find I still hate *benga* music. Everybody now is saying it is the true music of Kenya. Maybe in my heart I am a little Anglo-Kenyan, unable to appreciate *benga*.

I start watching the documentary, and somebody with a posh English accent is narrating the story of *benga*, and then I see a small group of traditional Luo musicians dancing and playing instruments on a patch of dust in a courtyard between grass huts. One man is playing the *nyatiti*. It sounds fine. No *kimay*. I am not thrilled. The music is coherent and complicated. The *nyatiti* and its younger cousin the lyre are two of the most ancient of stringed musical instruments. But it is the entry of the *orutu*—a wooden bow and string rubbing a fiddle made from a gourd—that scatters my senses and leaves me shifting uncomfortably, that bowel seesawing sound. I still can't make the connection between the wooden sounds of this instrument and the acoustic guitar sounds of *benga.*

In the 1940s, thousands of Kenyans, including one Barack Obama Senior, left their villages for the first time, in uniform for the British, and ended up watching their fellow Kenyans dying inelegantly, and buried inelegantly, and left to rot inelegantly in a foreign land. These soldiers lived a life of thrills and excitement, full of adventure and horror. They met and saw people from all over the colonies. They saw them shit; they saw them die. They saw them sing. They expanded, they recoiled, they measured themselves, and they found no mathematical principle to account for their designated roles back home. Here, a man who was just a white man's cook, barefoot and grateful, could start to push his son to be as good as the colonizer.

A certain taboo of superiority was broken as soldiers witnessed a mortally wounded Britain floundering in the jungles for its survival. Those lonely evenings, maybe even in ceremonies to mark the dead who were never to be brought home, some started to play Spanish acoustic guitar. They used the guitar to re-create the sounds of home. The man who sits and plays the *nyatiti* is a storyteller. A group of players will come to a homestead and stand near the granary—far from delicate ears. As he plays the *nyatiti,* he composes a song, full of local characters, and history, and raunchy scandals, and love, and jealousy. The *nyatiti,* the drums, the rattles, the ankle rattles, the *orutu* simply accompany the story.

It is a literary form, and the song, the tune of the song, does not follow a separate and parallel musical scale: it too is a slave to the story, its peaks and troughs, its moments of wisdom, its bad behavior. And people dance, moving enough around the music to inhabit the story. If in Kenya the Spanish guitar was an object to be revered, smooth and without kink, a thing for white people's music, in Burma—in bloodied uniforms, muddy, exhausted, and malarial—it was used with impunity, with no respect for the forms and scales and manners its brand name promised. To these soldiers, it became only an awkward pretender to the noble *nyatiti* and the noble *orutu.* It was weak, but it had to do the job of both. A good *orutu* or *nyatiti* player, like a jazz guitarist, will live up to the narrative improvisations of the singer. So they did, musicians like Olima Anditi and John Ogara found a way to make the Spanish guitar re-create the partnership of sounds between the *nyatiti* and the *orutu* as accompaniments to singing/storytelling. It became a whole new idea—carrying all of what came before, but a thing of its own.

Something calls my attention. I pause the documentary, stand up, my hands shaking, get a coffee, and come back and watch Dave Otieno, a Kenyan guitarist—and music genius—speaking. Here it is, the source of all *kimay*. The music of the *nyatiti* is all about the singer. The *nyatiti* and *orutu* do not create their own sounds. Their job is to follow the words, the intonation, the language and melody of the song, to maintain the integrity of the story. So, if you take the singer away, what they sound like is what the singer was saying. They mimic the singer. The *nyatiti* is plucked, not strummed, and this makes sounds very different from any other Spanish guitar sound. Because Nairobi in the 1960s was now full of Luo *benga* guitarists in this tradition, *benga* as an idea spread quickly to different tribes, and their new popular music. Any good *benga* guitarist can mimic the architecture and musical rhythms and verbal sounds of any Kenyan language. Stripped down, that is the intent of *benga*.

Kimay is people talking without words, exact languages, the guitar sounds of all of Kenya speaking Kenya's languages. If *kimay* brought me uncertainty, it was because I simply lacked the imagination to think that such a feat was possible. For *kimay* was part of a project to make people like us certain of our place in the world, to make us unable to see the past and our place in it. To make us a sort of Anglo-Kenyan. Right at the beginning, in our first popular Independence music, before the flag was up, Kenyans had already found a coherent platform to carry our diversity and complexity in sound.

We fail to trust that we knew ourselves to be possible from the beginning.

Acknowledgments

Over the past six years, while writing this book, I have been fortunate to receive the attention, support, and goodwill of many people.

I would like to thanks my muses and readers who all intervened with support and love during the many creative crises: Martin Kimani, Chimamanda Adichie, David Godwin, Ed Pavlic, Keguro Macharia, David Kaiza, Sara Holloway, the Secret Wambui, Dr. Wambui Mwangi, John Ryle, Muthoni Garland, Achal Prabhala, Sarah Chalfant.

Special thanks to Fiona McCrae, my editor at Graywolf Press.

Thanks to the Wingate Foundation, and the Ford Foundation team in Nairobi, Kenya, especially Rob Burnet and Dr. Joyce Nyairo, who have changed the arts landscape in Nairobi. I would like to thank the people at the Lannan Foundation, and Aslak and the team at the House of Literature in Oslo. The team at *Granta* magazine and Granta Books, and the Farafina community. Thanks to the Chimurenga community. Thanks to Tom Maliti, Kairo Kiarie, June Wainaina, Malla Mummo, Angela Wachuka, Billy Kahora and the *Kwani?* community. Thanks to Mikhail Iossel and the SLS team.

Many thanks to the Bard community for welcoming me here. Thanks to President Leon Botstein, Professor Chinua Achebe, our patron, Jesse Shipley, Dimitri B. Papadimitriou, Jim Brudvig, Michèle Dominy, Irene Zedlacher, Professor Mary Caponegro, Max Kenner, and Professor John Ryle of the Rift Valley Institute at Bard College. Many thanks to the English department at Union College, especially Professor Harry Merten and Stacey Barnum. Many thanks to Professor Kenda Mutongi of the Africana program at Williams College, where I spent a wonderful semester as the Sterling Brown Visiting Professor of African Studies. Many thanks to Professor Ngugi wa Thiong'o, Teju Cole, and Chris Abani. Many thanks to the team at Graywolf Press, and the team at the Wylie Agency.

Many thanks to Andy and Georgia Hanson for offering their home and friendship to me in 2007 when I needed to hide and finish writing this book.

I would like to pay tribute to the late Rod Amis, legendary editor of the amazing netzine g21.net, who published everything I sent, and always paid $100 by Western Union for each story—from his own pocket. Rod was the most generous and giving editor I have worked with.

Much love and good wishes to you all.

Binyavanga Wainaina
Annandale-on-Hudson, New York
May 2, 2011

Binyavanga Wainaina was a Kenyan author, publisher, and cultural worker. He was the founding editor of *Kwani?*, one of Africa's leading literary magazines. He won the 2002 Caine Prize for African Writing for his story "Discovering Home," and his essay "How to Write About Africa" attracted wide attention globally. His acclaimed memoir, *One Day I Will Write About This Place*, has been translated into several languages. He was a Sterling Brown Fellow at Williams College, a Lannan Fellow, and the director of the Chinua Achebe Center for African Writers and Artists at Bard College. In 2014, he came out publicly and was subsequently named one of *Time* magazine's 100 Most Influential People.

This book is made possible through a partnership with the College of Saint Benedict, and honors the legacy of S. Mariella Gable, a distinguished teacher at the College.

Previous titles in this series include:

Loverboy by Victoria Redel
The House on Eccles Road by Judith Kitchen
One Vacant Chair by Joe Coomer
The Weatherman by Clint McCown
Collected Poems by Jane Kenyon
Variations on the Theme of an African Dictatorship
    by Nuruddin Farah:
        Sweet and Sour Milk
        Sardines
        Close Sesame
Duende by Tracy K. Smith
All of It Singing: New and Selected Poems by Linda Gregg
The Art of Syntax: Rhythm of Thought, Rhythm of Song
    by Ellen Bryant Voigt
How to Escape from a Leper Colony by Tiphanie Yanique

Support for this series has been provided by the Manitou Fund as part of the Warner Reading Program.

The text of *One Day I Will Write About This Place* is set in Adobe Jenson Pro, a typeface drawn by Robert Slimbach and based on late-fifteenth-century types by the printer Nicolas Jenson. This book was designed by Ann Sudmeier. Composition by BookMobile Design and Publishing Services, Minneapolis, Minnesota. Manufactured by Versa Press on acid-free 30 percent postconsumer wastepaper.